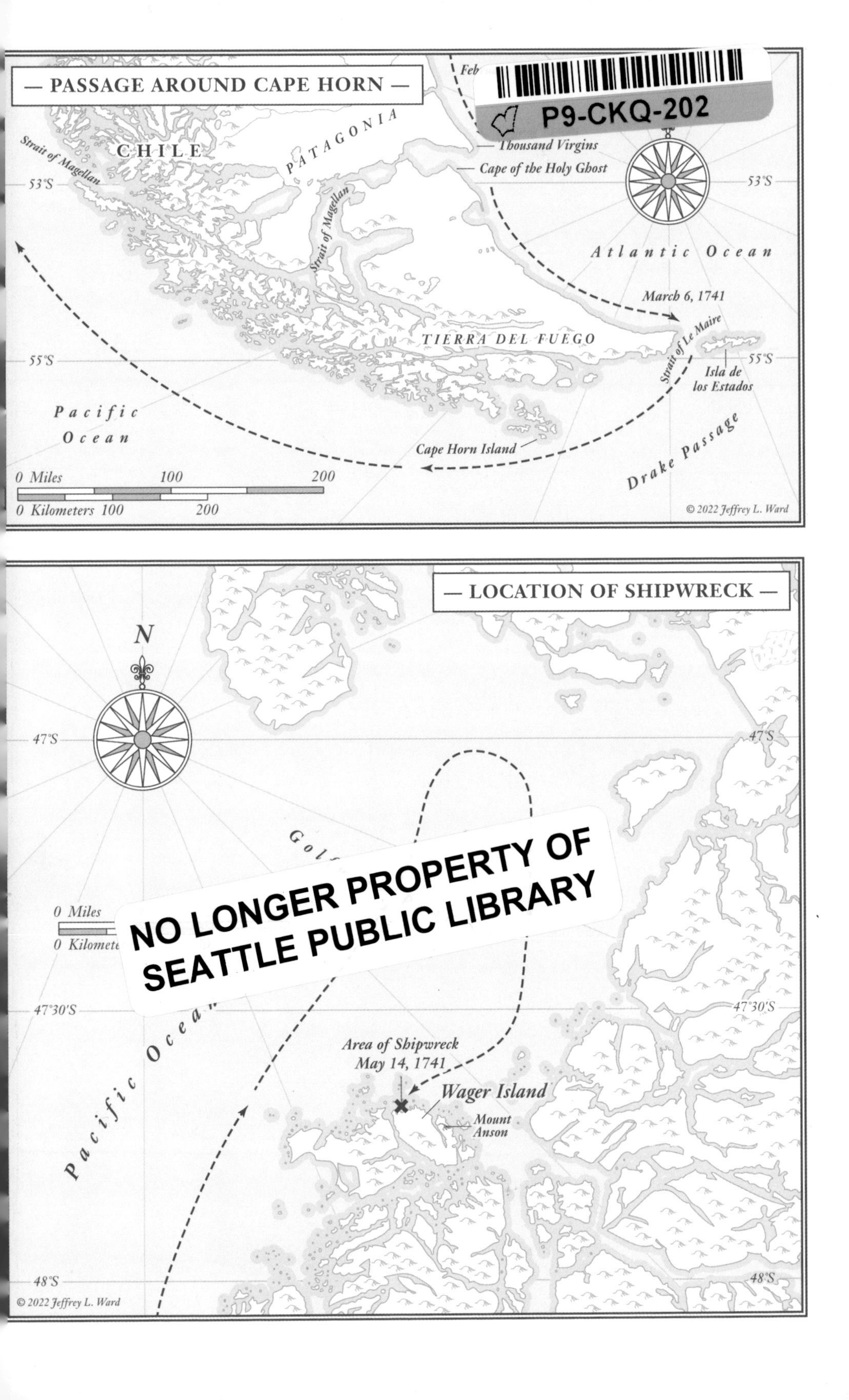
— PASSAGE AROUND CAPE HORN —
CHILE
PATAGONIA
Strait of Magellan
Strait of Magellan
Thousand Virgins
Cape of the Holy Ghost
53°S
53°S
Atlantic Ocean
March 6, 1741
TIERRA DEL FUEGO
Strait of Le Maire
55°S
55°S
Isla de
los Estados
Pacific
Ocean
Cape Horn Island
Drake Passage
0 Miles 100 200
0 Kilometers 100 200
© 2022 Jeffrey L. Ward
— LOCATION OF SHIPWRECK —
N
47°S
47°S
0 Miles
47°30'S
47°30'S
Pacific Ocean
Area of Shipwreck
May 14, 1741
Wager Island
Mount
Anson
48°S
48°S
© 2022 Jeffrey L. Ward

The WAGER

ALSO BY DAVID GRANN

The Lost City of Z:
A Tale of Deadly Obsession in the Amazon

The Devil and Sherlock Holmes:
Tales of Murder, Madness, and Obsession

Killers of the Flower Moon:
The Osage Murders and the Birth of the FBI

The White Darkness

Killers of the Flower Moon:
Adapted for Young Readers

The WAGER

A Tale of Shipwreck, Mutiny, and Murder

David Grann

DOUBLEDAY
New York

www.doubleday.com

Book design by Maria Carella
Maps designed by Jeffrey L. Ward
Jacket painting: *Ships in Distress in a Storm,* circa 1720–30,
by Peter Monamy © Tate, London / Art Resource, NY
Jacket design by John A. Fontana

Library of Congress Cataloging-in-Publication Data
Names: Grann, David, author.
Title: The Wager: a tale of shipwreck, mutin,y and murder / David Grann.
Description: First edition. | New York: Doubleday, 2023. |
Includes bibliographical references and index.
Identifiers: LCCN 2022028630 (print) | LCCN 2022028631 (ebook) |
ISBN 9780385534260 (hardcover) | ISBN 9780385534277 (ebk)
Subjects: LCSH: Wager (Ship) | Shipwrecks—Patagonia (Argentina and Chile) |
Shipwreck victims—Patagonia (Argentina and Chile) | Shipwreck victims—
Great Britain. | Mutiny—Great Britain.
Classification: LCC G530.W25 G73 2023 (print) | LCC G530.W25 (ebook) |
DDC 910.9164/1—dc23/eng20221202
LC record available at https://lccn.loc.gov/2022028630
LC ebook record available at https://lccn.loc.gov/2022028631

MANUFACTURED IN THE UNITED STATES OF AMERICA

1 3 5 7 9 10 8 6 4 2
First Edition

FOR KYRA, ZACHARY, AND ELLA

We are the hero of our own story.

—MARY McCARTHY

Maybe there is a beast.... Maybe it's only us.

—WILLIAM GOLDING, *Lord of the Flies*

Contents

Author's Note

I must confess that I did not witness the ship strike the rocks or the crew tie up the captain. Nor did I see firsthand the acts of deceit and murder. I have, however, spent years combing through the archival debris: the washed-out logbooks, the moldering correspondence, the half-truthful journals, the surviving records from the troubling court-martial. Most critically, I have studied the accounts published by those who were involved, who not only witnessed the events but also shaped them. I tried to gather all the facts to determine what really happened. Still, it's impossible to escape the participants' conflicting, and at times warring, perspectives. So instead of smoothing out every difference, or further shading the already shaded evidence, I've tried to present all sides, leaving it to you to render the ultimate verdict—history's judgment.

The WAGER

Prologue

THE ONLY IMPARTIAL WITNESS was the sun. For days, it watched as the strange object heaved up and down in the ocean, tossed mercilessly by the wind and the waves. Once or twice the vessel nearly smashed into a reef, which might have ended our story. Yet somehow—whether through destiny, as some would later proclaim, or dumb luck—it drifted into an inlet, off the southeastern coast of Brazil, where several inhabitants laid eyes upon it.

Above fifty feet long and ten feet wide, it was a boat of some sort—though it looked as if it had been patched together from scraps of wood and cloth and then battered into oblivion. Its sails were shredded, its boom shattered. Seawater seeped through the hull and a stench emanated from within. The bystanders, edging closer, heard unnerving sounds: thirty men were crammed onboard, their bodies almost wasted to the bone. Their clothes had largely disintegrated. Their faces were enveloped in hair, tangled and salted like seaweed.

Some were so weak they could not even stand. One soon gave out his last breath and died. But a figure who appeared to be in charge rose with an extraordinary exertion of will and announced that they were castaways from His Majesty's Ship the *Wager*, a British man-of-war.

When the news reached England, it was greeted with disbelief. In September 1740, during an imperial conflict with Spain, the *Wager*, carrying some 250 officers and crew, had embarked from Portsmouth in a squadron on a secret mission: to capture a treasure-filled Spanish galleon known as "the prize of all the oceans." Near Cape Horn, at the tip of South America, the squadron had been engulfed by a hurricane, and the *Wager* was believed to have sunk with all its souls. But 283 days after the ship had last been reported seen, these men miraculously emerged in Brazil.

They had been shipwrecked on a desolate island off the coast of Patagonia. Most of the officers and crew had perished, but eighty-one survivors had set out in a makeshift boat lashed together partly from the wreckage of the *Wager.* Packed so tightly onboard that they could barely move, they traveled through menacing gales and tidal waves, through ice storms and earthquakes. More than fifty men died during the arduous journey, and by the time the few remnants reached Brazil three and a half months later, they had traversed nearly three thousand miles—one of the longest castaway voyages ever recorded. They were hailed for their ingenuity and bravery. As the leader of the party noted, it was hard to believe that "human nature could possibly support the miseries that we have endured."

Six months later, another boat washed ashore, this one landing in a blizzard off the southwestern coast of Chile. It was even smaller—a wooden dugout propelled by a sail stitched from the rags of blankets. Onboard were three additional survivors, and their condition was even more frightful. They were half naked and emaciated; insects swarmed over their bodies, nibbling on what remained of their flesh. One man was so delirious that he had "quite lost himself," as a companion put it, "not recollecting our names... or even his own."

After these men recovered and returned to England, they leveled a shocking allegation against their companions who had surfaced in Brazil. They were not heroes—they were mutineers. In the controversy that followed, with charges and countercharges from both sides, it became clear that while stranded on the island the *Wager*'s officers and crew had struggled to persevere in the most extreme circumstances. Faced with starvation and freezing temperatures, they built an outpost and tried to re-create naval order. But as their situation deteriorated, the *Wager*'s officers and crew—those supposed apostles of the Enlightenment—descended into a Hobbesian state of depravity. There were warring factions and marauders and abandonments and murders. A few of the men succumbed to cannibalism.

Back in England, the principal figures from each group along with their allies were now summoned by the Admiralty to face a court-martial. The trial threatened to expose the secret nature not only of those charged but also of an empire whose self-professed mission was spreading civilization.

Several of the accused published their sensational—and wildly conflicting—accounts of what one of them called the "dark and intricate" affair. The philosophers Rousseau, Voltaire, and Montesquieu were influenced by reports of the expedition, and so, later, were Charles Darwin and two of the great novelists of the sea, Herman Melville and Patrick O'Brian. The suspects' main aim was to sway the Admiralty and the public. A survivor from one party composed what he described as a "faithful narrative," insisting, "I have been scrupulously careful not to insert one word of untruth: for falsities of any kind would be highly absurd in a work designed to rescue the author's character." The leader of the other side claimed, in his own chronicle, that his enemies had furnished an "imperfect narrative" and "blackened us with the greatest calumnies." He vowed, "We stand or fall by the truth; if truth will not support us, nothing can."

We all impose some coherence—some meaning—on the chaotic events of our existence. We rummage through the raw images of our memories, selecting, burnishing, erasing. We emerge as the heroes of our stories, allowing us to live with what we have done—or haven't done.

But these men believed their very lives depended on the stories they told. If they failed to provide a convincing tale, they could be secured to a ship's yardarm and hanged.

Part One

THE WOODEN WORLD

CHAPTER 1

The First Lieutenant

EACH MAN IN THE squadron carried, along with a sea chest, his own burdensome story. Perhaps it was of a scorned love, or a secret prison conviction, or a pregnant wife left on shore weeping. Perhaps it was a hunger for fame and fortune, or a dread of death. David Cheap, the first lieutenant of the *Centurion*, the squadron's flagship, was no different. A burly Scotsman in his early forties with a protracted nose and intense eyes, he was in flight—from squabbles with his brother over their inheritance, from creditors chasing him, from debts that made it impossible for him to find a suitable bride. Onshore, Cheap seemed doomed, unable to navigate past life's unexpected shoals. Yet as he perched on the quarterdeck of a British man-of-war, cruising the vast oceans with a cocked hat and spyglass, he brimmed with confidence—even, some would say, a touch of haughtiness. The wooden world of a ship—a world bound by the Navy's rigid regulations and the laws of the sea and, most of all, by the hardened fellowship of men—had provided him a refuge. Suddenly he felt a crystalline order, a clarity of purpose. And Cheap's newest posting, despite the innumerable risks that it carried, from plagues and drowning to enemy cannon fire, offered what he longed for: a chance to finally claim a wealthy prize and rise to captain his own ship, becoming a lord of the sea.

The problem was that he could not get away from the damned land. He was trapped—cursed, really—at the dockyard in Portsmouth, along the English Channel, struggling with feverish futility to get the *Centurion* fitted out and ready to sail. Its massive wooden hull, 144 feet long and 40 feet wide, was moored at a slip. Carpenters, caulkers, riggers, and joiners combed over its decks like rats (which were also plentiful). A cacophony of hammers and saws. The cobblestone streets past the shipyard were congested with rattling wheelbarrows and horse-drawn wagons, with porters, peddlers, pickpockets, sailors, and prostitutes. Periodically, a boatswain blew a chilling whistle, and crewmen stumbled from ale shops, parting from old or new sweethearts, hurrying to their departing ships in order to avoid their officers' lashes.

It was January 1740, and the British Empire was racing to mobilize for war against its imperial rival Spain. And in a move that had suddenly raised Cheap's prospects, the captain under whom he served on the *Centurion*, George Anson, had been plucked by the Admiralty to be a commodore and lead the squadron of five warships against the Spanish. The promotion was unexpected. As the son of an obscure country squire, Anson did not wield the level of patronage, the grease—or "interest," as it was more politely called—that propelled many officers up the pole, along with their men. Anson, then forty-two, had joined the Navy at the age of fourteen, and served for nearly three decades without leading a major military campaign or snaring a lucrative prize.

Tall, with a long face and a high forehead, he had a remoteness about him. His blue eyes were inscrutable, and outside the company of a few trusted friends he rarely opened his mouth. One statesman, after meeting with him, noted, "Anson, as usual, said little." Anson corresponded even more sparingly, as if he doubted the ability of words to convey what he saw or felt. "He loved reading little, and writing, or dictating his own letters less, and that seeming negligence . . . drew upon him the ill will of many," a relative wrote. A diplomat later quipped that Anson was so unknowing about the world that he'd been "round it, but never in it."

Nevertheless, the Admiralty had recognized in Anson what Cheap had also seen in him in the two years since he'd joined the

Centurion's crew: a formidable seaman. Anson had a mastery of the wooden world and, equally important, a mastery of himself—he remained cool and steady under duress. His relative noted, "He had high notions of sincerity and honor and practiced them without deviation." In addition to Cheap, he had attracted a coterie of talented junior officers and protégés, all vying for his favor. One later informed Anson that he was more obliged to him than to his own father and would do anything to "act up to the good opinion you are pleased to have of me." If Anson succeeded in his new role as commodore of the squadron, he would be in a position to anoint any captain he wanted. And Cheap, who'd initially served as Anson's second lieutenant, was now his right-hand man.

Like Anson, Cheap had spent much of his life at sea, a bruising existence he'd at first hoped to escape. As Samuel Johnson once observed, "No man will be a sailor who has contrivance enough to get himself into a jail; for being in a ship is being in a jail, with the chance of being drowned." Cheap's father had possessed a large estate in Fife, Scotland, and one of those titles—the second Laird of Rossie—that evoked nobility even if it did not quite confer it. His motto, emblazoned on the family's crest, was *Ditat virtus*: "Virtue enriches." He had seven children with his first wife, and, after she died, he had six more with his second, among them David.

In 1705, the year that David celebrated his eighth birthday, his father stepped out to fetch some goat's milk and dropped dead. As was custom, it was the oldest male heir—David's half brother James—who inherited the bulk of the estate. And so David was buffeted by forces beyond his control, in a world divided between first sons and younger sons, between haves and have-nots. Compounding his upheaval, James, now ensconced as the third Laird of Rossie, frequently neglected to pay the allowance that had been bequeathed to his half brothers and half sister: some blood was apparently thicker than others'. Driven to find work, David apprenticed to a merchant, but his debts mounted. So in 1714, the year he turned seventeen, he ran off to sea, a decision that was evidently welcomed by his family—as his guardian wrote to his older brother, "The sooner he goes off it will be better for you and me."

After these setbacks, Cheap seemed only more consumed by his festering dreams, more determined to bend what he called an "unhappy fate." On his own, on an ocean distant from the world he knew, he might prove himself in elemental struggles—braving typhoons, outdueling enemy ships, rescuing his companions from calamities.

But though Cheap had chased a few pirates—including the one-handed Irishman Henry Johnson, who fired his gun by resting the barrel on his stump—these earlier voyages had proved largely uneventful. He'd been sent to patrol the West Indies, generally considered the worst assignment in the Navy because of the specter of disease. The Saffron Scourge. The Bloody Flux. The Breakbone Fever. The Blue Death.

But Cheap had endured. Wasn't there something to be said for that? Moreover, he'd earned the trust of Anson and worked his way up to first lieutenant. No doubt it helped that they shared a disdain for reckless banter, or what Cheap deemed a "vaporing manner." A Scottish minister who later became close to Cheap noted that Anson had employed him because he was "a man of sense and knowledge." Cheap, the once-forlorn debtor, was but one rung from his coveted captaincy. And with the war with Spain having broken out, he was about to head into full-fledged battle for the first time.

The conflict was the result of the endless jockeying among the European powers to expand their empires. They each vied to conquer or control ever larger swaths of the earth, so that they could exploit and monopolize other nations' valuable natural resources and trade markets. In the process, they subjugated and destroyed innumerable indigenous peoples, justifying their ruthless self-interest—including the reliance on the ever-expanding Atlantic slave trade—by claiming that they were somehow spreading "civilization" to the benighted realms of the earth. Spain had long been the dominant empire in Latin America, but Great Britain, which already possessed colonies along the American eastern seaboard, was now on the ascendance—and determined to break its rival's hold.

Then, in 1738, Robert Jenkins, a British merchant captain, was summoned to appear in Parliament, where he reportedly claimed that a Spanish officer had stormed his brig in the Caribbean and, accusing him of smuggling sugar from Spain's colonies, cut off his left ear. Jenkins reputedly displayed his severed appendage, pickled in a jar, and pledged "my cause to my country." The incident further ignited the passions of Parliament and pamphleteers, leading people to cry for blood—an ear for an ear—and a good deal of booty as well. The conflict became known as the War of Jenkins' Ear.

British authorities soon devised a plan to launch an attack on a hub of Spain's colonial wealth: Cartagena. A South American city on the Caribbean, it was where much of the silver extracted from Peruvian mines was shipped in armed convoys to Spain. The British offensive—involving a massive fleet of 186 ships, led by Admiral Edward Vernon—would be the largest amphibious assault in history. But there was also another, much smaller operation: the one assigned to Commodore Anson.

With five warships and a scouting sloop, he and some two thousand men would sail across the Atlantic and round Cape Horn, "taking, sinking, burning, or otherwise destroying" enemy ships and weakening Spanish holdings from the Pacific coast of South America to the Philippines. The British government, in concocting its scheme, wanted to avoid the impression that it was merely sponsoring piracy. Yet the heart of the plan called for an act of outright thievery: to snatch a Spanish galleon loaded with virgin silver and hundreds of thousands of silver coins. Twice a year, Spain sent such a galleon—it was not always the same ship—from Mexico to the Philippines to purchase silks and spices and other Asian commodities, which, in turn, were sold in Europe and the Americas. These exchanges provided crucial links in Spain's global trading empire.

Cheap and the others ordered to carry out the mission were rarely privy to the agendas of those in power, but they were lured by a tantalizing prospect: a share of the treasure. The *Centurion*'s twenty-two-year-old chaplain, Reverend Richard Walter, who later compiled an account of the voyage, described the galleon as "the most desirable prize that was to be met with in any part of the globe."

If Anson and his men prevailed—"if it shall please God to bless our arms," as the Admiralty put it—they would continue circling the earth before returning home. The Admiralty had given Anson a code and a cipher to use for his written communication, and an official warned that the mission must be carried out in the "most secret, expeditious manner." Otherwise, Anson's squadron might be intercepted and destroyed by a large Spanish armada being assembled under the command of Don José Pizarro.

Cheap was facing his longest expedition—he might be gone for three years—and his most perilous. But he saw himself as a knight-errant of the sea in search of "the greatest prize of all the oceans." And along the way, he might become a captain yet.

Yet if the squadron didn't embark quickly, Cheap feared, the entire party would be annihilated by a force even more dangerous than the Spanish armada: the violent seas around Cape Horn. Only a few British sailors had successfully made this passage, where winds routinely blow at gale force, waves can climb to nearly a hundred feet, and icebergs lurk in the hollows. Seamen thought that the best chance to survive was during the austral summer, between December and February. Reverend Walter cited this "essential maxim," explaining that during winter not only were the seas fiercer and the temperatures freezing; there were fewer hours of daylight in which one could discern the uncharted coastline. All these reasons, he argued, would make navigating around this unknown shore the "most dismaying and terrible."

But since war had been declared, in October 1739, the *Centurion* and the other men-of-war in the squadron—including the *Gloucester,* the *Pearl,* and the *Severn*—had been marooned in England, waiting to be repaired and fitted out for the next journey. Cheap watched helplessly as the days ticked by. January 1740 came and went. Then February and March. It was nearly half a year since the war with Spain had been declared; still, the squadron was not ready to sail.

It should have been an imposing force. Men-of-war were among the most sophisticated machines yet conceived: buoyant wooden castles powered across oceans by wind and sail. Reflecting the dual nature of their creators, they were devised to be both murderous instruments and the homes in which hundreds of sailors lived together as a family. In a lethal, floating chess game, these pieces were deployed around the globe to achieve what Sir Walter Raleigh had envisioned: "Whosoever commands the seas commands the trade of the world; whosoever commands the trade of the world commands the riches of the world."

Cheap knew what a cracking ship the *Centurion* was. Swift and stout, and weighing about a thousand tons, she had, like the other warships in Anson's squadron, three towering masts with crisscrossing yards—wooden spars from which the sails unfurled. The *Centurion* could fly as many as eighteen sails at a time. Its hull gleamed with varnish, and painted around the stern, in gold relief, were Greek mythological figures, including Poseidon. On the bow rode a sixteen-foot wooden carving of a lion, painted bright red. To increase the chances of surviving a barrage of cannonballs, the hull had a double layer of planks, giving it a thickness of more than a foot in places. The ship had several decks, each stacked upon the next, and two of them had rows of cannons on both sides—their menacing black muzzles pointing out of square gunports. Augustus Keppel, a fifteen-year-old midshipman who was one of Anson's protégés, boasted that other men-of-war had "no chance in the world" against the mighty *Centurion.*

Yet building, repairing, and fitting out these watercraft was a herculean endeavor even in the best of times, and in a period of war it was chaos. The royal dockyards, which were among the largest manufacturing sites in the world, were overwhelmed with ships—leaking ships, half-constructed ships, ships needing to be loaded and unloaded. Anson's vessels were laid up on what was known as Rotten Row. As sophisticated as men-of-war were with their sail propulsion and lethal gunnery, they were largely made from simple, perishable materials: hemp, canvas, and, most of all, timber. Constructing a single large warship could require as many as four thousand trees; a hundred acres of forest might be felled.

Most of the wood was hard oak, but it was still susceptible to the pulverizing elements of storm and sea. *Teredo navalis*—a reddish shipworm, which can grow longer than a foot—ate through hulls. (Columbus lost two ships to these creatures during his fourth voyage to the West Indies.) Termites also bored through decks and masts and cabin doors, as did deathwatch beetles. A species of fungus further devoured the ship's wooden core. In 1684, Samuel Pepys, a secretary to the Admiralty, was stunned to discover that many new warships under construction were already so rotten they were "in danger of sinking at their very moorings."

The average man-of-war was estimated by a leading shipwright to last only fourteen years. And to survive that long, a ship had to be virtually remade after each extensive voyage, with new masts and sheathing and rigging. Otherwise, it risked disaster. In 1782, while the 180-foot *Royal George*—for a time the largest warship in the world—was anchored near Portsmouth, with a full crew onboard, water began flooding its hull. It sank. The cause has been disputed, but an investigation blamed the "general state of decay of her timbers." An estimated nine hundred people drowned.

Cheap learned that an inspection of the *Centurion* had turned up the usual array of sea wounds. A shipwright reported that the wooden sheathing on its hull was "so much worm eaten" that it had to be taken off and replaced. The foremast, toward the bow, contained a rotten cavity a foot deep, and the sails were, as Anson noted in his log, "much rat eaten." The squadron's other four warships faced similar problems. Moreover, each vessel had to be loaded with tons of provisions, including some forty miles of rope, more than fifteen thousand square feet of sails, and a farm's worth of livestock—chickens, pigs, goats, and cattle. (It could be fiercely difficult to get such animals onboard: steers "do not like the water," a British captain complained.)

Cheap pleaded with the naval administration to finish readying the *Centurion.* But it was that familiar story of wartime: though much of the country had clamored for battle, the people were unwilling to pay enough for it. And the Navy was strained to a breaking point. Cheap could be volatile, his moods shifting like the winds, and here he was, stuck as a landsman, a pen pusher! He badgered dockyard officials to replace the *Centurion*'s damaged mast, but they insisted the cavity could simply be patched. Cheap wrote to the Admiralty decrying this "very strange way of reasoning," and officials eventually relented. But more time was lost.

And where was that bastard of the fleet, the *Wager*? Unlike the other men-of-war, it was not born for battle but had been a merchant vessel—a so-called East Indiaman, because it traded in that region. Intended for heavy cargo, it was tubby and unwieldy, a 123-foot eyesore. After the war began, the Navy, needing additional ships, had purchased it from the East India Company for nearly four thousand pounds. Since then, it had been sequestered eighty miles northeast of Portsmouth, at Deptford, a royal dockyard on the Thames, where it was undergoing a metamorphosis: cabins were torn apart, holes cut into the outer walls, and a stairwell obliterated.

The *Wager's* captain, Dandy Kidd, surveyed the work being done. Fifty-six years old, and reportedly a descendant of the infamous buccaneer William Kidd, he was an experienced seaman, and a superstitious one—he saw portents lurking in the winds and the waves. Only recently had he obtained what Cheap dreamed of: the command of his own ship. At least from Cheap's perspective, Kidd had earned his promotion, unlike the captain of the *Gloucester*, Richard Norris, whose father, Sir John Norris, was a celebrated admiral; Sir John had helped to secure his son a position in the squadron, noting that there would be "both action and good fortune to those who survived." The *Gloucester* was the only vessel in the squadron being swiftly repaired, prompting another captain to complain, "I lay three weeks in the dock and not a nail drove, because Sir John Norris's son must first be served."

Captain Kidd bore his own story. He'd left behind, at a boarding school, a five-year-old son, also named Dandy, who had no mother to raise him. What would happen to him if his father didn't survive the voyage? Already Captain Kidd feared the omens. In his log, he wrote that his new ship nearly "tumbled over," and he warned the Admiralty that she might be a "crank"—a ship that heeled abnormally. To give the hull ballast so the ship wouldn't capsize, more than four hundred tons of pig iron and gravel stones were lowered through the hatches into the dark, dank, cavernous hold.

The workers toiled through one of England's coldest winters on record, and just as the *Wager* was ready to sail, Cheap learned to his dismay, something extraordinary happened: the Thames froze, shimmering from bank to bank with thick, unbreakable waves of ice. An official at Deptford advised the Admiralty that the *Wager* was imprisoned until the river melted. Two months passed before she was liberated.

In May, the old East Indiaman finally emerged from the Deptford Dockyard as a man-of-war. The Navy classified warships by their number of cannons, and, with twenty-eight, she was a sixth-rate—the lowest rank. She was christened in honor of Sir

Charles Wager, the seventy-four-year-old First Lord of the Admiralty. The ship's name seemed fitting: weren't they all gambling with their lives?

As the *Wager* was piloted down the Thames, drifting with the tides along that central highway of trade, she floated past West Indiamen loaded with sugar and rum from the Caribbean, past East Indiamen with silks and spices from Asia, past blubber hunters returning from the Arctic with whale oil for lanterns and soaps. While the *Wager* was navigating this traffic, her keel ran aground on a shoal. Imagine being shipwrecked here! But it soon dislodged, and in July the ship arrived at last outside Portsmouth harbor, where Cheap laid eyes upon her. Seamen were merciless oglers of passing ships, pointing out their elegant curves or their hideous flaws. And though the *Wager* had assumed the proud look of a man-of-war, she could not completely conceal her former self, and Captain Kidd beseeched the Admiralty, even at this late date, to give the vessel a fresh coat of varnish and paint so that she could shine like the other ships.

By the middle of July, nine bloodless months had gone by since the war began. If the squadron left promptly, Cheap was confident that it could reach Cape Horn before the end of the austral summer. But the men-of-war were still missing the most important element of all: men.

Because of the length of the voyage and the planned amphibious invasions, each warship in Anson's squadron was supposed to carry an even greater number of seamen and marines than it was designed for. The *Centurion*, which typically held four hundred people, was expected to sail with some five hundred, and the *Wager* would be packed with about two hundred and fifty—nearly double its usual complement.

Cheap had waited and waited for crewmen to arrive. But the Navy had exhausted its supply of volunteers, and Great Britain had no military conscription. Robert Walpole, the country's first prime minister, warned that the dearth of crews had rendered a third of the Navy's ships unusable. "Oh! seamen, seamen, seamen!" he cried at a meeting.

While Cheap was struggling with other officers to scrounge up sailors for the squadron, he received more unsettling news: those men who had been recruited were falling sick. Their heads throbbed and their limbs were so sore they felt as if they'd been pummeled. In severe cases, these symptoms were compounded by diarrhea, vomiting, bursting blood vessels, and fevers reaching as high as 106 degrees. (This led to delirium—"catching at imaginary objects in the air," as a medical treatise put it.)

Some men succumbed even before they had gone to sea. Cheap counted at least two hundred sick and more than twenty-five dead on the *Centurion* alone. He had brought his young nephew Henry to apprentice on the expedition... and what if he perished? Even Cheap, who was so indomitable, was suffering from what he called a "very indifferent state of health."

It was a devastating epidemic of "ship's fever," now known as typhus. No one then understood that the disease was a bacterial infection, transmitted by lice and other vermin. As boats transported unwashed recruits crammed together in filth, the men became lethal vectors, more deadly than a cascade of cannonballs.

Anson instructed Cheap to have the sick rushed to a makeshift hospital in Gosport, near Portsmouth, in the hope that they would recover in time for the voyage. The squadron still desperately needed men. But as the hospital became overcrowded, most of the sick had to be lodged in surrounding taverns, which offered more liquor than medicine, and where three patients sometimes had to squeeze into a single cot. An admiral noted, "In this miserable way, they die very fast."

After peaceful efforts to man the fleets failed, the Navy resorted to what a secretary of the Admiralty called a "more violent" strategy. Armed gangs were dispatched to press seafaring men into service—in effect, kidnapping them. The gangs roamed cities and towns, grabbing anyone who betrayed the telltale signs of a mariner: the familiar checkered shirt and wide-kneed trousers and round hat; the fingers smeared with tar, which was used to make virtually everything on a ship more water-resistant and durable. (Seamen were known as tars.) Local authorities were ordered to "seize all straggling seamen, watermen, bargemen, fishermen and lightermen."

A seaman later described walking in London and having a stranger tap him on the shoulder and demand, "What ship?" The seaman denied that he was a sailor, but his tar-stained fingertips betrayed him. The stranger blew his whistle; in an instant a posse appeared. "I was in the hands of six or eight ruffians whom I soon found to be a press gang," the seaman wrote. "They dragged me hurriedly through several streets, amid bitter execrations bestowed on them from passers-by and expressions of sympathy directed towards me."

Press gangs headed out in boats as well, scouring the horizon for incoming merchant ships—the most fertile hunting ground. Often, men seized were returning from distant voyages and hadn't seen their families for years; given the risks of a subsequent long voyage during war, they might never see them again.

Cheap became close to a young midshipman on the *Centurion* named John Campbell, who had been pressed while serving on a merchant ship. A gang had invaded his vessel, and when he saw them hauling away an older man in tears he stepped forward and offered himself up in his place. The head of the press gang remarked, "I would rather have a lad of spirit than a blubbering man."

Anson was said to have been so struck by Campbell's gallantry that he'd made him a midshipman. Most sailors, though, went to extraordinary lengths to evade the "body snatchers"—hiding in cramped holds, listing themselves as dead in muster books, and abandoning merchant ships before reaching a major port. When a press gang surrounded a church in London, in 1755, in pursuit of a seaman inside, he managed, according to a newspaper report, to slip away disguised in "an old gentlewoman's long cloak, hood and bonnet."

Sailors who got snatched up were transported in the holds of small ships known as tenders, which resembled floating jails, with gratings bolted over the hatchways and marines standing guard with muskets and bayonets. "In this place we spent the day and following night huddled together, for there was not room to sit or stand separate," one seaman recalled. "Indeed, we were in a pitiable plight, for numbers of them were sea-sick, some retching, others were smoking, whilst many were so overcome by the stench, that they fainted for want of air."

Family members, upon learning that a relative—a son, or a brother, or a husband, or a father—had been apprehended, would often rush to where the tenders were departing, hoping to glimpse their loved ones. Samuel Pepys describes, in his diary, a scene of pressed sailors' wives gathered on a wharf near the Tower of London: "In my life, I never did see such a natural expression of passion as I did here in some women's bewailing themselves, and running to every parcel of men that were brought, one after another, to look for their husbands, and wept over every vessel that went off, thinking they might be there, and looking after the ship as far as ever they could by moon-light, that it grieved me to the heart to hear them."

Anson's squadron received scores of pressed men. Cheap processed at least sixty-five for the *Centurion*; however distasteful he might have found the press, he needed every sailor he could get. Yet the unwilling recruits deserted at the first opportunity, as did volunteers who were having misgivings. In a single day, thirty men vanished from the *Severn*. Of the sick men sent to Gosport, countless took advantage of the lax security to flee—or, as one admiral put it, "go off as soon as they can crawl." Altogether, more than 240 men absconded from the squadron, including the *Gloucester*'s chaplain. When Captain Kidd dispatched a press gang to find new recruits for the *Wager*, six members of the gang itself deserted.

Anson ordered the squadron to moor far enough outside Portsmouth harbor that swimming to freedom was impossible—a frequent tactic that led one trapped seaman to write his wife: "I would give all I had if it was a hundred guineas if I could get on shore. I only lays on the deck every night... There is no hopes of my getting to you... do the best you can for the children and God prosper you and them till I come back."

Cheap, who believed that a good sailor must possess "honour, courage... steadiness," was undoubtedly appalled by the quality of the recruits who lingered. It was common for local authorities, knowing the unpopularity of the press, to dump their undesirables. But these conscripts were wretched, and the volunteers were little better. An admiral described one bunch of recruits as being "full of the pox, itch, lame, King's evil, and all other distempers, from the hospitals at London, and will serve only to breed an infection in the ships; for the rest, most of them are thieves, house breakers, Newgate [Prison] birds, and the very filth of London." He concluded, "In all the former wars I never saw a parcel of turned over men half so bad, in short they are so very bad, that I don't know how to describe it."

To at least partly address the shortage of men, the government sent to Anson's squadron 143 marines, who in those days were a branch of the Army, with their own officers. The marines were supposed to help with land invasions and also lend a hand at sea. Yet they were such raw recruits that they had never set foot on a ship and didn't even know how to fire a weapon. The Admiralty admitted that they were "useless." In desperation, the Navy took the extreme step of rounding up for Anson's squadron five hundred invalid soldiers from the Royal Hospital, in Chelsea, a pensioner's home established in the seventeenth century for veterans who were "old, lame, or infirm in ye service of the Crowne." Many were in their sixties and seventies, and they were rheumatic, hard of hearing, partially blind, suffering from convulsions, or missing an assortment of limbs. Given their ages and debilities, these soldiers had been deemed unfit for active service. Reverend Walter described them as the "most decrepit and miserable objects that could be collected."

As these invalids made their way to Portsmouth, nearly half slipped away, including one who hobbled off on a wooden leg. "All those who had limbs and strength to walk out of Portsmouth deserted," Reverend Walter noted. Anson pleaded with the Admiralty to replace what his chaplain called "this aged and diseased detachment." No recruits were available, though, and after Anson dismissed some of the most infirm men, his superiors ordered them back onboard.

Cheap watched the incoming invalids, many of them so weak they had to be lifted onto the ships on stretchers. Their panicked faces betrayed what everyone secretly knew: they were sailing to their deaths. As Reverend Walter acknowledged, "They would in all probability uselessly perish by lingering and painful diseases; and this, too, after they had spent the activity and strength of their youth in their country's service."

On August 23, 1740, after nearly a year of delays, the battle before the battle was over with "everything being in readiness to proceed on the voyage," as an officer of the *Centurion* wrote in his journal. Anson ordered Cheap to fire one of the guns. It was the signal for the squadron to unmoor, and at the sound of the blast the entire force—the five men-of-war and an eighty-four-foot scouting sloop, the *Trial*, as well as two small cargo ships, the *Anna* and the *Indus-*

try, which would accompany them partway—stirred to life. Officers emerged from quarters; boatswains piped their whistles and cried "All hands! All hands!"; crewmen raced about extinguishing candles, lashing hammocks, and loosening sails. Everything around Cheap—Anson's eyes and ears—seemed to be in motion, and then the ships began to move, too. Farewell to the debt collectors, the invidious bureaucrats, the endless frustrations. Farewell to all of it.

As the convoy made its way down the English Channel toward the Atlantic, it was surrounded by other departing ships, jockeying for wind and space. Several vessels collided, terrifying the uninitiated landsmen onboard. And then the wind, as fickle as the gods, abruptly shifted in front of them. Anson's squadron, unable to bear that close to the wind, was forced to return to its starting point. Twice more it embarked, only to retreat. On September 5, the London *Daily Post* reported that the fleet was still "waiting for a favourable wind." After all the trials and tribulations—Cheap's trials and tribulations—they seemed condemned to remain in this place.

Yet on September 18, as the sun was going down, the seamen caught a propitious breeze. Even some of the recalcitrant recruits were relieved to be finally underway. At least they would have tasks to distract them, and now they could pursue that serpentine temptation: the galleon. "The men were elevated with hopes of growing immensely rich," a seaman on the *Wager* wrote in his journal, "and in a few years of returning to Old England loaded with the wealth of their enemies."

Cheap assumed his commanding perch on the quarterdeck—an elevated platform by the stern that served as the officers' bridge and that housed the steering wheel and a compass. He inhaled the salted air and listened to the splendid symphony around him: the rocking of the hull, the snapping of the halyards, the splashing of waves against the prow. The ships glided in elegant formation, with the *Centurion* leading the way, her sails spread like wings.

After a while, Anson ordered a red pendant, signifying his rank as commodore of the fleet, to be hoisted on the *Centurion*'s mainmast.

The other captains fired their guns thirteen times each in salute—a thunderous clapping, a trail of smoke fading in the sky. The ships emerged from the Channel, born into the world anew, and Cheap, ever vigilant, saw the shore receding until, at last, he was surrounded by the deep blue sea.

CHAPTER 2

A Gentleman Volunteer

JOHN BYRON WAS AWAKENED by the maniacal cries of the *Wager*'s boatswain and his mates summoning the morning watch: "Rouse out, you sleepers! Rouse out!" It was not quite four a.m., and still dark out, though from his berth in the bowels of the ship Byron couldn't discern whether it was day or night. As a midshipman on the *Wager*—he was only sixteen—he was given a spot below the quarterdeck, below the upper deck, and even below the lower deck, where the ordinary sailors slept in hammocks, their bodies dangling from the beams. Byron was stuck down in the aft part of the orlop deck—a damp, airless hole devoid of natural light. The only place beneath it was the ship's hold, where dirty bilge water pooled, its foul scent harassing Byron, who slept just above it.

The *Wager* and the rest of the squadron had been at sea for barely two weeks, and Byron was still acclimating to his environs. The height of the orlop deck was under five feet, and if he didn't duck while standing he would smack his head. He shared this oaken vault with the other young midshipmen. They were each allowed a space no wider than twenty-one inches in which to sling their hammocks, and at times their elbows and knees jostled with the sleepers beside them; this was still a glorious seven inches more room than was allotted to ordinary seamen—though less than what officers had in their private berths, especially the captain, whose great cabin off the quarterdeck included a sleeping chamber, dining area, and a balcony overlooking the sea. As on land, there was a premium on real estate, and where you lay your head marked your place in the pecking order.

The oaken vault contained the few items that Byron and his companions had been able to cram into their sea chests, wooden trunks that held all their possessions for the voyage. Onboard, these boxes doubled as chairs, card tables, and desks. A novelist depicted one eighteenth-century midshipman's berth as being cluttered with heaps of soiled clothing and "plates, glasses, books, cocked hats, dirty stockings, tooth-combs, a litter of white mice and a caged parrot." The totem of any midshipman's quarters, though, was a wooden table long enough for a body to lie on. This was for amputating limbs. The berth served double duty as the surgeon's operating room, and the table was a reminder of the dangers that lay ahead: once the *Wager* was in battle, Byron's home would be filled with bone saws and blood.

The boatswain and his mates, the town criers, continued bellowing and blowing their whistles. They moved through the decks, holding lanterns and leaning over slumbering seamen, shouting, "Out or down! Out or down!" Anyone who didn't rise would have his hammock cut free from the rope suspending it, sending his body crashing onto the deck. The *Wager*'s boatswain, a burly figure named John King, would not likely touch a midshipman. But Byron knew to stay clear of him. Boatswains, who were responsible for herding crews and administering punishments—including lashing the unruly with a bamboo cane—were notorious bruisers. Yet there was something especially unnerving about King. A crew member noted that King suffered from "so perverse and turbulent a temper," and was "so abusive in speech, that we could not bear with him."

Byron needed to rise quickly. There was no time to bathe, which was rarely done anyway, because of the limited supply of water; and he began to dress, overcoming whatever discomfort he felt baring himself before strangers and living amid such squalor. He came from one of the oldest lines in England—his ancestry could be traced to the Norman Conquest—and he had been born into nobility on both sides of his family. His father, now deceased, had been the fourth

Lord Byron, and his mother was the daughter of a baron. His older brother, the fifth Lord Byron, was a peer in the House of Lords. And John, being the younger son of a nobleman, was, in the parlance of the day, an "honorable" gentleman.

How far the *Wager* seemed from Newstead Abbey, the Byron family estate, with its breathtaking castle, part of which had been built as a monastery in the twelfth century. The property, totaling three thousand acres, was surrounded by Sherwood Forest, the fabled haunt of Robin Hood. Byron's mother had etched his name and birthdate—November 8, 1723—on a window in the monastery. The *Wager*'s young midshipman was destined to become the grandfather of the poet Lord Byron, who frequently evoked Newstead Abbey in his Romantic verses. "The mansion's self was vast and venerable," he wrote, adding that it "left a grand impression on the mind, / At least of those whose eyes are in their hearts."

Two years before Anson launched his expedition, John Byron, then fourteen, had left the elite Westminster School and volunteered for the Navy. This was partly because his older brother, William, had inherited the family estate, along with the mania that infected so many Byrons—one that eventually caused him to squander the family fortune, reducing Newstead Abbey to ruins. ("The hall of my fathers, art gone to decay," the poet wrote.) William, who staged fake naval battles on a lake, and fatally stabbed a cousin in a sword duel, was nicknamed the Wicked Lord.

John Byron had been left with few means to earn a respectable living. He could enter the Church, as one of his younger brothers later did, but that was far too dull for his sensibilities. He could serve in the Army, which many gentlemen preferred, because they could frequently sit idly on a horse looking debonair. Then there was the Navy, in which you actually had to work and get your hands dirty.

Samuel Pepys had tried to encourage young noblemen and gentlemen to think of going to sea as "honourable service." In 1676, he established a new policy to make this path more attractive to privileged youths: if they apprenticed on a warship for at least six years, and passed an oral examination, they would be commissioned as an officer in His Majesty's Royal Navy. These volunteers, who often began as either a captain's servant or what was known as a King's Letter boy, were eventually rated as midshipmen, which gave them an ambiguous status on a man-of-war. Forced to toil like ordinary seamen so they could "learn the ropes," they were also recognized as officers-in-training, future lieutenants and captains, possibly even admirals, and were allowed to walk the quarterdeck. Despite these enticements, a naval career was considered somewhat unseemly for a person of Byron's pedigree—a "perversion," as Samuel Johnson, who knew Byron's family, called it. Yet Byron was enraptured by the mystique of the sea. He was fascinated by books about sailors, like Sir Francis Drake, so much so that he brought them onboard the *Wager*—the stories of maritime exploits stashed in his sea chest.

Yet, even for young nobles drawn to a life at sea, their sudden change in circumstances could be shocking. "Ye gods, what a difference!" one such midshipman recalled. "I had anticipated a kind of elegant house with guns in the windows; an orderly set of men; in short, I expected to find a species of Grosvenor Place, floating around like Noah's ark." Instead, he noted, the deck was "dirty, slippery and wet; the smells abominable; the whole sight disgusting; and when I remarked the slovenly attire of the midshipmen, dressed in shabby round jackets, glazed hats, no gloves, and some without shoes, I forgot all the glory... and, for nearly the first time in my life, and I wish I could say it was the last, took the handkerchief from my pocket, covered my face, and cried like the child I was."

Though poor and pressed sailors were given a basic set of clothing, known as "slops," to avoid what was deemed "unwholesome ill smells" and "nasty beastliness," the Navy had yet to institute official uniforms. Although most men of Byron's station could afford a flourish of lace and silk, their outfits generally had to conform to the demands of shipboard life: a hat, to shield them from the sun; a jacket (usually blue), to stay warm; a neckerchief, to mop the brow; and trousers—that curious fashion started by sailors. These pants, like his jacket, were cut short to keep them from getting caught in the ropes, and during foul weather they were coated with protective sticky tar. Even in these humble garments, Byron cut a striking figure, with pale, luminous skin; large, curious brown eyes; and ringlets of hair. One observer later described him as irresistibly handsome—"the champion of his form."

He took down his hammock and rolled it up for the day, along with his bedding. Then he hurriedly climbed a series of ladders between decks, making sure not to get lost in the interior wilderness of the ship. At last, he emerged, like a blackened miner, through a hatch onto the quarterdeck, sucking in the fresh air.

Most of the ship's company, including Byron, had been divided into two alternating watch parties—about a hundred people in each—and while he and his group worked topside, those previously on duty were resting, wearily, below. In the darkness, Byron heard scampering footsteps and a babel of accents. There were men from all strata of society, from dandies to city paupers, who had to have their wages garnished to pay the purser, Thomas Harvey, for their slops and eating utensils. In addition to the professional naval craftsmen—the carpenters and the coopers and the sailmakers—there were people from a dizzying array of vocations.

At least one member of the crew, John Duck, was a free Black seaman from London. The British Navy protected the slave trade, but captains in need of skilled sailors often enlisted free Black men. Although the society on a ship was not always as rigidly segregated as its counterpart on land, there was widespread discrimination. And Duck, who didn't leave behind any written records, faced a threat that no white seaman did: if captured overseas, he might be sold into slavery.

Onboard were also dozens of boys—some, perhaps, as young as six—training to become ordinary seamen or officers. And there were wizened old men: the cook, Thomas Maclean, was in his eighties. Several crew members were married with children; Thomas Clark, the ship's master and chief navigator, had even brought his young son with him on the voyage. As one seaman observed, "A man-of-war may justly be styled an epitome of the world, in which there is a sample of every character, some good men as well as bad." Among the latter, he noted, were "highwaymen, burglars, pickpockets, debauchees, adulterers, gamesters, lampooners, bastard-getters, imposters, panders, parasites, ruffians, hypocrites, threadworn beaux jack-a-dandies."

The British Navy was known for its ability to coalesce fractious individuals into what Vice-Admiral Horatio Nelson called a "band of Brothers." But the *Wager* had an unusual number of unwilling and troublesome crewmen, including the carpenter's mate James Mitchell. He frightened Byron even more than the boatswain, King; he seemed to burn with murderous rage. Byron could not yet know for certain the true nature lurking inside his fellow seamen or even himself: a long, dangerous voyage inexorably exposed one's hidden soul.

Byron assumed his position on the quarterdeck. Those on watch did more than keep lookout: they had a hand in managing the complex ship, a leviathan that never slept and was constantly in motion. As a midshipman, Byron was expected to help with everything from trimming the sails to carrying officers' messages. He quickly discovered that each person had his own distinct station—one that designated not only where he worked on the ship but also where he stood in its hierarchy. Captain Kidd, who presided from the quarterdeck, was at the pinnacle of this structure. At sea, beyond the reach of any government, he had enormous authority. "The captain had to be father and confessor, judge and jury, to his men," one historian wrote. "He had more power over them than the King—for the King could not order a man to be flogged. He could and did order them into battle and thus had the power of life and death over everyone on board."

The lieutenant, Robert Baynes, was second-in-command on the *Wager.* About forty years old, he'd served in the Navy for nearly a decade and presented certifications from two former captains attesting to his abilities. Yet many of the crew found him maddeningly indecisive. Though he came from a notable family—his grandfather Adam Baynes had been a member of Parliament—they repeatedly referred to him as Beans, which, whether intentional or not, seemed apropos. He and other ranking officers on duty supervised the watch and made sure that the captain's orders were being followed. As navigators, Master Clark and his mates plotted the ship's course and instructed the quartermaster on the proper heading; the quartermaster, in turn, directed the two helmsmen who gripped the double wheel and steered.

The nonseamen who specialized in trades formed their own social unit—the sailmaker mending canvases, the armorer sharpening swords, the carpenter repairing masts and plugging dangerous leaks in the hull, the surgeon attending to the sick. (His helpers were known as loblolly boys, for the porridge they served.)

The seamen, too, were separated into divisions that reflected their abilities. The topmen, who were young and agile and admired for their fearlessness, scurried up the masts to unfurl and roll up sails, and to keep lookout, hovering in the sky like birds of prey. Then came those assigned to the forecastle, a partial deck toward the bow, where they controlled the headsails and also heaved and dropped the anchors, the largest of which weighed about two tons. The forecastle men tended to be the most experienced, their bodies bearing the stigmata of years at sea: crooked fingers, leathery skin, lash scars. On the bottom rung, situated on deck alongside the squawking, defecating livestock, were the "waisters"—pitiful landlubbers with no sea experience who were relegated to unskilled drudgery.

Finally, in their own special category, were the marines: soldiers detached from the Army who were equally pathetic landlubbers. While at sea, they were governed by naval authority and had to obey the *Wager*'s captain, but they were commanded by two Army officers: a sphinxlike captain named Robert Pemberton and his hot-headed lieutenant, Thomas Hamilton. Hamilton had originally been assigned to the *Centurion*, but he was relocated after he got in a knife fight with another marine and threatened to duel him to the death. On the *Wager*, the marines mostly helped with heaving and hauling. And if there was ever an insurrection onboard, the captain would order them to suppress it.

For the ship to thrive, each of these elements needed to be integrated into one crisp organization. Inefficiency, missteps, stupidity, drunkenness—any could lead to disaster. One sailor described a man-of-war as a "set of *human* machinery, in which every man is a wheel, a band, or a crank, all moving with wonderful regularity and precision to the *will* of its machinist—the all-powerful captain."

In the morning hours, Byron would observe these components busily at work. He was still learning the art of seamanship, being initiated into a mysterious civilization so strange that it seemed to one boy as if he were "always asleep or in a dream." Moreover, Byron, as a gentleman and a future officer, was expected to learn how to draw, fence, and dance—and to at least feign some understanding of Latin.

One British captain recommended that a young officer in training bring onboard a small library with the classics by Virgil and Ovid and poems by Swift and Milton. "It is a mistaken notion that any blockhead will make a seaman," the captain explained. "I don't know one situation in life that requires so accomplished an education as the sea officer.... He should be a man of letters and languages, a mathematician, and an accomplished gentleman."

Byron also needed to learn how to steer and splice and brace and tack, how to read the stars and the tides, how to use a quadrant to fix his position, and how to measure the ship's speed by casting a line ribbed with evenly spaced knots into the water and then counting the number that slipped through his hands over a period of time. (One knot equaled a little more than a land mile per hour.)

He had to decipher a new, mystifying language, cracking a secret code—or he would be ridiculed as a landlubber. When he was ordered to pull sheets, he'd better seize the ropes instead of his bedding. He must not speak of the privy but, rather, the head—essentially a hole on the deck through which the waste plunged into the ocean. And God forbid he should say he was *on* a ship rather than in one. Byron himself was baptized with a new name. The men began to call him Jack. John Byron had become Jack Tar.

During the age of sail, when wind-powered vessels were the only bridge across the vast oceans, nautical language was so pervasive that it was adopted by those on terra firma. To "toe the line" derives from when boys on a ship were forced to stand still for inspection with their toes on a deck seam. To "pipe down" was the boatswain's whistle for everyone to be quiet at night, and "piping hot" was his call for meals. A "scuttlebutt" was a water cask around which the seamen gossiped while waiting for their rations. A ship was "three sheets to the wind" when the lines to the sails broke and the vessel pitched drunkenly out of control. To "turn a blind eye" became a popular expression after Vice-Admiral Nelson deliberately placed his telescope against his blind eye to ignore his superior's signal flag to retreat.

Not only did Byron have to learn to talk like a sailor—and curse like one—but also to endure a punishing regimen. His day was governed by the sound of bells, which measured each passing half hour during a four-hour watch. (A half hour was calculated by the emptying of a sandglass.) Day after day, night after night, he heard the bells tolling and scrambled to his station on the quarterdeck—his body shivering, his hands calloused, his eyes bleary. And if he violated the rules, he might be tied to the rigging or, worse, flogged with the cat-o'-nine-tails—a whip with nine long lashes that cut into the skin.

Byron was also learning the pleasures of life at sea. During mealtimes, the food—consisting largely of salted beef and pork, dried peas, oatmeal, and biscuits—was surprisingly plentiful, and he enjoyed dining in his berth with his fellow midshipmen, Isaac Morris and Henry Cozens. Meanwhile, seamen gathered on the gun deck, unhooking wooden planks that hung down from ropes from the ceiling to form tables, and sitting in groups of eight or so. Because the sailors chose their own messmates, these units were like families, and members would reminisce and confide in one another as they relished their daily ration of beer or spirits. Byron was beginning to form those deep friendships that emerged from being in such tight quarters, and he grew especially close to his messmate Cozens. "I never knew a better natured man," Byron wrote—"when sober."

There were other moments of merriment, especially on Sundays, when an officer might yell, "All hands to play!" A ship of war would then transform into a recreational park, with men playing backgammon and boys skylarking in the rigging. Anson liked to gamble and earned a reputation as a crafty card player, his blank eyes masking his intentions. The commodore was also passionately fond of music, and every muster had at least a fiddler or two, and sailors would do jigs and reels across the deck. One popular song was about the War of Jenkins' Ear:

They cut off his ears and slit his nose . . .
Then with a jeer, they gave him his ear,
Saying "Take it to your master" in disdain.
But our King I can tell, loves his subjects so well,
That he'll curb the haughty pride of Spain.

Perhaps Byron's fondest diversion was sitting on the *Wager*'s deck and listening to the old salts tell tales about the sea—tales of lost loves and near-wrecks and glorious battles. These stories pulsed with life, the life of the teller, the life that had escaped death before and might escape it again.

Swept up in the romance of it all, Byron began what would become a habit of excitedly filling his journals with his own observations. Everything seemed "the most surprising" or "astonishing." He noted unfamiliar creatures, such as an exotic bird—"the most surprising one I ever saw"—with a head like an eagle and feathers that were "as black as jet and shined like the finest silk."

One day Byron heard that petrifying order eventually given to every midshipman: "Aloft you go!" Having trained on the smaller mizzenmast, he now had to clamber up the mainmast, the tallest of the three, which rose some hundred feet into the sky. A plunge from such a height would undoubtedly kill him, as it had another seaman on the *Wager.* A British captain recalled that once when two of his finest boys were climbing, one lost his grip and hit the other, sending them both plummeting: "They struck with their heads upon the muzzles of the guns.... I was walking the quarter-deck and presented with this most horrid spectacle. It is impossible to tell you what I feel on the occasion, or even to describe the general grief of the ship's company."

Byron had an artistic sensibility (a friend said that he was drawn to connoisseurs), and he was sensitive about seeming like a delicate fop. Once, he told a member of the crew, "I can bear hardships as well as the best of you, and must use myself to them." Now he began his ascent. It was critical for him to climb on the windward side of the mast, so that when the ship heeled his body would at least be pressed against the ropes. He slipped over a rail and placed his feet on some ratlines—small horizontal ropes that were fastened to the shrouds, the near-vertical ropes holding up the mast. Using this mesh of rope as a wobbly ladder, Byron hoisted himself upward. He went up ten feet, then fifteen, then twenty-five. With each roll of the sea, the mast swayed back and forth, while the ropes trembled in his hands. About a third of the way up, he came abreast of the main yard, the wooden spar that extended from the mast like the arms of a cross, and from which the mainsail unfurled. It was also where, on the foremast, a condemned mutineer got hanged from a rope—or, as the saying went, took "a walk up Ladder Lane, and down Hemp Street."

Not far above the mainyard was the maintop—a small platform used for lookouts, where Byron could rest. The simplest and safest way to get there was to slip through a hole in the middle of the platform. Yet this so-called lubber hole was considered strictly for cowards. Unless Byron wanted to be ridiculed for the rest of the voyage (and would it not be better to plunge to his death?), he had to go around the rim of the platform by holding on to cables known as futtock shrouds. These cables were slanted on an angle, and as he shinnied along them his body would tilt farther and farther until his back was nearly parallel to the deck. Without panicking, he had to feel with his foot for a ratline and pull himself onto the platform.

When he stood on the maintop, he had little time to celebrate. The mast was not a single long wooden pole; rather, it consisted of three great "sticks" stacked on top of one another. And Byron had ascended only the first section. As he continued upward, the shroud ropes converged, the gaps between them growing narrower and narrower. An inexperienced climber would fumble to find a perch for his feet, and at this height there was no longer any space between the horizontal ratlines to wrap his arm around for a rest. With the wind buffeting him, Byron went past the main-topmast yard, from which the second large canvas sail was fastened, and past the crosstrees—wooden struts where a lookout could sit and get a clearer view. He kept ascending, and the higher he went, the more he felt the mast, and his body, lurching from side to side, as if he were clinging to the tip of a giant pendulum. The shrouds he gripped shook violently. These ropes were coated in tar against the elements, and the boatswain was responsible for making sure that they remained in good condition. Byron confronted an inescapable truth of the wooden world: each man's life depended on the performance of the others.

They were akin to the cells in a human body; a single malignant one could destroy them all.

At last, nearly a hundred feet above the water, Byron reached the main topgallant yard, where the highest sail on the mast was set. A line was attached to the base of the yard, and he had to shuffle along it, while leaning his chest over the yard to balance himself. Then he awaited his orders: to furl the sail or reef it—roll it up partly to reduce the amount of canvas spread in heavy winds. Herman Melville, who served on a US warship in the 1840s, wrote in *Redburn,* "The first time we reefed top-sails of a dark night, and I found myself hanging over the yard with eleven others, the ship plunging and rearing like a mad horse.... But a few repetitions, soon made me used to it." He continued, "It is surprising, how soon a boy overcomes his timidity about going aloft. For my own part, my nerves became as steady as the earth's diameter.... I took great delight in furling the top-gallant sails and royals in a hard blow, which duty required two hands on the yard. There was a wild delirium about it, a fine rushing of the blood about the heart; and a glad, thrilling, and throbbing of the whole system, to find yourself tossed up at every pitch into the clouds of a stormy sky, and hovering like a judgment angel between heaven and earth."

As Byron now stood at the peak, high above all the strife on the decks below, he could see the other great ships in the squadron. And beyond them the sea—a blank expanse on which he was ready to write his own story.

At five in the morning on October 25, 1740, thirty-seven days after the squadron's departure from England, a lookout on the *Severn* spotted something in the emerging light. After the crew flashed lanterns and fired several guns to alert the rest of the squadron, Byron saw it, too—a jagged outline on the rim of the sea. "Land ahoy!" It was Madeira, an island off the northwest coast of Africa that was known for its perennial spring climate and superb wine, wine that seemed, as Reverend Walter noted, "designed by Providence for the refreshment of the inhabitants of the torrid zone."

The squadron anchored in a bay on the eastern side of the island—the expedition's last stop before the nearly five-thousand-mile crossing of the Atlantic to the southern Brazilian coast. Anson ordered the crews to quickly replenish their water and wood, and to load up on copious amounts of the prized wine. He was eager to move on. He had wanted to complete the passage to Madeira in no more than two weeks, but because of contrary winds it had taken three times that. Any lingering hopes of circling South America during the austral summer seemed to evaporate. "The difficulties and dangers of the passage round Cape Horn in the winter season filled our imaginations," Reverend Walter confessed.

Before they weighed anchor, on November 3, two events sent further shudders throughout the fleet. First, Richard Norris, the captain of the *Gloucester* and the son of Admiral John Norris, abruptly asked to resign his post. "Having been extremely ill ever since I left England," he wrote in a message to Anson, "I am apprehensive my constitution will not permit me to proceed upon so long a voyage." The commodore granted his request, though he despised any lack of valor—so much so that he later persuaded the Navy to add a regulation specifying that any person found guilty of "Cowardice, Negligence or Disaffection" during battle "shall suffer Death." Even Reverend Walter, whom a colleague described as "rather a puny, weakly, and sickly man," said of fear, "Fye upon it! It is an ignoble passion, and beneath the dignity of man!" Walter noted starkly that Norris "quit" his command. Later in the war, when Richard Norris was captaining another ship, he would be accused of betraying the "greatest signs of fear" by retreating in battle, and ordered to face a court-martial. In a letter to the Admiralty, he insisted that he welcomed the opportunity to "remove that infamy which malice and falsehood have thrown upon me." But before the hearing he deserted and was not heard from again.

Norris's departure initiated a cascade of promotions among the commanding officers. The captain of the *Pearl* was appointed to the *Gloucester*, a more powerful warship. The *Wager*'s captain, Dandy Kidd—whom another officer described as a "worthy and humane commander, and universally respected onboard his ship"—moved to the *Pearl*. Taking his place on the *Wager* was George Murray, a nobleman's son who had been in charge of the *Trial* sloop.

The *Trial* was the one ship with an empty commanding-officer's chair. There were no more captains for Anson to choose from, and a fierce competition broke out among the junior officers. A naval surgeon once compared the jealous rivalries on ships to palace intrigue, where everyone is "courting the favour of a despot, and trying to undermine his rivals." Ultimately, Anson chose his dogged first lieutenant, David Cheap.

Cheap's luck had turned, turned at last. The eight-gun *Trial* was no man-of-war, yet it was a ship of his own. In the *Trial*'s muster book, his name was now enshrined as Captain David Cheap.

Different captains meant different rules, and Byron would have to adjust to his new commander on the *Wager*. Moreover, because of the shifts, a stranger was now invading Byron's jammed sleeping quarters. He introduced himself as Alexander Campbell. Only about fifteen, and speaking with a thick Scottish accent, he was a midshipman whom Murray had brought from the *Trial*. Unlike the other midshipmen with whom Byron had become friends, Campbell seemed haughty and mercurial. Lording his status as a future officer over ordinary seamen, he came off as a petty tyrant who went about ruthlessly enforcing the captain's orders, sometimes with his fists.

While the shakeup of commanders unsettled Byron and the other men, a second development was even more worrisome. The governor of Madeira informed Anson that lurking off the western coast of the island was a Spanish armada of at least five massive warships, including a sixty-six-gun man-of-war with some seven hundred combatants, a fifty-four-gunner with five hundred men, and a vessel with a whopping seventy-four cannons and seven hundred fighters. Word of Anson's mission had leaked out—a breach that was later confirmed when a British captain in the Caribbean seized a ship with Spanish documents detailing all the "intelligence" that had been gathered on Anson's expedition. The enemy knew everything and had dispatched the armada led by Pizarro. Reverend Walter noted that this force was "intended to put a stop to our expedition," adding, "In strength they were greatly superior."

The squadron waited until dark to slip away from Madeira, and Byron and his companions were ordered to extinguish lanterns onboard, to prevent detection. No longer were they prowling the sea in secret. They were themselves being hunted.

CHAPTER 3

The Gunner

ONE OF THE MARINES on the *Wager* pounded a drum, the ominous "beating to quarters," and the men and boys, whether half asleep or half clothed, rushed through the darkness to their battle stations. They cleared the decks of loose items—anything that could splinter into lethal shards during an attack. A fourteen-year-old boy who served on a British man-of-war recalled that he had "never seen a man killed before"—until, during a skirmish, a splinter struck a companion in the "crown of the head, and when he fell the blood and brains came out, flowing over the deck." The prospect of the wooden world turning into flames was an even graver threat. The men on the *Wager* filled buckets with water and readied the ship's great guns, those two-ton iron beasts with snouts extending eight feet or more. A single cannon required a crew of at least six people to unleash its destructive force.

Each team member moved according to his own hidden design. The "powder monkey," culled from the ranks of the boys, hurried across the gun deck to retrieve a cartridge that was being passed up from the subterraneous magazine room, where all the explosive materials were stored under lock and key. Marines stood guard. No burning candles were allowed inside.

The boy collected the cartridge, which held several pounds of powder, and then scurried to his appointed gun, careful not to stumble on the tangle of men and machinery and spark an explosive fire. Another member of his team took the cartridge and shoved it down the muzzle. Then a loader thrust inside an eighteen-pound cast-iron ball, followed by a wad of rope to hold it in place. Each gun was mounted on a carriage with four wooden wheels, and the men, using tackles and blocks and dense cables, heaved the weapon forward until the muzzle protruded from a porthole. One after another, on both sides of the ship, the guns emerged.

Trimmers and topmen, meanwhile, tended to the sails. Unlike on a battlefield, there was no fixed position at sea: a ship was always shifting with the wind and the waves and the currents. A captain had to adjust to these unpredictable forces as well as to the movements of a cunning adversary, and all this required enormous tactical skills—the skills of an artilleryman and a seaman. In the fury of combat, with cannonballs and grapeshot and musket shot and two-foot-long splinters flying in all directions, the captain might need to hoist extra sails or lower them, to tack or jibe, to give chase or flee. And he might have to ram his prow over an enemy ship, so that his men could storm it with boarding axes and cutlasses and swords, as gunplay gave way to hand-to-hand combat.

The men on the *Wager* worked in silence so that they could hear the orders being barked out: "Prick the cartridge.... Point the gun.... Take your match.... Fire!"

The head of the team, who was also the matchman, stabbed a slow-burning wick into a touchhole at the closed end of the gun, and then jumped out of the way with the rest of the crew as the flash ignited the cartridge and the shot exploded with such force that the cannon reared violently backward, until the breeching rope restrained it. If a man did not move in time, he'd be crushed. All through the ship the great guns were blazing, the eighteen-pound balls whirring through the air at about 1,200 feet per second, the smoke blinding, the roar deafening, and the decks shuddering as if the sea were boiling.

Standing amid the heat and light was the *Wager*'s gunner, John Bulkeley. He was among the few in the ship's ragtag company who seemed ready for a potential attack. But the call to arms turned out to be only a drill—Commodore Anson, after the recent intelligence about the lurking Spanish armada, had grown ever more fanatical about preparing everyone for battle.

Bulkeley performed his tasks with the ruthless efficiency of one of his cold black guns. He was a true seaman, having served more than a decade in the Navy. He'd begun his career doing dirty chores, dipping his hands in the tar bucket and pumping the bilge, learning with the downtrodden to "laugh at vindictive malice," in the words of one seaman, "hate oppression, support misfortune." He worked his way up from the lower deck until, a few years before Anson's voyage, he went before a board of experts and passed an oral examination to become a gunner.

Whereas the captain and the lieutenant received their commissions from the Crown and often changed ships after a voyage, the technical specialists, such as the gunner and the carpenter, were issued warrants from the Navy Board and were supposed to be permanently assigned to one vessel, making it more or less their home. They ranked below commissioned sea officers, but were, in many ways, the heart of a ship: a professional corps that kept it running smoothly. Bulkeley was responsible for all the *Wager*'s instruments of death. It was a crucial role, especially in times of conflict, and this was reflected in the Navy's regulations: there were more articles concerned with the duties of the gunner than with those of the master, or even the lieutenant. As one commander put it, "A gunner at sea ought to be skillful, careful, and courageous; for the strength of the ship is put into his hands." The *Wager* was transporting munitions for the entire squadron, and Bulkeley presided over a vast arsenal that included enough gunpowder to detonate a small town.

A devout Christian, he hoped one day to discover what he called the "Garden of the Lord." Although the *Wager* was supposed to hold Sunday religious services, Bulkeley complained that "prayer had been entirely neglected on board," and that in the Navy "devotion, in so solemn a manner, is so rarely performed that I know but one instance of it during the many years I have belonged." He had brought with him a book entitled *The Christian's Pattern: or, A Treatise of the Imitation of Jesus Christ,* and he seemed to approach the treacherous journey at least partly as a way of getting closer to himself and to God. Suffering can "make a man enter into himself," the book instructed, but in this world of temptation, "the life of man is a warfare upon earth."

Despite his beliefs, or perhaps because of them, Bulkeley had mastered the dark arts of gunnery, and was determined to make the *Wager,* to use one of his preferred phrases, "the terror of all her enemies." He knew the precise point on a cresting wave when a crew should unleash fire. He expertly mixed cartridges and packed grenades with corn powder, and when necessary, he pulled the fuses with his teeth. Most important, he fiercely guarded the munitions entrusted to him, knowing that if they fell into careless or mutinous hands, they could destroy a ship from within. A 1747 naval manual stressed that a gunner must be a "sober, careful, honest man," and it seemed to describe Bulkeley exactly when it noted that some of the best gunners had come from the "lowest station on board, raising themselves to preferment by pure dint of diligence and industry." Bulkeley was so skilled and trusted that, unlike most gunners on men-of-war, he was placed in charge of one of the *Wager*'s watch parties. In his journal, he wrote with a touch of pride, "Tho' I was gunner of the ship, I had the charge of a watch during the whole voyage."

Bulkeley seemed, as a naval officer noted, an instinctive leader. Yet he was stuck in his station. Unlike his new captain, George Murray, or the midshipman John Byron, he was no silk-stocking dandy. He didn't have a baron as a father, or some powerful patron greasing his path to the quarterdeck. He might outrank Byron—and might serve as his guide on the ways of a man-of-war—but he was still considered socially inferior to him. Though there were instances of gunners becoming lieutenants or captains, they were rare, and Bulkeley was too blunt, too certain of himself, to flatter his superiors, which he deemed a "degenerate" practice. As the historian N. A. M. Rodger observed, "In the time-honoured English fashion, the experts were kept in their place; it was the commissioned officers, educated only as seamen, who took command."

Bulkeley was no doubt physically imposing. He once fought with an associate of the *Wager*'s bullying boatswain, John King. "He compelled me to stand in my own defense, and I soon mastered him," Bulkeley wrote in his journal. Yet there is no record of what Bulkeley looked like, whether he was tall or short, bald or thick-haired, blue-eyed or dark-eyed. He couldn't afford to have the celebrated artist Joshua Reynolds paint a portrait of him posing in a regal naval costume and a powdered wig, the way Anson and Byron and the *Centurion*'s midshipman Augustus Keppel did. (Keppel's portrait, modeled on the classical image of Apollo, depicted him striding across a beach in front of a foaming sea.) Bulkeley's past, too, is largely obscure, as if dabbed in tar along with his calloused hands. In 1729, he married a woman named Mary Lowe. They had five children—the oldest, Sarah, was ten, and the youngest, George Thomas, was less than a year old. They lived in Portsmouth. That is about all we know of Bulkeley's early background. He emerges in our story like one of those settlers who arrives on the American frontier with no discernable history—a man to be reckoned with by his present deeds alone.

Yet we can glimpse some of his private thoughts, because he could write—and write well. He wasn't required, like more senior officers, to maintain a logbook, but he kept one for himself anyway. These volumes, written on thick sheets of paper with quills and ink—ink that sometimes smudged as the ship rocked or was sprayed with seawater—were formatted in columns, under which were noted, each day, the direction of the wind, the ship's location or bearing, and any "remarkable observations and accidents." The entries were supposed to be impersonal, as if the wild elements could be contained by codifying them. Daniel Defoe complained that sailors' logbooks were often no more than "tedious accounts of... how many leagues they sailed every day; where they had the winds, when it blew hard, and when softly." Nevertheless, these journals, mirroring a voyage, had an inherent narrative momentum, with a beginning, middle, and end, with unforeseen twists and turns. And some log keepers inserted personal notes. Bulkeley, in one of his journals, transcribed a verse from a poem:

> *Bold were the Men who on the Ocean first*
> *Spread the new Sails, when Ship wreck was the worst:*
> *More Dangers Now from MAN alone we find,*
> *Than from the Rocks, the Billows, and the Wind.*

After a voyage, the captain of a ship turned over the requisite logbooks to the Admiralty, providing reams of information for building an empire—an encyclopedia of the sea and of unfamiliar lands. Anson and his officers would frequently consult the journals of the few seamen who had ventured around Cape Horn.

Moreover, these "logbooks of memory," as one historian coined them, created a record of any controversial actions or mishaps that occurred during a voyage. If need be, they could be submitted as evidence at courts-martial; careers and lives might depend on them. A nineteenth-century treatise on practical seamanship advised that each logbook be "carefully kept, and all interlineations and erasures should be avoided, as they always raise suspicion." It went on, "The entries should be made as soon as possible after each event takes place, and nothing should be entered which the mate would not be willing to adhere to in a court of justice."

These logbooks were also becoming the basis of popular adventure tales for the public. Fueled by printing presses and growing literacy, and by a fascination with realms previously unknown to Europeans, there was an insatiable demand for the kind of yarns that seamen had long spun on the forecastle. In 1710, the Earl of Shaftesbury observed that tales of the sea were "in our present days what books of chivalry were in those of our forefathers." The books—which stoked the fervid imaginations of youths like Byron—typically resembled the chronological format of a log, but featured more personal reflection; individualism was creeping into them.

Bulkeley did not plan to publish his own journal—the authorship of this growing body of literature was still largely limited to commanding officers or to men of certain standing and class. But in contrast to the *Trial*'s purser, Lawrence Millechamp, who confessed in his journal how "unequal" he was to the task of "writing the following sheets," Bulkeley relished recording what he saw. It gave him a voice, even if no one but him would ever hear it.

One early morning in November, not long after Bulkeley and his companions had left Madeira, a lookout perched in the masthead spied a ship rising on the horizon. He sounded the alarm: "Sail ho!"

Anson made sure that all five of his men-of-war stayed close together, so they could quickly establish a line of battle—the ships spread out evenly, like an elongated chain, in order to consolidate their power and make it easier to assist any weakened link. This formation was the way two fleets usually squared off, but that would gradually change, culminating in 1805 when Vice-Admiral Horatio Nelson defied the rigid line of battle at Trafalgar to, as he put it, "surprise and confound the enemy" so "they won't know what I am about." Even in Anson's time, shrewd captains often concealed their intentions, using trickery and deception. A captain might creep up in the fog and steal his opponent's wind by blocking his sails. Or he might feign distress before springing an attack. Or pretend to be a friend, perhaps by beckoning in a foreign language, in order to get within point-blank range.

After Anson's lookout sighted the vessel, it was imperative to determine whether she was a friend or a foe. One seaman described the protocol that ensued when an alien ship was detected. The captain rushed forward and yelled to the lookout, "Masthead there!"

"Sir!"

"What does she look like?"

"A square-rigged vessel, sir."

The captain demanded silence fore and aft, and after a while he cried again, "Masthead there!"

"Sir!"

"What does she look like?"

"A large ship, sir, standing toward us."

The *Wager's* officers and crew strained to make out the ship, to discern her nationality and purpose. But she was too far away, no more than a menacing shadow. Anson signaled to Captain Cheap, newly enthroned on the quarterdeck of the speedy *Trial*, to give chase and gather more intelligence. Cheap and his men set off with their canvas spread. Bulkeley and the others waited and prepared the guns once more in nervous expectation—that constant stress of fighting a war on a vast ocean with limited means of surveillance and communication.

After two hours, Cheap bore down on the ship and fired a warning shot. She came about, allowing Cheap to approach. It turned out that she was merely a Dutch vessel bound for the East Indies. The men in the squadron returned to their watches—for the enemy, like the hidden power of the sea, might yet emerge on the horizon.

Not long after, there came an invisible siege. Though no guns were fired, many of Bulkeley's companions began to collapse, as though struck by some malignant force. Boys could no longer muster the energy to climb the masts. The pressed invalids suffered the most, writhing in their hammocks, feverish and sweating, vomiting into pails or on themselves. Some were delirious and had to be watched so that they didn't stumble into the sea. The bacterial bomb of typhus, planted in the ships before they set sail, was now erupting throughout the fleet. "Our men grew distempered and sickly," an officer observed, adding that the fever was "beginning to reign amongst us."

At least when the squadron was in England the infected could be brought ashore to be treated; now they were trapped on the over-crowded ships—social distancing, had they even understood the concept, was impossible—and their lice-speckled bodies pressed against unsuspecting new victims. The lice would crawl from one seaman to another, and though their bites weren't dangerous, the traces of feces they deposited in the resulting wound were laden with bacteria. When a seaman innocently scratched the bite—the louse's saliva made it itch—he became an unwitting participant in his own bodily invasion. The pathogens entered his bloodstream like a stealth boarding party, then spread the contagion from louse to louse and into the lifeblood of the squadron.

Bulkeley was uncertain how to protect himself—except to devote himself even more intensely to God. The *Wager*'s surgeon, Henry Ettrick, set up a sick bay on the lower deck, which had more room to sling hammocks than the operating area in the midshipmen's berth. (When ailing seamen were shielded belowdecks from the adverse elements outside, they were said to be "under the weather.") Ettrick was committed to his patients and a capable knifeman, able to amputate a limb in a few minutes. He'd designed what he called a "machine for reducing fractures of the thigh"—a fifteen-pound contraption with a wheel and pinion, which he promised would ensure a patient recovered without limping.

Despite such innovations, Ettrick and other doctors of his era had little scientific understanding of disease, and they had no idea how to stop a typhus outbreak. The *Centurion*'s schoolmaster, Pascoe Thomas, grumbled that Ettrick's theories of infection consisted of a vain "flow of words, with little or no meaning." Because the concept of germs had not yet emerged, surgical instruments were not sterilized, and paranoia over the source of the epidemic ate at sailors like the disease itself. Did typhus spread through the water or through dirt? Through a touch or a look? One prevailing medical theory held that certain stagnant environments, like those on a ship, emitted noxious smells that caused disease in humans. Something, it was believed, really was "in the air."

As members of Anson's squadron became sick, the officers and surgeons roamed the decks, sniffing out potential culprits: foul bilge, moldy sails, rancid meat, human sweat, rotten timber, dead rats, piss and excrement, unwashed livestock, dirty breath. The fetidness had unleashed a plague of bugs—one so biblical that it was unsafe, as Millechamp noted, "for a man to open his mouth for fear of having them fly down his throat." Some crew members carved wooden boards into makeshift fans. "These a certain number of men were employed to wave backwards and forwards, in order to agitate the infected air," an officer recalled.

Captain Murray and the other senior officers held an emergency conference with Anson. Bulkeley was not included—there were certain rooms where he wasn't allowed. He soon learned that the officers had debated how to let in more air belowdecks. Anson ordered the carpenters to cut six additional openings in the hull of each man-of-war, just above the waterline. Still, the plague accelerated, with scores more infected.

Ettrick and other doctors stationed in the sick bays grew overwhelmed. Tobias Smollett, whose picaresque novel *The Adventures of Roderick Random* drew on his experiences as a naval surgeon's mate during the war against Spain, wrote of an epidemic, "I was much less surprised that people should die on board than that any sick person should recover. Here I saw about fifty miserable distempered wretches, suspended in rows, so huddled upon another... and deprived of the light of the day, as well as the fresh air; breathing nothing but... their own excrements and diseased bodies." As a sick patient fought for his life on the lonely seas far from home, his mates might visit him, holding a lantern over his vacant eyes and trying to cheer him up—or perhaps, as a chaplain on a man-of-war described it, "dropping silent tears on him, or in the most heart-rending accents calling him."

One day on the *Wager*, several men emerged from the sick bay carrying a long, shrouded package. It was the dead body of one of their companions. According to tradition, a body to be buried at sea was wrapped in a hammock, along with at least one cannonball. (When the hammock was sewn together, the final thread was often stitched through the victim's nose, to ensure that he was dead.) The stiffening corpse was placed on a plank and a Union Jack was draped over it, making it seem less like a mummy. Any of the deceased's personal effects, his clothes, his trinkets, his sea chest, were collected for auction, to raise money for his widow or other family members; even the most hardened seamen often offered exorbitant bids. "Death is at all times solemn, but never so much so as at sea," one sailor recalled. "The man is near you—at your side—you hear his voice, and in an instant he is gone, and nothing but a vacancy shows his loss.... There is always an empty berth in the forecastle, and one man wanting when the small night watch is mustered. There is one less to take the wheel, and one less to lay out with you upon the yard. You miss his form, and the sound of his voice, for habit had made them almost necessary to you, and each of your senses feels the loss."

The *Wager*'s bell tolled, and Bulkeley, Byron, and the other men gathered on the deck and on the gangways and booms. The officers and crews of the other ships drew up nearby as well, forming a kind of funeral procession. The boatswain cried, "Off hats," and the mourners bared their heads. They prayed for the dead, and perhaps for themselves, too.

Captain Murray recited the words "We therefore commit his body to the deep." After the flag was removed, the plank was lifted up and the body slid over the railing. A splash broke the silence. Bulkeley and his mates watched their companion sinking under the weight of the cannonball until he vanished, on that last unknown voyage, into the depths of the ocean.

On November 16, the captains of the *Anna* and the *Industry*, the pair of cargo ships accompanying the squadron, informed Anson that they had fulfilled their contract with the Navy and wanted to return home—a desire no doubt heightened by the growing epidemic and the looming Cape Horn. Because the squadron lacked the space to store the two ships' remaining provisions, including tons of brandy, Anson decided to release only the *Industry,* which had not been very seaworthy.

Each man-of-war carried onboard at least four small transport crafts to ferry goods and people to shore or between ships. The largest was the longboat, at about thirty-six feet, and like the others it could be rowed or sailed. These little boats were kept strapped to a ship's deck, and to commence the hazardous process of transferring the *Industry*'s leftover supplies, Anson's men began lowering them into the turbulent sea. Meanwhile, many of the officers and crew hastily composed missives to be sent back to England on the *Industry.* It could be months, if not years, before they would have another chance to communicate with loved ones.

Bulkeley could let his wife and children know that, even though death had stalked the squadron across the sea, he remained miraculously healthy. If the surgeons were right, and the fever was caused by poisonous smells, why were some people on the ship affected and others untouched? Many of the devout believed that life-obliterating diseases were rooted in the fallen nature of humans—their idleness, their dissolution, their debauchery. The first medical textbook for sea surgeons, published in 1617, warned that plagues were God's way of cutting "sinners from off the Earth." Maybe Anson's seamen were being smitten like the Egyptians, and Bulkeley had been spared for some righteous purpose.

On the night of November 19, the transfer of the *Industry*'s cargo was complete. Bulkeley wrote succinctly, in his journal, "The *Industry* store-ship parted company." Unbeknownst to him and the other members of the squadron, she would soon be captured by the Spanish. Their letters would never arrive.

By December, more than sixty-five members of the squadron had been buried at sea. The disease, Reverend Walter reported, was "not only terrible in its first instance, but even the remains of it often proved fatal to those who considered themselves as recovered from it," for it "always left them in a very weak and helpless condition." Although the *Centurion*'s chief surgeon, the squadron's most experienced doctor, had only limited means at his disposal, he worked valiantly to save lives. Then, on December 10, he, too, succumbed.

The squadron sailed on. Bulkeley scoured the horizon for South America, for terra firma. Yet there was nothing to behold but the sea. He was a connoisseur of its varying hues and shapes. There were glassy waters and ragged, white-capped waters and brackish waters and transparent blue waters and rolling waters and sunlit waters glittering like stars. One time, Bulkeley wrote, the sea was so crimson it "looked like blood." Each time the squadron crossed a swath of the immense liquid expanse, another appeared before them, as if all of Earth had been submerged.

On December 17—six weeks after leaving Madeira, and three months since their departure from England—Bulkeley glimpsed an unmistakable smudge on the horizon: a strip of land. "We saw the island of St. Catherine, at noon," he wrote excitedly in his logbook. Situated just off the southern coast of Brazil, St. Catherine was under Portuguese control. (In 1494, in the wake of Columbus's breakthrough voyage, Pope Alexander VI had, with an imperious wave of his hand, divided the world beyond Europe in half, bestowing the western side to Spain and the eastern regions, including Brazil, to Portugal.) Cape Horn was two thousand miles south of St. Catherine, and with the prospect of winter still looming, Anson was anxious to press on. Yet he knew that his men needed to recuperate, and the wooden ships had to be patched up before entering hostile regions under Spanish control.

As they approached the island, they could discern lush forests and mountains sliding into the sea. A branch of the Guaraní Indians had once thrived there, hunting and fishing, but after European explorers made contact, in the sixteenth century, and after Portuguese settlers arrived, in the seventeenth century, they'd been decimated by disease and persecution—that endless toll of imperialism rarely, if ever, recorded in logbooks. The island was now overrun with bandits who, according to Schoolmaster Thomas, had "fled hither from other parts of the Brazils to shelter themselves from justice."

The squadron anchored in a harbor, and Anson immediately sent ashore the hundreds of sick. Those who were fit set up a camp in a clearing and constructed shelters from old sails, the white canvas billowing in the breeze. While the surgeons and loblolly boys attended to the ailing, Bulkeley, Byron, and others hunted monkeys and wild boars and what Lieutenant Philip Saumarez described as a "very singular bird, called the Toucan, whose plumage is red and yellow, with a long beak resembling tortoise-shell." The seamen also discovered an abundance of medicinal plants. "One might imagine oneself in a druggist's shop," the lieutenant observed in wonder.

Nevertheless, the sickness did not release its grip, and at least eighty men and boys died on the island, their bodies buried in shallow, sandy graves. In a report to the Admiralty, Anson noted that since the squadron had left England 160 of its roughly 2,000 members had perished. And the fleet had not even begun the most perilous part of the journey.

Bulkeley spent Christmas on the island. Three sailors died that day, casting a pall over the occasion, and whatever celebration occurred was so cursory that none of the men mentioned it in their journals. The next morning, they pressed on with their tasks—replenishing supplies, repairing masts and sails, washing the decks with disinfecting vinegar. Charcoal also burned inside the hulls to smoke out the proliferating cockroaches and rats, a procedure that Schoolmaster Thomas described as "absolutely necessary, these creatures being extremely troublesome." On January 18, 1741, at the break of dawn, the squadron shoved off for Cape Horn.

Before long, the men were engulfed in a blinding squall—the first hint of the ominous weather to come. On the *Trial* sloop, eight young topmen were aloft reefing a sail when the mast snapped in the wind, catapulting them into the sea. Seven were rescued, Millechamp noted, though all were "cut and bruised in a most terrible manner." The eighth man had become entangled in the rope tentacles of the rigging and drowned.

After the storm lifted, Bulkeley noticed that the *Pearl*, under the command of Dandy Kidd, was nowhere to be found. "We lost sight of" her, he wrote in his journal. For days, he and his colleagues searched for the ship, but she was gone, along with her people. After nearly a month the worst was almost certain. Then, on February 17, a lookout spotted the ship's masts scraping the sky. Anson instructed the seamen on the *Gloucester* to sail after her, but the *Pearl* darted away, as though its crew were terrified of them. At last, the *Gloucester* caught up to the *Pearl*, and its officers revealed why they'd been so wary. Several days earlier, while they had been looking for the squadron, they had detected five men-of-war, one of which had hoisted a broad red pendant, signifying that it was Anson's flagship. In excitement, the *Pearl* had raced toward the fleet, but while its crew was lowering a longboat, to send a party to greet the commodore, someone shouted that the pendant didn't look quite right. The ships weren't Anson's—they were the Spanish armada led by Pizarro, who had made a replica of Anson's pendant. "They came within gunshot of us, when we found out the cheat," an officer on the *Pearl* reported.

The *Pearl*'s seamen immediately tightened their sails and tried to flee. As they were being chased, five ships against one, they began to chuck tons of supplies overboard—casks of water, oars, even the longboat—in order to clear the decks for battle and to go faster. The enemy ships, with guns primed, were closing in. Ahead of the *Pearl*, the ever-changing sea darkened and rippled—a sign, the men feared, of a reef lurking below. If the *Pearl* turned back, it would be pulverized by the Spanish; if it kept going, it might run aground and sink.

Pizarro signaled for his ships to stop. The *Pearl* forged onward. As it crossed the rippling, the men onboard braced for impact, for destruction, but there was not a jolt. Not even a shudder. The water had simply been stirred by spawning fish, and the ship glided over them. Pizarro's squadron resumed its chase, but the *Pearl* had amassed too great a lead, and that evening she escaped into the darkness.

While Bulkeley and his colleagues were assessing the implications of this encounter (how would they cope with the loss of provisions? how far away was Pizarro's squadron?), one of the officers on the *Pearl* informed Anson that something else had happened during their separation. "I regret to report to Your Honor," he said, "that our commander, Captain Dandy Kidd, died" of fever. Bulkeley had known Kidd from his time on the *Wager*, and he was a fine captain and a good soul. According to one officer's journal, shortly before Kidd passed he had hailed his men as "brave fellows" and had beseeched them to be dutiful to their next commander. "I cannot live long," he muttered. "I hope I have made my peace with God." Fretting over the fate of his five-year-old son, who seemingly had nobody else to look after him, he composed his last will and testament, setting aside money for the boy's education and "advancement in the World."

The death of Captain Kidd provoked another round of changes to the captaincies. Bulkeley was told that the *Wager*'s recently appointed commander, Murray, was being promoted again—this time to the larger *Pearl*. As for the *Wager*, it would be getting yet another new leader, someone who had never been in charge of a man-of-war: David Cheap. The men wondered whether Cheap, like Captain Kidd and Commodore Anson, understood that the secret to establishing command was not tyrannizing men but convincing, sympathizing, and inspiring them—or if he would be one of those despots who ruled by the lash.

Bulkeley rarely betrayed emotion, and in his journal he coolly noted this turn of events, as if it were just another trial in that eternal "warfare upon earth." (As his book on Christianity asked, "How shall thy patience be crowned, if no adversity happen unto thee?") But his entry did dwell on one unsettling detail. He wrote that Captain Kidd, on his deathbed, had delivered a prophecy concerning the expedition: "It would end in poverty, vermin, famine, death and destruction."

Part Two

INTO THE STORM

CHAPTER 4

Dead Reckoning

AS DAVID CHEAP STEPPED onboard the *Wager*, the ship's officers and crew gathered on deck, greeting him with all the pomp accorded to a captain of a man-of-war. Whistles were blown, hats removed. Yet there was an inevitable uneasiness. Just as Cheap was scrutinizing his new men—including the intense gunner, Bulkeley, and the eager midshipman Byron—they were eyeing their new captain. No longer was he one of *them;* he was in charge of them, responsible for every soul onboard. His position required, another officer wrote, "command of temper, integrity of purpose, vigour of mind, and abnegation of self.... He—and he alone—is expected, and exhorted, to bring a set of unruly and discordant beings into a state of perfect discipline and obedience, so that... the safety of the ship may be staked upon." Having long dreamed of this moment, Cheap could take comfort in knowing that many aspects of the wooden world were stable: a sail was a sail, a rudder a rudder. But others were unpredictable—and how would he handle surprises? As a newly appointed captain in Joseph Conrad's story "The Secret Sharer" wondered, how far would he prove "faithful to that ideal conception of one's own personality every man sets up for himself secretly"?

Cheap had no time for philosophizing, though: he had a ship to run. With the help of his devoted steward, Peter Plastow, he quickly settled into his spacious great cabin, a mark of his newfound status. He tucked away his sea chest, which contained his prized letter from Anson appointing him captain of the *Wager.* Then he mustered the crew and stood before them on the quarterdeck. It was his duty to recite the Articles of War—thirty-six rules regulating the behavior of every man and boy onboard. He went through the usual litany—no cursing, no drunkenness, no scandalous action in derogation of God's honor—until he came to Article 19. Its words held new meaning for him as he uttered them with finality: "No person in or belonging to the fleet shall utter any words of sedition or mutiny... upon pain of death."

Cheap began to prepare the *Wager* for the passage round Cape Horn, the rocky, barren island marking the southernmost tip of the Americas. Because the far-southern seas are the only waters that flow uninterrupted around the globe, they gather enormous power, with waves building over as much as thirteen thousand miles, accumulating strength as they roll through one ocean after another. When they arrive, at last, at Cape Horn, they are squeezed into a narrowing corridor between the southernmost American headlands and the northernmost part of the Antarctic Peninsula. This funnel, known as the Drake Passage, makes the torrent even more pulverizing. The currents are not only the longest-running on earth but also the strongest, transporting more than four billion cubic feet of water per second, more than six hundred times the discharge of the Amazon River. And then there are the winds. Consistently whipping eastward from the Pacific, where no lands obstruct them, they frequently accelerate to hurricane force, and can reach two hundred miles per hour. Seamen refer to the latitudes in which they blow with names that capture the increasing intensity: the Roaring Forties, the Furious Fifties, and the Screaming Sixties.

Moreover, a sudden shallowing of the seabed in the region—it goes from thirteen hundred feet deep to barely three hundred—combines with the other brute forces to generate waves of frightening magnitude. These "Cape Horn rollers" can dwarf a ninety-foot mast. Floating on some of these waves are lethal bergs cleaved from pack ice. And the collision of cold fronts from the Antarctic and warm fronts from near the equator produce an endless cycle of rain and fog, sleet and snow, thunder and lightning.

When a British expedition discovered these waters in the sixteenth century, it turned back after battling what a chaplain onboard described as "the most mad seas." Even those ships that completed the journey around the Horn lost countless lives, and so many expeditions ended in annihilation—shipwreck, sinking, disappearing—that most Europeans abandoned the route altogether. Spain preferred to sail cargo to one coast of Panama and then haul it more than fifty miles across the sweltering, disease-ridden jungle to ships waiting on the opposite coast. Anything to avoid tempting the Horn.

Herman Melville, who made the passage, compared it, in *White-Jacket*, to the descent into hell in Dante's Inferno. "At those ends of the earth are no chronicles," Melville wrote, except for the ruins of spars and hulls that hint of dark endings—"of ships that have sailed from their ports, and never more have been heard of." He went on, "Impracticable Cape! You may approach it from this direction or that—in any way you please—from the east or from the west; with the wind astern, or abeam, or on the quarter; and still Cape Horn is Cape Horn.... Heaven help the sailors, their wives and their little ones."

Over the years, seamen have strained to find a fitting name for this watery graveyard at the ends of the earth. Some call it the "Terrible," others "Dead Men's Road." Rudyard Kipling dubbed it the "blind Horn's hate."

Cheap pored over his sketchy charts. The names of other places in the region were equally unnerving: The Island of Desolation. The Port of Famine. Deceit Rocks. The Bay of the Severing of Friends.

Like the other captains in the squadron, Cheap was approaching this vortex partially blind. To determine his location, he needed to calculate his degrees of latitude and longitude, relying on those imaginary lines drawn onto the globe by cartographers. Latitudinal lines, which run parallel to one another, indicate how far north or south one is from the equator. Cheap could ascertain his latitude relatively easily, by determining his ship's position in relation to the stars. But, as Dava Sobel documents in *Longitude*, calculating that east-west position was a conundrum that baffled scientists and seamen for ages. During Ferdinand Magellan's expedition—the first to circumnavigate the globe, in 1522—a scribe onboard wrote that the pilots "will not speak of the longitude."

Longitudinal lines, which run perpendicular to the parallels of latitude, have no fixed reference point, like the equator. And so navigators must establish their own demarcation—their home port or some other arbitrary line—from which to gauge how far east or west they are. (Today, Greenwich, England, is designated the prime meridian, marking zero degrees longitude.) Because longitude represents a distance in the direction of the earth's daily rotation, measuring it is further complicated by time. Each hour of the day corresponds to fifteen degrees of longitude. If a seaman compares the exact time on his ship to that of his selected reference point, he can calculate his longitude. But eighteenth-century timepieces weren't reliable, especially at sea. As Isaac Newton wrote, "By reason of the motion of the ship, the variation of heat and cold, wet and dry, and the difference of gravity in different latitudes, such a watch hath not yet been made." Cheap carried with him a gold pocket watch, which, despite his debts, he had held on to, guarding it closely. But it was too imprecise to be of help.

How many ships, with precious lives and cargo, had wrecked because mariners hadn't known precisely where they were? A lee shore—a shore lying in the direction that a ship was being blown—might suddenly emerge before them in the darkness or a dense fog. In 1707, four British men-of-war smashed into a rocky isle just off the southwestern tip of England—their own homeland. More than thirteen hundred people perished. As the deaths caused by wayward navigation mounted over the years, some of the greatest scientific minds tried to crack the mystery of longitude. Galileo and Newton thought that the clocklike stars held the key to the riddle, whereas others came up with cockamamie plans involving everything from the "yelps of wounded dogs" to the "cannon blasts of signal ships." In 1714, the British Parliament passed the Longitude Act, offering a prize of twenty thousand pounds—the equivalent today of some three and a half million dollars—for a "Practicable and Useful" solution.

Cheap's former vessel the *Centurion* had played a role in testing a potentially revolutionary new method. Four years before this voyage, it had carried onboard a forty-three-year-old inventor named John Harrison, whom the First Lord of the Admiralty, Charles Wager, had recommended as a "very ingenious and sober man." Harrison was given free rein of the ship to conduct a trial of his latest contraption—a timepiece about two feet high, with ball weights and oscillating arms. The clock was in its developmental stages, but when Harrison used it to gauge the *Centurion*'s longitude, he correctly announced that the ship was off course by . . . sixty miles! Harrison continued to hone his timekeeper until, in 1773, at the age of eighty, he garnered the prize.

But Cheap and his colleagues had no such miraculous device. They were forced instead to rely on "dead reckoning"—a process using a sandglass to estimate time, and a knotted line dropped in the sea to approximate the ship's speed. The method, which also incorporated intuition about the effects of winds and currents, amounted to informed guesswork and a leap of faith. Too often for a commander, as Sobel put it, "the technique of dead reckoning marked him for a dead man."

Cheap was heartened, at least, by the calendar. It was February, which meant that the squadron would reach the seas around Cape Horn in March, before the austral winter descended. Against all odds, the party had done it. But what Cheap did not know—what none of the men knew—was that summer was not actually the safest time to round the Horn from east to west. Though in May and the winter months of June and July, the air temperature is colder and there is less light, the winds are tempered and sometimes blow from the east, making it easier to sail toward the Pacific. During the rest of the year, the conditions are more brutal. In fact, in the equinoctial month of March, when the sun is directly above the equator, the westerly winds and waves tend to be at their violent peak. And so Cheap was heading into the "blind Horn's hate" not only by dead reckoning but at the most dangerous time.

Cheap guided the *Wager* southward, along the coast of what is now Argentina. He hugged the squadron's other six ships and kept the decks cleared for battle, in case the Spanish armada appeared, and he had the sails reefed and the hatches battened down. "We had here uncertain boisterous weather, with . . . so much wind and sea, as made us ride very hard," Schoolmaster Thomas wrote.

The *Trial* still had a snapped mast, and in order to repair it the squadron paused for several days at St. Julian, a harbor along the coast. Previous explorers had recounted seeing inhabitants in the region, but it now appeared forsaken. "The only things we met with remarkable here are the armadillos, or what the seamen call hogs in armour," the *Trial*'s purser, Millechamp, wrote. "They are about the size of a large cat, their nose like a hog's, with a thick shell . . . hard enough to resist a strong blow with a hammer."

St. Julian was not just a place of desolation; it also stood, in the eyes of Cheap and his men, as a grisly memorial to the toll that a long, claustrophobic voyage could wreak upon a ship's company. When Magellan anchored there, on Easter Day in 1520, several of his increasingly resentful men tried to overthrow him, and he had to quash a mutiny. On a tiny island in the harbor, he ordered one of the rebels beheaded—his body quartered and hung from a gibbet for everyone to see.

Fifty-eight years later, when Francis Drake paused at St. Julian during his round-the-world voyage, he also suspected a simmering plot, and accused one of his men, Thomas Doughty, of treason. (The charge was likely false.) Doughty pleaded to be brought back to England for a proper trial, but Drake responded that he had no need for "crafty lawyers," adding, "Neither care I for the laws." At the same execution site that Magellan had used, Doughty was decapitated with an axe. Drake ordered that the head, still pouring blood, be held up before his men, and cried out, "Lo! This is the end of traitors!"

While Cheap and Anson's other captains were waiting for the *Trial*'s mast to be fixed, an officer identified the spot where the executions had taken place. The area, Lieutenant Saumarez fretted, seemed to be the "seat of infernal spirits." And, on February 27, Cheap and the rest of the men were relieved to leave behind what Drake had named the Island of True Justice and Judgment—or what his crew had called the Island of Blood.

The currents pulled these pilgrims on to the world's end. The air became colder, rawer; snow sometimes dusted the planks. Cheap stood exposed on the quarterdeck, bundled in his self-styled captain's uniform. He remained vigilant, peering at times through his spyglass. There were penguins, which Millechamp described as "half fish, half fowl," and there were southern right whales and humpbacks, blowing their spouts. The impressionable Byron later wrote of these southern seas, "It is incredible the number of whales that are here, it makes it dangerous for a ship, we were very near striking upon one, and another blew the water in upon the quarterdeck and they are of the largest kind we ever have seen." Then there was the sea lion, which he considered "rather a dangerous animal," noting: "I was attacked by one when I least expected it, and had much ado to get clear of him; they are of a monstrous size and when angered make a dreadful roaring."

The men sailed on. As the squadron traced the South American coastline, Cheap beheld the Andes mountain range, which extended the length of the continent, the snow-blown peaks rising, in places, more than twenty thousand feet. Soon a mist wafted over the sea, like a ghostly presence. It gave everything, Millechamp wrote, "a pleasing dreadful effect." Objects seemed to mutate. "The land sometimes would appear of a prodigious height with huge broken mountains," Millechamp wrote, before magically stretching and bending and flattening. "The ships underwent the same transformation, sometimes appearing like huge ruinous castles, sometimes in their proper shapes, and sometimes like large logs of timber floating on the water." He concluded, "We really seemed to be in the midst of enchantments."

As Cheap and his men headed farther south, they went past the mouth of an alternate route to the Pacific, the Strait of Magellan, which Anson decided to avoid because it was so narrow and twisting in places. They went past the Cape of Eleven Thousand Virgins and the Cape of the Holy Ghost. They slipped beyond the continental mainland, unmoored. Their only signpost was an island to the west, which spanned nearly twenty thousand square miles and featured more Andean peaks. Schoolmaster Thomas complained that the frozen slopes contained not "one cheerful green through all the dismal scene."

The island was the largest of the archipelago Tierra del Fuego—that Land of Fire where Magellan and his company had reported seeing the flames from native camps. The conquistadores had claimed that the inhabitants of these bottomlands were a race of giants. According to Magellan's scribe, one was "so tall that the tallest of us only came up to his waist." Magellan called the region Patagonia. The name may have derived from the inhabitants' feet—*pata* means "paw" in Spanish—which, as legend has it, were mammoth; or perhaps the name was borrowed from a medieval saga that featured a monstrous figure known as "the Great Patagon." There was a sinister design to these fictions. By portraying the natives as both magnificent and less than human, Europeans tried to pretend that their brutal mission of conquest was somehow righteous and heroic.

By the night of March 6, the squadron was off Tierra del Fuego's eastern extremity. For Cheap and the men, the supreme test of seamanship had arrived. Anson ordered the crews to wait till the morning light. Let them, if nothing else, see. The *Wager* drifted alongside the other ships, bow toward the wind, rocking back and forth, as if keeping beat to some metronome. The sky above them seemed as vast and black as the sea. The stays and shrouds vibrated in the wind.

Cheap ordered his men to make final preparations. They replaced the worn sails with fresh ones and secured the guns and anything else that might become a lethal projectile in rough seas. The bells counted down each half hour. Few men slept. Despite Anson's abhorrence of paperwork, he'd carefully written out instructions for Cheap and the other captains, who were told to destroy these plans, along with any other confidential documents, if their ships were about to fall into enemy hands. During the passage, Anson stressed, the captains needed to do everything possible to avoid being separated from the squadron—or "you will answer the contrary at your utmost peril." If they were forced apart, they were to proceed around the Horn and rendezvous on the Chilean side of Patagonia, where they were to wait for Anson for fifty-six days. "If not joined by me in that time, you are to conclude some accident has befallen me," Anson wrote. One point he made especially clear: should he perish, they must continue the mission and adhere to the chain of command, putting themselves under the control of the new senior officer.

At the first crack of light, Anson fired the *Centurion*'s guns and the seven ships set off into the dawn. The *Trial* and the *Pearl* led the way, their lookouts perched in the crosstrees in order to scour, as one officer put it, "for islands of ice" and to "make timely signals of danger." The *Anna* and the *Wager*, the slowest and least sturdy ships, drew up the rear. By ten a.m., the squadron had approached the Strait of Le Maire, a roughly fifteen-mile-wide opening between Tierra del Fuego and Isla de los Estados, or Staten Island—the gateway to Cape Horn. As the ships entered the strait, they bore close to Staten Island. The sight unnerved the men. "Though Tierra del Fuego had an aspect extremely barren and desolate," Reverend Walter noted, this island "far surpasses it, in the wildness and horror of its appearance." It consisted of nothing but rocks cloven by lightning and earthquakes, and stacked precariously on top of one another, rising three thousand feet in pinnacles of icy solitude. Melville wrote that these mountains "loomed up, like the border of some other world. Flashing walls and crystal battlements, like the diamond watch-towers along heaven's furthest frontier." In his journal, Millechamp described the island as the most horrid thing he had ever seen—"a proper nursery for desperation."

Occasionally, a white-bellied albatross soared through the air, flaunting its enormous wingspan, the largest of any bird—as much as eleven feet. On a previous British expedition, an officer had spotted an albatross by Staten Island and, fearing that it was a bad omen, shot it, and the ship later wrecked on an island. The incident inspired Samuel Taylor Coleridge's *Rime of the Ancient Mariner.* In the poem, the killing of the albatross brings a curse upon the seaman, causing his companions to die of thirst:

Instead of the cross, the Albatross
About my neck was hung.

Anson's men hunted these birds nonetheless. "I remember one caught with a hook and line... baited with a piece of salt pork," Millechamp wrote. Though the albatross weighed about thirty pounds, he added, "the captain, lieutenant, surgeon and myself eat him all up for dinner."

Cheap and his companions seemed to have escaped any curse. Despite a few close calls, they'd avoided Pizarro's ships, and the sky was now bright blue and the seas stunningly serene. "The morning of this day, in its brilliancy and mildness," Reverend Walter reported, was more pleasing than any "we had seen since our departure from England." The ships were being swept easily, peacefully, toward the Pacific. It was "a prodigious fine passage," one thrilled captain wrote in his logbook. Convinced that Captain Kidd's dying prophecy had been wrong, the men began boasting of their prowess and planning what they would do with their eventual treasure. "We could not help persuading ourselves that the greatest difficulty of our voyage was now at an end, and that our most sanguine dreams were upon the point of being realized," Reverend Walter noted.

And then the clouds blackened, blotting out the sun. The winds began to wail, and angry waves emerged from nowhere, exploding against the hulls. The ships' prows, including the *Centurion*'s red-painted lion, plunged into the deep hollows, before rearing upward pleadingly toward the heavens. The sails convulsed and the ropes whipped and the hulls creaked as if they might splinter. Although the other ships gradually made headway, the *Wager*, loaded down with cargo, was caught in the furious currents and was being driven eastward, as if by some magnetic force, toward Staten Island. She was on the verge of being dashed to pieces.

As the rest of the squadron looked on helplessly, Cheap summoned every able man on the *Wager* to his station, shouting commands. To reduce sail, the topmen labored up the teetering masts. As one topman who experienced a gale recalled, "The force of the wind was literally breathtaking. Up on the yardarm, our feet on the footrope, we clutched whatever we could hold on to. We had to turn our heads to take a breath, or the wind simply jammed the air down our throats. The rain stung our faces and our bare legs like hard pellets. It was almost impossible to open my eyes."

Cheap instructed his topmen to furl the uppermost sails and reef the main. He needed the perfect balance: enough canvas to propel the ship from the rocks but not so much as to capsize it. Even trickier, he needed every member of the ship to perform flawlessly: Lieutenant

Baynes showing some rare gumption; the confident gunner, Bulkeley, proving his seamanship; the boyish Midshipman Byron mustering his courage and lending a hand with his pal Henry Cozens; the often unruly boatswain, John King, dutifully keeping the crew at their posts; the helmsmen maneuvering the bow amid the vise of currents; the forecastle men controlling the sails; and the carpenter, John Cummins, and his mate James Mitchell preventing damage to the hull. Even the inexperienced waisters must join the efforts.

As Cheap braced himself on the quarterdeck, his face doused by the freezing spray, he marshaled these forces, struggling to save the ship. *His* ship. Each time the *Wager* began to edge away from the island, the currents heaved her back toward it. The waves burst against the towering rocks, grinding and spewing. The roar was deafening. As a seaman put it, the island seemed to have been designed for one purpose—"crushing the lives of fragile mortals." But Cheap remained composed and harnessed every element of the ship, until gradually, remarkably, he coaxed the *Wager* to safety.

Unlike victories in battles, such feats against the natural elements, which were often more dangerous, garnered no laurels—that is, none beyond what a captain described as that pride among the ship's company over having performed a vital duty. Byron marveled that they were "very near being wrecked upon the rocks," and yet "we endeavoured all in our power to make up our lost way and regain our station." The hard-bitten Bulkeley appraised Cheap an "excellent seaman," adding, "As for personal bravery, no man had a larger share of it." In that moment, the final surge of joy most of them would ever experience, Cheap had become the man he always pictured himself—a lord of the sea.

CHAPTER 5

The Storm Within the Storm

STORMS CONTINUED TO BATTER the ships day and night. John Byron stared in awe at the waves that broke over the *Wager*, bandying the 123-foot vessel about as if it were no more than a pitiful rowboat. Water seeped through virtually every seam of the hull, flooding the lower decks and causing the officers and crewmen to abandon their hammocks and berths; there was no longer any realm "under the weather." The men's fingers would burn from gripping the wet ropes, and the wet yards, and the wet shrouds, and the wet steering wheel, and the wet ladders, and the wet sails. Byron, drenched by the pouring rains as well as the waves, was unable to keep a dry thread on his body. Everything seemed to drip, to shrivel, to decompose.

During that March of 1741, as the squadron plowed through the howling darkness toward the elusive Cape Horn (where were they exactly on the map?), Byron endeavored to maintain his station on watch. He spread his feet like a bowlegged gaucho and held on to anything secure—otherwise he would be hurled into the frothing sea. Lightning blitzed the sky, flashing before him and then turning the world even blacker.

The temperature kept dropping until the rains hardened into sleet and snow. Cables became encrusted with ice and some of the men succumbed to frostbite. "Below forty degrees latitude, there is no law," a sailors' adage went. "Below fifty degrees, there is no God." And Byron and the rest of the crew were now in the Furious Fifties.

The wind in these parts, he noted, blows with "such violence that nothing can withstand it, and the sea runs so high that it works and tears a ship to pieces." It was, he concluded, "the most disagreeable sailing in the world."

He knew that the squadron needed every man and boy to persevere. But almost immediately after the *Wager* passed through the Strait of Le Maire, on March 7, he noticed that many of his companions could no longer rise from their hammocks. Their skin began to turn blue, and then as black as charcoal—"a luxuriance," as Reverend Walter put it, "of fungous flesh." Their ankles swelled hideously, and whatever was consuming them progressed up their bodies, into their thighs and their hips and their shoulders, like some corrosive poison. When Schoolmaster Thomas suffered from the affliction, he recalled, he initially felt just a small pain in his left big toe, but soon noticed hard nodes and ulcerous sores spreading across his body. This was accompanied, he wrote, "with such excessive pains in the joints of the knees, ankles and toes, as I thought, before I experienced them, that human nature could never have supported." Byron later caught the dreadful disorder, and found that it engendered "the most violent pain imaginable."

As the scourge invaded the sailors' faces, some of them began to resemble the monsters of their imaginations. Their bloodshot eyes bulged. Their teeth fell out, as did their hair. Their breath reeked of what one of Byron's companions called an unwholesome stench, as if death had already come upon them. The cartilage that glued together their bodies seemed to be loosening. In certain cases, even old injuries reemerged. A man who had been injured at the Battle of the Boyne, which took place in Ireland more than fifty years earlier, had his ancient wounds suddenly break out anew. "Still more astonishing," Reverend Walter observed, one of this man's bones that had healed after fracturing at the Boyne now dissolved again, "as if it had never been consolidated."

Then there were the effects on the senses. One moment, the men might be overcome with visions of bucolic streams and pastures; then, realizing where they were, they would sink into complete despair. Reverend Walter noted that this "strange dejection of the spirits" was marked by "shiverings, tremblings, and . . . the most dreadful terrors." One medical expert compared it to "the falling down of the whole soul." Byron saw some of the men descend into lunacy—or, as one of his companions wrote, the disease "got into their brains, and they ran raving mad."

They were suffering from what a British captain had dubbed "the plague of the sea": scurvy. Like everyone else, Byron didn't know what caused it. Striking a company after at least a month at sea, it was the great enigma of the Age of Sail, killing more mariners than all other threats—including gun battles, tempests, wrecks, and other diseases—combined. On Anson's ships, scurvy appeared after the men were already ailing, leading to one of the most severe maritime outbreaks. "I cannot pretend to describe that terrible distemper," the ordinarily phlegmatic Anson reported, "but no plague ever equaled the degree we had of it."

One night, during the endless storm, as Byron struggled to sleep in his soaked, rattling berth, he heard the eight bells and strove to get on deck for another watch. As he staggered through the labyrinth of the ship, it was difficult to see—lamps had been extinguished for fear that they might topple and catch fire. Even the cook was not permitted to light his stove, forcing the men to eat their meat raw.

When Byron emerged on the quarterdeck, feeling the cold blast of wind, he was startled to find only a few dozen people on watch. "The greatest part of the men," Bryon wrote in his account, had been "disabled through fatigue and sickness."

The ships were in danger of running out of hands to operate them. The surgeon Henry Ettrick—who, after the *Centurion*'s chief surgeon died, was relocated there from the *Wager*—tried to stanch the outbreak. Down on the *Centurion*'s orlop deck, cloaked in a smock, he took out his saw and cut open several corpses, trying to pinpoint the cause of the disease. Perhaps the dead would save the living. According to reports of his findings, the victims' "bones, after the flesh was scraped off, appeared quite black," and their blood seemed to have a peculiar color, like that of a "black and yellow liquor." After several dissections, Ettrick proclaimed that the disease was induced by the frigid climate. Yet when it was pointed out to Ettrick that scurvy was just as prevalent in tropical climates, he conceded that the cause might remain an "entire secret."

The outbreak raged on, a storm within the storm. After Ettrick had moved to the *Centurion*, the *Trial*'s surgeon, Walter Elliot, had been relocated to the *Wager*. Byron described him as a generous, active, and very strong young man, who seemed destined to survive the longest. Elliot was devoted to Captain Cheap, who was now battling scurvy himself. "It was a very great misfortune," Elliot remarked, that their captain "should be ill at such a time."

The doctor did everything in his power to help Cheap and Byron and the other ailing men. But what remedies existed were as worthless as the theories behind them. A number of people, believing there must be something in the nature of land vital to humans, claimed that the only cure was burying the sick up to their chins in soil. An officer on another voyage recalled the bizarre sight of "twenty men's heads stuck out of the ground."

While Anson's expedition was trapped at sea, the main medicine prescribed was Dr. Joshua Ward's "pill and drop"—a purgative that was advertised as performing "many marvelous and sudden cures." Anson, who refused to let his men undergo what he would not endure himself, took the pills first. Thomas wrote that most of the men who consumed them were seized "very violently, both by vomit and stool." One sailor, after a single pill, began to pour blood from his nostrils and lay near the point of death. Ward turned out to be a quack; his potion contained poisonous amounts of the metalloid antimony and, some suspected, arsenic. The pills purged the sick of needed nutrients, likely contributing to many deaths. The surgeon Ettrick, who would later die of illness on the voyage, conceded despairingly that all his available treatments were useless.

Yet the solution was so simple. Scurvy is brought on by a deficiency of vitamin C, owing to a lack of raw vegetables and fruits in one's diet. Such a deprived person stops producing the fibrous protein known as collagen, which holds bones and tissues together, and which is used to synthesize dopamine and other hormones that can affect moods. (Anson's men also appear to have been suffering from other vitamin deficiencies, such as insufficient levels of niacin, which can lead to psychosis, and of vitamin A, which causes night blindness.) Lieutenant Saumarez later sensed the power of certain nutrients. "I could plainly observe," he wrote, "that there is a *Je ne sais quoi* in the frame of the human system that cannot be renewed, cannot be preserved, without the assistance of certain earthly particles, or in plain English, the land is man's proper element, and vegetables and fruit his only physic." All Byron and his companions needed to combat scurvy was some citrus, and when they had stopped at St. Catherine to gather supplies, there had been an abundance of limes. The cure—that unforbidden fruit which decades later would be furnished to all British seamen, giving them the nickname Limeys—had been right within their grasp.

As the squadron sailed on, Byron watched in anguish as many of the sick gasped for air. They appeared to be dry drowning. One after the other, they died—far from their families and from the graves of their ancestors. Some who attempted to stand, Reverend Walter reported, "died before they could well reach the deck; nor was it an uncommon thing for those who were able to walk the deck, and to do some kind of duty, to drop down dead in an instant." Even those who were carried in their hammocks from one part of the ship to another died suddenly. "Nothing was more frequent than to bury eight or ten men from each ship every morning," Millechamp wrote in his journal.

Altogether, nearly 300 of the *Centurion*'s some 500 men were eventually listed as "DD"—Discharged Dead. Of the roughly 400 people on the *Gloucester* who had departed from England, three quarters were reported to have been buried at sea, including all its share of the invalid recruits. The captain, who was himself extremely ill, wrote in his logbook, "So miserable was the scene, that words cannot express the misery that some of the men died in." The *Severn* had buried 290 men and boys, the *Trial* nearly half its crew. On the *Wager*, Byron saw the original company of some 250 officers and crew dwindle to fewer than 220, and then fall below 200. And those who were alive were nearly indistinguishable from the dead—"so weak and so much reduced," as one officer put it, "that we could hardly walk along the deck."

The disease had consumed not only the bonds that glued together the seamen's bodies but their vessels' companies. The once-mighty squadron resembled ghost ships, where, according to one account, only vermin thrived: "So great a number of rats were seen between decks, as would appear incredible to any but an eye witness." They infested sleeping quarters, ran across meal tables, and disfigured the dead, which lay about the deck awaiting burial. On one corpse the eyes were eaten out, on another the cheeks.

Each day, Byron and other officers inscribed, in their records, the names of their companions who had just "departed this life." The captain of the *Severn* wrote, in a report to the Admiralty, that after the death of his ship's master he had filled the role by promoting a seaman named Campbell—who had shown "great diligence and resolute behavior under all our difficulties and dangers"; moments later, the captain added to the same dispatch, "I have just received notice that Mr. Campbell is this day dead." The *Centurion*'s midshipman Keppel, whose diseased, toothless mouth resembled a dark cave, grew so weary of cataloging the dead that he wrote apologetically, "I have omitted to insert in my log the deaths of several men."

One later passing was not neglected in the records. The entry, truncated with the standard abbreviations of "AB" for "Able Seaman" and "DD" for "Discharged Dead," is now smudged but still legible, like a faded epitaph. It reads, "Henry Cheap, AB, DD... at sea." It was Captain Cheap's young nephew and apprentice. His death no doubt rattled the *Wager*'s new captain more than any storm.

Byron tried to offer his deceased companions a proper sea burial, but there were so many corpses, and so few hands to assist, that the bodies often had to be heaved overboard unceremoniously. As the poet Lord Byron—who drew on what he referred to as "my granddad's 'Narrative'"—would put it, "Without a grave, unknelled, uncoffined, and unknown."

By late March, after nearly three weeks of futile attempts to get through the Drake Passage, the squadron was on the verge of what Reverend Walter called "total destruction." Its only hope was to quickly get around the Horn and reach the nearest secure landfall: the Juan Fernández Islands, an uninhabited archipelago in the Pacific 350 miles off the western coast of Chile. "Getting thither was the only chance we had left to avoid perishing at sea," Reverend Walter noted.

For John Byron, that lover of sea literature, the archipelago offered more than a refuge: it was burnished in lore. In 1709, the English captain Woodes Rogers had stopped there while his crew was being ravaged by scurvy. As he detailed in his journal, later published as *A Cruising Voyage Round the World*, which Byron had eagerly read, Rogers was astonished to discover on one island a Scottish sailor named Alexander Selkirk, who had been a castaway there for more than four years after being left behind by his ship. Through extraordinary ingenuity, he had managed to survive—learning to make a fire by scraping sticks together, and hunting animals and foraging for wild turnips. "When his clothes wore out," Rogers explained, "he made himself a coat and cap of goat-skins, which he stitched together with . . . no other needle but a nail." Selkirk read from a Bible that he had with him, "so that he said he was a better Christian while in this solitude than ever he was before." Rogers called Selkirk "the absolute monarch of the island." As a tale gets passed from one person to another, it ripples out until it is as wide and mythic as the sea. And Selkirk's story provided the germ for Daniel Defoe's 1719 fictional account of Robinson Crusoe—a paean not only to British ingenuity but also to the country's colonial mastery of distant realms.

As Byron and his shipmates were being pounded by the forces of nature, they became entranced by visions of Juan Fernández, visions no doubt made more dazzling by their scorbutic dreams. On that "long wished for island," as Millechamp called it, they would find emerald fields and streams of pure water. Thomas, in his journal, compared the island to the Eden of John Milton's *Paradise Lost.*

One night in April, Byron and others in the squadron determined they'd made it far enough through the Drake Passage, and to the west of Cape Horn Island, that they could finally turn north—and head safely to Juan Fernández. But not long after the ships tacked north, the lookout on the *Anna* noticed, through the glancing moonlight, strange formations: rocks. The *Anna*'s crewmen fired their guns, twice, in warning, and soon the other ships' watches also discerned the jutting lee shore, the glistening rocks rising, as one captain wrote in his logbook, "like two black towers of an extraordinary height."

Once more, the navigators' dead reckoning had been wrong—this time by hundreds of miles. The ships were not west of the tip of the continent; rather, they were, having been driven eastward by the winds and the currents, pinned against it. The crew members managed to turn just in time and avoid being wrecked. But more than a month after entering the Drake Passage, they had still not escaped the "blind Horn's hate." Millechamp wrote in his journal, "Our seamen now almost all despairing of ever getting on shore voluntarily gave themselves up to their fatal distemper." And they envied "those whose good fortune it was to die first."

Byron's spirits were crushed. To get clear of the land, they were heading back south, in the opposite direction of the island of Robinson Crusoe—and back into the vortex of the storms.

CHAPTER 6

Alone

AS THE SQUADRON TRIED to claw past the rim of South America, the storms intensified into what Byron dubbed the "perfect hurricane," though there were really many tempests, each succeeding the other with an escalating force that seemed destined to destroy the entire expedition, once and for all. Because of the depletion of men, the *Wager*'s gunner, John Bulkeley, was now regularly in charge of two consecutive watches—eight straight hours of being hammered by the winds and waves. Sounding like the neophyte Byron, he wrote in his journal, "We had... the largest swell I ever saw." The *Severn*'s veteran captain similarly observed, in a report to the Admiralty, that it was a "greater sea than I ever saw before"—virtually the exact phrase used by the *Pearl*'s commander, George Murray. Suddenly these men of the sea lacked not only the power to manage it but even to describe it.

Each time the *Wager* went over a wave, Bulkeley felt the ship hurtling on an avalanche of water, cascading into a chasm devoid of light. All he could discern behind him was a looming mountain of water; in front of him nothing but another terrifying mountain. The hull rocked from gunwale to gunwale, tipping so far over that the yards sometimes dipped underwater as the topmen aloft clung spiderlike to the web of ropes.

One night, at eleven p.m., a wave overwhelmed the squadron. "A raging sea took us on the starboard bow, and broke in clear fore and aft," the *Centurion*'s Schoolmaster Thomas wrote in his journal, adding that the wave struck with such violence that the ship lay completely on her side, before slowly righting. "It threw down and half drowned all the people on the deck."

If Bulkeley didn't keep himself fastened at all times, he would be catapulted through the air. One seaman, thrown into the hold, snapped his femur. A boatswain's mate was upended and shattered his collarbone, then shattered it again during a subsequent fall. Another seaman broke his neck. When Thomas was on the *Centurion*'s quarterdeck, trying to observe the dim stars in order to fix their position, a wave knocked him off his feet. "Down I came on my head and right shoulder with such violence as quite stunned me," he wrote. Barely conscious, he was carried to his hammock, where he lay for more than two weeks—a convalescence that was anything but peaceful, his bed a menacing swing.

One morning, when Bulkeley was at the *Wager*'s helm, he was also nearly swept away by a monstrous wave—a wave that, as he put it, "carried me over the wheel." In the deluge one of the four transport boats, the cutter, was sent careening across the deck. The boatswain, John King, wanted to heave it overboard. But Bulkeley ordered him, "Do nothing with her," not until he'd consulted Captain Cheap.

Cheap was in his great cabin, where it was as if a tornado had passed through, everything tossed about. Bulkeley, in his journal, often carped about the *Wager*'s officers—the boatswain was wicked, the master useless, the lieutenant more useless—and he'd begun to harbor certain reservations about his new captain. Pacing with a silver-headed cane, which clacked like a pirate's wooden leg, Cheap seemed increasingly hell-bent on conquering the elements and fulfilling his glorious mission. Bulkeley didn't trust this aspect of Cheap, complaining in his journal that the captain often did not consult with his officers, and would lash out at anyone who expressed misgivings.

After Bulkeley apprised him of the situation with the cutter,

Cheap ordered him to try to salvage it, and to lower the boom for the jib, which was swinging dangerously. Bulkeley later noted with satisfaction in his journal that he was the one who rescued the cutter and secured the jibboom.

Because of the ferocity of the winds, the *Wager* and the other ships sometimes had to furl their sails, tossing for days with bare poles at the mercy of the waves. The vessels were uncontrollable in such a state, and at one point Commodore Anson, in order to turn the *Centurion*, was forced to send several topmen to stand on the yards, hold on to ropes, and use their bodies to catch the wind. The gale blew against their faces and chests and arms and legs, each a threadbare sail. With extraordinary daring, the men resisted the wind with their frosted, concaved bodies long enough to allow Anson to maneuver the ship. But one topman lost his grip and was cast into the churning ocean. It was impossible to come about in time to rescue him, and the men watched as he stroked after them, trying frantically to catch up, waging a heroic, solitary war against the waves, until he receded in the distance—though they knew he was still out there, swimming after them. "He might continue sensible for a considerable time longer, of the horror attending his irretrievable situation," Reverend Walter noted.

The celebrated eighteenth-century poet William Cowper later read Walter's account and penned "The Castaway," in which he imagined the seaman's fate:

Wash'd headlong from on board,
Of friends, of hope, of all bereft,
His floating home for ever left.

. . . .

His comrades, who before
Had heard his voice in ev'ry blast.
Could catch the sound no more:
For then, by toil subdued, he drank
The stifling wave, and then he sank.

No poet wept him; but the page
Of narrative sincere,
That tells his name, his worth, his age,
Is wet with Anson's tear.

Bulkeley and the other survivors sailed on. Not only were they suffering from scurvy; they were now running low on fresh supplies. Each biscuit had become "so much worm-eaten," Thomas wrote, that "it was scarce anything but dust, and a little blow would reduce it to that immediately." No livestock remained, and the salted "beef and pork was likewise very rusty and rotten, and the surgeon endeavored to hinder us from eating any of it, alleging it was, though a slow, yet a sure poison." Some of the ships had only a few remaining casks of drinking water, and Captain Murray confessed that "if it had not pleased God" to take so many of his people from disease they would all be dead from thirst. One sailor on the *Centurion* became so demented that he had to be chained in irons. And the men's ships—their last protection against the forces of nature—began to break apart.

On the *Centurion*, it was the topsail that first split, blowing almost to pieces. Then several of the shrouds, the thick vertical ropes supporting the masts, snapped, and soon after that the heads—the box-like toilets on the deck—were destroyed by waves, forcing the men to relieve themselves in buckets or by leaning dangerously over the railing. Then a bolt of lightning hit the ship. "A quick, subtle fire ran along our deck," Midshipman Keppel wrote, "which, bursting, made a report like a pistol, and struck several of our men and officers, who with the violence of the blow were black and blue." The "crazy ship," as Reverend Walter called the *Centurion*, had begun to heel abnormally. Even the proud lion was loosening from its mount, trembling.

On the other ships, the officers catalogued their own "list of defects," which went on for pages, citing broken backstays, clew lines, buntlines, leech lines, halyards, braces, tackles, ladders, stoves, hand pumps, gratings, and gangways. The captain of the *Severn* reported that his ship was in the utmost distress—all her sails torn and the sailmaker needed to repair them dead.

One day Bulkeley heard the *Gloucester* firing its guns in alarm: a yard on its mainmast had cracked in two. Anson ordered Captain Cheap to send John Cummins, the *Wager*'s talented carpenter, to help repair it. Cummins was Bulkeley's closest friend, and the gunner watched as Cummins set out in one of the small transport boats, bouncing about in the harrowing waves, until he was hauled, half-drowned, onboard the *Gloucester*.

Though the *Wager* was an eyesore, she was sacred to Bulkeley, and every day she was being devoured even more than the other ships. She was pelted and gouged. She pitched, she heaved, she groaned, she splintered. Then one day, after colliding with a wave, the mizzen, a vital mast, toppled over like an axed tree, crashing down with its rigging and sails into the sea. All that was left was a stump. Thomas predicted that a ship in such a condition would inevitably perish in these waters. The *Wager*, laboring in the waves, fell farther and farther behind the rest of the squadron. The *Centurion* circled back to the *Wager*, and Anson—using a speaking trumpet that allowed him to communicate with Captain Cheap across the waves and over the roar of the wind—hollered to ask why he didn't set the topsail on another mast to help propel the ship.

"My rigging is all gone, and broke fore and aft, and my people almost all taken ill and down," Cheap shouted back. "But I will set him as soon as possible."

Anson said he would make sure that the *Wager*'s carpenter, Cummins, who had been trapped on the *Gloucester* because of the weather, was sent back. When Cummins arrived, he immediately went to work with his mates, attaching a forty-foot boom to the stump and jury-rigging a sail. This steadied the ship some, and the *Wager* sailed on.

Amid these travails, the one superior whom Bulkeley never criticized was Anson. From the outset, the commodore had been dealt a sinister hand—a woefully organized expedition—but he had done all he could to preserve the squadron and bolster the men's spirits. Ignoring stifling naval hierarchies, he toiled alongside the crew, assisting with the most arduous tasks. He shared his private stores of brandy with the ordinary seamen to relieve their suffering and cheer them up. When a bilge pump on a vessel broke, he sent over the one from his own ship. And when he had no more supplies to dole out, he encouraged the men and boys with his words—which, given his taciturn nature, seemed all the more stirring.

But there were simply too few healthy men and boys to manage the ships. The *Centurion*, which once had more than two hundred people serving on each watch, was reduced to six seamen per watch. Captain Cheap reported of the *Wager*, "My ship's company at that unhappy juncture were almost all sick ... and they so fatigued with the excessive length of the voyage, the long course of bad weather, and the scarcity of fresh water that they were very little able to do their duty." Some vessels could not even raise a sail. Captain Murray wrote that his crew had resisted the elements with a "resolution not to be met with in any but English seamen," yet now, being "quite jaded and fatigued with continual labour and watching, and pinched with the cold and want of water ... they became so dejected as to lay themselves down in despair, bewailing their misfortunes, wishing for death as the only relief to their miseries."

On April 10, 1741, seven months after the squadron had departed England and more than four weeks since it had entered the Drake Passage, the *Severn* and the *Pearl* began to trail behind the other ships. Then they disappeared. "Lost sight of the *Severn* and *Pearl*,"

Bulkeley wrote in his journal. Some suspected that these ships' officers had given up and turned back around Cape Horn, retreating to safety. Thomas claimed they seemed to "lag designedly."

The squadron—down to five ships, of which only three were men-of-war—strove to stay together. To signal their location, they hung lantern lights and fired their guns nearly every half hour. Bulkeley knew that if the *Wager* became separated from the fleet, not to mention Commodore Anson, there would be nobody to rescue them from sinking or from a shipwreck. They might be forced to spend their days, as Reverend Walter put it, "on some desolate coast, without any reasonable hope of ever getting off again."

The *Centurion* was the first to disappear in the murk. After Bulkeley spotted its flickering lights on the night of April 19, he wrote in his account, "This was the last time I ever saw the Commodore." He discerned the other ships in the distance, but they, too, were soon "gone," the sound of their booming guns smothered by the wind. The *Wager* was alone at sea, left to its own destiny.

CHAPTER 7

The Gulf of Pain

DAVID CHEAP, COMMANDER OF His Majesty's Ship the *Wager*, would never turn back. His company continued to wither, and his own body was hollowed out by what he, to avoid the stigma of scurvy, preferred to call "rheumatism" and "asthma." His ship, the first man-of-war under his charge, was not just deformed, with its missing mast, torn sails, and bad leaks; it was alone upon the quaking sea. Despite all this, he sailed on, determined to find Anson at the rendezvous. If Cheap failed at this challenge, was he truly a captain after all?

Once this goal had been achieved, and once the remaining men in Cheap's party recuperated, they would proceed with the plan that Commodore Anson had confided in him: an assault on Valdivia, a town on the southwestern coast of Chile. Because the *Wager* was carrying much of the squadron's armaments, the success of the first strike against the Spanish—and perhaps of the entire expedition—depended on him miraculously making it to the rendezvous. The very hopelessness of the situation offered a peculiar human appeal: if Cheap prevailed, he would become a hero, his feats celebrated in the yarns and ballads of seamen. Never again would those landlubbers back home doubt what he was made of.

Watch after watch, bell after bell, he continued sailing, scraping, battling, until three weeks had passed since his separation from the squadron. With skill and daring, and a touch of ruthlessness, he had navigated the *Wager* around Cape Horn, joining that elite club, and he was now hastening along the Pacific, heading northeast off the Chilean coast of Patagonia. In several days, he would arrive at the rendezvous. Imagine Anson's expression when he saw the lost *Wager* and realized that his former lieutenant had saved the day!

Yet the Pacific did not live up to its peaceful name. As the *Wager* headed north off the coast of Chile, all the previous storms seemed to have combined into one climatic fury. God was ever the yarn spinner. Some of the men appeared ready to "cut and run," just as the officers and crews of the *Pearl* and the *Severn* were suspected of doing. But Cheap—his eyes inflamed, his teeth loosening—was unwavering. He demanded that his crew brace the sails, clamber up the masts amid vicious gusts of wind, and work the manual pump, which required lowering saucers on a long chain into the water-filled hold and then hauling them upward—a backbreaking ritual that had to be repeated over and over again. Cheap relied on the midshipman Alexander Campbell to strong-arm the crew and enforce his orders. "My attachment to the Captain was zealous," Campbell acknowledged. One seaman later shouted curses at the midshipman and vowed retribution.

Cheap relentlessly drove the men onward—drove them even as they dumped overboard a growing number of corpses. "Let the fate of particular persons be what it will," Cheap proclaimed, "but let the honour of our country be immortal."

As they forged on, John Byron—who noted Cheap's "stubborn defiance of all difficulties," and how he was unfazed by the "apprehensions which so justly alarmed all"—peered over the edge of the quarterdeck. Ever alert to nature, he noticed, floating on the rushing water, little green strands. *Seaweed.* He anxiously told the gunner, Bulkeley, "We can't be far off the land."

John Bulkeley thought that their course was madness. According to Master Clark, the navigator, they remained safely west of the Patagonian coast of Chile, but his dead reckoning had been wrong before. And if they kept on a northeast tack they might become entangled with an unknown lee shore and not be able turn around in time to avoid wrecking. The carpenter, Cummins, remarked that given the "condition the ship was in, she was not fit to come in with the land," especially with "all our men being sick." Bulkeley went and asked Lieutenant Baynes, the superior officer on duty, why they did not alter their course and turn west back out to sea.

The lieutenant seemed evasive. When Bulkeley pressed him again, Baynes replied that he had spoken to Cheap, and that the captain was intent on making it to the rendezvous in time. "I would have you go to him, he may be persuaded by you," Baynes said fecklessly.

Bulkeley had no need to seek a meeting with Cheap. The captain, undoubtedly hearing of the gunner's grumblings, soon summoned him and asked, "What distance do you reckon yourself off the land?"

"About sixty leagues," Bulkeley responded, which was roughly two hundred miles. But the currents and swells were driving them rapidly eastward toward the coastline, he noted, adding, "Sir, the ship is a perfect wreck. Our mizzenmast gone . . . and all our people down."

For the first time, Cheap divulged Anson's secret orders, and he insisted that he would not deviate from them and threaten the operation. He believed a captain must fulfill his duties: "I am obliged and determined."

Bulkeley thought that the decision was "a very great misfortune." But he bowed to his superior's orders, leaving the captain alone with his clacking cane.

On May 13, at eight in the morning, Byron was on watch when several of the pulleys for the foresails broke. As the carpenter, Cummins, hurried forward to inspect them, thunderclouds cloaking the horizon parted ever so slightly, and in the distance he could see something shadowy and misshapen. Was it land? He approached Lieutenant Baynes, who squinted but didn't see anything. Maybe Baynes was suffering from blindness induced by lack of vitamin A. Or maybe it was Cummins's eyes that had been deceived. After all, Baynes reckoned that the ship was still more than 150 miles from shore. He told Cummins that it was "impossible" for him to have discerned land, and he made no report of the sighting to the captain.

By the time Cummins told Byron about what he thought he had seen, the sky was again subsumed in darkness, and Byron couldn't see any land himself. He wondered whether he should inform the captain, but Baynes was second-in-command and Byron was a mere midshipman. It's not my place, he thought.

Later that day, at two in the afternoon, with only three seamen on the watch, Bulkeley had to go aloft himself to help lower one of the yards on the foremast. While the ship bucked like some stupendous wild creature, he slithered up the rigging. The gale whipped against his body and the rain pricked his eyes. Up he went—up, up, up—until he reached the yard, which rocked with the ship, nearly plunging him into the water before lifting him back into the sky. He held on desperately, looking out at the world before him. And that's when, as he recalled it, "I saw the land very plain." There were enormous craggy hills—and the *Wager* was barreling toward them, propelled by westerly winds. Bulkeley raced down the mast and across the slippery deck to warn the captain.

Cheap moved immediately into action. "Sway the foreyard up and set the foresail!" he cried to the half-human figures wandering about. Then he ordered the men to execute a jibe—turning the ship around by swinging its bow away from the wind. The helmsman (there was only one available) cranked the double wheel. The bow began arcing downwind, but then the gale caught the sails from behind at full force and the hull surfed the enormous waves. Cheap looked on in alarm as the ship headed faster and faster toward the rocks. He ordered the helmsman to keep cranking the wheel and the other men to tend to the rigging. And just before a collision was inevitable, the bow swung farther around—a full 180 degrees—and the sails flung violently to the opposite side of the ship, completing the jibe.

The *Wager* was now running parallel to the coastline on a southward trajectory. Yet, because of the westerly direction of the winds, Cheap was unable to point farther out to sea, and the *Wager* was being dragged toward the shore by the waves and the currents. The landscape of Patagonia revealed itself, jagged and jumbled, with rocky islets and gleaming glaciers, with wild forests creeping up mountainsides and cliffs plunging straight into the ocean. Cheap and his men were trapped in a bay known as the Golfo de Penas—the Gulf of Sorrows or, as some prefer, the Gulf of Pain.

Cheap thought that they could claw their way out, but the topsails suddenly blew right off the yards. Seeing his despairing men struggling to fix the rigging in the forecastle, he decided to go and help, to show them there was still a way out. Rashly, bravely, he rushed toward the bow—a bull storming into the gale and spray. And it was then, unsteadied by a wave, that he made a misstep (one small misstep) and began to fall into an abyss. He had tumbled through a ripped-open hatchway, plummeting about six feet before smacking the oaken deck below. He hit so hard that the bone in his left shoulder snapped and protruded from his armpit. The men carried him into the surgeon's cabin. "I was taken up very much stunned and hurt with the violence of the fall," Cheap noted. He wanted to get up, so that he could save the ship and his men, but the pain was overwhelming, and it was the first moment in so long that he had laid down to rest. The surgeon, Walter Elliot, gave him opium, and for once Cheap was at peace, sailing into the ether of his dreams.

At 4:30 a.m. on May 14, Byron, who was on deck, felt the *Wager* judder in the darkness. Midshipman Campbell, sounding suddenly like the child that he was, asked, What was that? Byron peered into the storm; it was now so dense—"dreadful beyond description," as he put it—that he could no longer make out even the ship's bow. He wondered whether the *Wager* had been blindsided by a massive wave, but the blow had come from underneath the hull. It was, he realized, a sunken rock.

The carpenter, Cummins, jolted awake in his cabin, had come to the same conclusion. He hurried to inspect the damage with his mate James Mitchell—who, for once, was not surly. While Cummins waited by a hatch, Mitchell scurried down a ladder into the hold, shining his lantern over the planks. No burst of water, he yelled up. The planks were intact!

As the waves thumped the ship, though, it lunged forward and struck more rocks. The rudder shattered and an anchor weighing more than two tons crashed through the ship's hull, leaving a gaping hole in the *Wager*. The ship began to teeter, rolling farther and farther over, and panic took hold. Some of the sick men who had not appeared on watch for two months staggered onto the deck with blackened skin and bloodshot eyes, rising from one deathbed to another. "In this dreadful situation," Byron observed, the *Wager* "lay for some little time, every soul on board looking upon the present minute as his last."

Another mountainous wave swept the ship, and she lurched onward, stumbling through a minefield of rocks, with no rudder to steer her and with the sea pouring through the hole. The carpenter's mate Mitchell cried, "Six foot of water in the hold!" An officer reported that the ship was now "full of water up to the hatches."

Byron glimpsed—and, perhaps more terrifyingly, heard—the surrounding breakers, thunderous waves crushing everything in their jaws. They were all around the ship. Where was the romance now?

Many of the men prepared to die. Some fell to their knees, reciting prayers in the spray. Lieutenant Baynes retreated with a bottle of liquor. Others, Byron noted, became "bereaved of all sense, like inanimate logs, and were bandied to and fro by the jerks and rolls of the ship, without exerting any efforts to help themselves." He added, "So terrible was the scene of foaming breakers around us that one of the bravest men we had could not help expressing his dismay at it, saying it was too shocking a sight to bear." The man tried to throw himself over the railing but was restrained. Another seaman stalked the deck waving his cutlass and screaming that he was the King of England.

One veteran sailor, John Jones, tried to galvanize the men. "My friends," he shouted, "let us not be discouraged: did you never see a ship amongst breakers before? Let us try to push her through them. Come, lend a hand; here is a sheet, and here is a brace; lay hold. I don't doubt but we may . . . save our lives." His courage inspired several officers and crewmen, including Byron. Some grabbed ropes to set the sails; others frantically pumped and bailed the water. Bulkeley attempted to maneuver the ship by manipulating the sails, pulling them one way and then the other. Even the helmsman, despite his inoperable wheel, remained at his post, insisting that it would be unbecoming to desert the *Wager* as long as it stayed afloat. And, astonishingly, that much-maligned ship kept going. Hemorrhaging water, she sailed on through the Gulf of Pain—without a mast, without a rudder, without a captain on the quarterdeck. The men quietly cheered her on. Her fate was theirs, and she fought with all she was worth, proudly, defiantly, nobly.

At last, she crashed into a cluster of rocks and began ripping apart. The two remaining masts started to fall and were cut down by the men before they could pull the ship entirely over. The bowsprit cleaved, windows burst, treenails popped, planks shattered, cabins collapsed, decks caved in. Water flooded the lower portions of the ship, snaking from chamber to chamber, filling nooks and crannies. Rats scurried upward. The men who had been too sick to leave their hammocks drowned before anyone could rescue them. As the poet Lord Byron wrote, in *Don Juan*, of a sinking ship, it "made a scene men do not soon forget," for they always remember what "breaks their hopes, or hearts, or heads, or necks."

The *Wager*, having improbably survived this far, offered one final gift to its inhabitants. "Providentially we stuck fast between two great rocks," John Byron noted. Sandwiched, the *Wager* did not sink completely—at least not yet. And as Byron climbed to a high point on the vessel's ruins, the sky cleared enough for him to see beyond the breakers. There, shrouded in mist, was an island.

Part Three

CASTAWAYS

CHAPTER 8

Wreckage

THE SEAWATER BUBBLED UP toward the surgeon's cabin, where Captain David Cheap lay motionless. Confined there since his injury, he had not witnessed the collision, but he'd recognized the loud scraping sound, the sound that every commander dreads—a hull grinding on rocks. And he knew that the *Wager*, that vessel of his voracious dreams, was lost. If he survived, he would face a court-martial to determine whether he had run His Majesty's Ship aground because of "willfulness, negligence, or other defaults." Would he be found guilty—guilty in the eyes of the court, guilty in the eyes of Anson, guilty in the eyes of himself—for wrecking the first man-of-war under his command, thus ending his naval career? Why had the lieutenant not alerted him to the danger earlier? Why had the surgeon knocked him out with opium—"contrary to my knowledge," Cheap would insist, "telling me it was only something to prevent fever"?

As the inexhaustible army of waves continued their assault, he felt the *Wager*'s remaining husk thudding among the rocks, making a death rattle. Bulkeley recalled, "We expected every moment that the ship would part," and the violent tremors "shocked every person aboard." The bone in Cheap's shoulder had been reset, during a nearly three-hour operation, and he was still in great pain.

Soon Byron and Campbell approached the surgeon's cabin doorway, dripping, ghostly figures seemingly from another world. The midshipmen apprised Cheap of what had happened and told him about the island. About a musket shot away, it appeared swampy, barren, and storm-swept, with scrubby woodlands and mountains rising into the gloomy mist. The island offered no "sign of culture," according to Byron. But it offered an escape: "We now thought of nothing but saving our lives."

Cheap instructed them to immediately deploy the four vessels that were strapped on the deck: the thirty-six-foot longboat, the twenty-five-foot cutter, the twenty-four-foot barge, and the eighteen-foot yawl. "Go and save all the sick," he said.

Byron and Campbell beseeched Cheap to get into a transport vessel with them. But he was resolved to abide by the code of the sea: a captain must be the last to leave his sinking ship, even if it means going down with it. "Don't mind me," he insisted. The seaman John Jones also attempted to persuade the captain to depart. Cheap responded, according to Jones, that "if the people's lives were saved, he had no regard to his own."

Byron was awed by Cheap's bravery: "He gave his orders at that time with as much coolness as ever he had done." Still, there was something unnerving about his resolution, as if he believed that only in death could he reclaim his honor.

The water continued creeping upward, sloshing and gurgling. One could hear men and boys scrambling on deck, and that awful, sickening sound of wood grinding on rocks.

John Bulkeley tried to help lower the transport boats, but there were no longer any masts from which to hoist them, and the once orderly crew had devolved into chaos. Most of the men couldn't swim and were engaged in a grim calculus: jump amid the breakers and attempt to make it to shore, or linger as the ship disintegrated?

The longboat—the largest, heaviest, and most essential of

the transport vessels—was cracked and buried under debris. But the men realized that the lighter barge could be dragged across the deck. Come on, come on! Grab hold and heave! It was now or never. Bulkeley, along with several strong sailors, lifted the barge over the gunwale and, using ropes, lowered it into the sea. Men began clamoring to get onboard, pushing and shoving, and several leapt inside, nearly capsizing it. Bulkeley watched the men as they rowed across the perilous waves, through the mist, and around the rocks, until they reached a beach on a corner of the island. It was the first solid ground they'd touched in two and a half months, and they collapsed.

Back on the *Wager*, Bulkeley waited for some of them to return with the barge. None did. It was raining hard, and the wind now hissed from the north, bringing forth a tumbling sea. The deck quaked, stirring Bulkeley and the others as only the prospect of death can, and they eventually succeeded in heaving the yawl and cutter into the water. The sickest were ferried first. The twenty-five-year-old purser, Thomas Harvey, responsible for the ship's provisions, made sure the crew grabbed whatever supplies they could. These included a few pounds of flour stashed in an uncleaned tobacco bag; guns and ammunition; cooking and eating utensils; a compass, maps, and chronicles of early explorers for navigation; a medicine chest; and a Bible.

After several hours, most of the company had been evacuated, but the carpenter's mate Mitchell, who'd always had a murderous glint about him, refused to depart, as did a dozen or so of his cohorts. They were joined by the boatswain, King, the very officer who was supposed to be enforcing discipline. This faction began to break open casks of liquor and indulge themselves, preferring, it seemed, to die in one last orgy of revelry. "We had several in the ship so thoughtless of their danger, so stupid and insensible of their misery," Bulkeley recalled, that "they fell into the most violent outrage and disorder."

Before Bulkeley left the ship, he tried to retrieve some of the ship's records. Logbooks were supposed to be preserved from a wreck so that the Admiralty could later determine the potential culpability of not only the captain but also the lieutenant, the master, and other officers. Bulkeley was shocked to discover that many of the *Wager*'s records had disappeared or were shredded, and not by mere accident. "We have good reason to apprehend there was a person employed to destroy them," he recalled. Somebody, whether a navigator or perhaps even a more senior officer, wanted to shield his actions from scrutiny.

John Byron hoped to collect some of his clothing before abandoning the ship. He went below, creeping through the detritus as water rose around him. Remnants of his old home—chairs, tables, candles, letters, mementos—floated past, as did the bodies of the dead. As he went deeper, the hull buckled and water rushed in. "I was forced to get upon the quarterdeck again, without saving a single rag but what was upon my back," he noted.

Despite the danger, he felt compelled to return for Captain Cheap, and along with a few officers he waded through the watery onslaught until he arrived at the surgeon's cabin. Byron and the others pleaded with Cheap to come with them.

He inquired whether all the other men had been ferried off. Yes, they explained, except for a small unruly gang that was intent on staying. Cheap indicated that he would wait. But after they swore that they had done all they could to remove these lunatics—and there was nothing more that could be done—Cheap finally, reluctantly, rose from his bed. Using his cane, he struggled to walk, and while Byron and some of the men steadied him, others carted off his sea chest, which, among the few belongings, contained the letter from Anson naming him the captain of the *Wager*. "We helped him into the boat," Campbell recalled, "and carried him ashore."

The castaways huddled on the beach in the cold, slashing rain. Cheap calculated that of the *Wager*'s original complement of some 250 men and boys, 145 had survived. They were a haggard, sickly, scantily clad bunch, who looked as if they'd been shipwrecked for ages. They included Byron, who was now seventeen, and Bulkeley; the spineless Lieutenant Baynes; the haughty Midshipman Campbell; Byron's messmates Cozens, who couldn't keep himself from the bottle, and Isaac Morris; the skillful carpenter, Cummins; the purser, Harvey; the young, strong surgeon, Elliot, whom Cheap, despite his flare of anger over the opium, considered a friend; and the veteran sailor Jones. There were also Master Clark and his son; the octogenarian cook and a twelve-year-old boy; the free Black seaman, John Duck; and Cheap's faithful steward, Peter Plastow. Many of the marines had perished, but their captain, Robert Pemberton, had survived, and so had his knife-fighting lieutenant, Thomas Hamilton, who was one of Cheap's closest allies. A few invalids also lay on the island.

Cheap didn't know exactly where he and his men were, or what lurked around them. It was extremely doubtful that any European ships would ever pass near enough to the island to spot them. They were cut off, lost. "It is natural to think that to men thus upon the point of perishing by shipwreck the getting to land was the highest attainment of their wishes," Byron wrote, adding, "This was a great and merciful deliverance from immediate destruction; but then we had wet, cold, and hunger to struggle with, and no visible remedy against any of these evils." Cheap believed that the only way they might see England again was by preserving the cohesion of the ship. Already he was dealing with the fact that a group of drunks remained on the unsubmerged part of the wreck... and were the men on the beach looking at him differently? Did they blame him for being marooned?

Night was quickly coming on, and it was getting colder. The thin strip of beach offered no protection from the stinging winds and rains. Though Byron and his companions were "faint, benumbed, and almost helpless," they exerted themselves to look for shelter. They dragged themselves inland through tangled, marshy grass and then up steep hills crowded with trees that were permanently bent over from the gales, as hunched and beaten as the castaways themselves.

After trekking a short distance, Byron noticed, tucked amid these woodlands, a dome-shaped structure. About ten feet across and six feet tall, it was covered with brush and had an opening in the front. It was some sort of dwelling, which Byron described as a wigwam. He looked around. No sign of the inhabitants, but they must be out there, either on the island or on the mainland. Inside the shelter were some lances and other weaponry, and the men feared being ambushed once it was dark. "Our uncertainty of their strength and disposition gave alarm to our imagination, and kept us in continual anxiety," Byron noted.

Several men squeezed into the shelter, seeking refuge from the storm, and they cleared a space for Captain Cheap, who had to be helped inside. In his condition, he would have "certainly lost his life without such a shelter," Campbell wrote.

There was no room for Byron, and along with most of the others he lay down in the mud. The stars, which had once guided them across the sea, were blotted out by the clouds, and Byron was cast in total darkness as he listened to the crashing surf and the jostling branches and the moaning sick.

It stormed all night. By morning it was still storming, and he had not slept. Though he and the rest of the castaways were drenched and half frozen, they forced themselves to their feet—except for one of the invalids and two other ailing men who had been sleeping beside Byron. Nothing awoke them, and it dawned on Byron that they were dead.

Near the shore, Cheap leaned on his cane. The mist hung over the sea, enclosing him and his men in a gray netherworld. Through the vaporous light, he could make out the remnants of the *Wager* still wedged between the rocks—a grotesque reminder of what had befallen them. It was obvious that King, Mitchell, and the other renegades who had refused to abandon the ship would soon be drowned. Determined to rescue them, Cheap dispatched young Campbell and a small party to fetch them in the yawl.

Campbell set off, and upon boarding the *Wager*, he was stunned by the bedlam. Mitchell and his gang, abetted by the boatswain, King, had commandeered what remained of the ship, pirating the wreckage like the survivors of an apocalypse. "Some were singing psalms," Campbell noted, "others fighting, others swearing, and some lay drunk on the deck." A few of the inebriates had fallen into the pooling waters and drowned, and their corpses were strewn among the revelers, along with empty casks of liquor and debris.

Campbell spotted a barrel of gunpowder and went to salvage it. But two of the seamen, embittered by his mistreatment of them during the voyage, came at him, screaming, "Damn ye!" A third seaman charged toward him with a bayonet, the blade shimmering. Campbell fled with his party, leaving the renegades on their doomed prize.

That evening, while Cheap was in the shelter, he was awakened by a blast, which was so loud it echoed over the blaring winds. Suddenly a metallic ball screeched right above his roof, smashing into the surrounding trees and cratering in the earth. Then came another blast—a burst of light radiating through the darkness. Cheap realized that the men on the wreck, fearing that it was about to fully sink, were firing shots from a cannon on the quarterdeck—a signal that they were *now* ready to come ashore.

The stragglers were successfully retrieved. As they paraded onto the island, Cheap fixated on their appearance. Over their tarred trousers and checkered shirts, they were wearing clothes of the finest silk and lace, which they had pilfered from the abandoned sea chests of the officers.

Because King was the boatswain, Cheap held him most responsible, and as the other castaways looked on, Cheap stepped toward him. King, in his regal outfit, was acting like a lord paramount. Cheap's left arm dangled lamely, but with his right one he raised his cane and struck King with such fury that the burly boatswain crumpled to the ground. Cheap cursed him as a rogue. Then he forced King and the rest of the lot, including Mitchell, to remove the officers' clothing until they looked, as Bulkeley put it, "like a parcel of transported felons." Cheap had made clear that he was still their captain.

CHAPTER 9

The Beast

BYRON WAS HUNGRY. In the few days since he and his companions had been cast on the island, they had come across virtually nothing to eat. "We had most of us fasted" forty-eight hours, Byron wrote, and some even longer than that. They had yet to spot a single animal on land to hunt—not even a rat. More surprisingly, perhaps because of the tremendous breakers, the waters near the shore seemed empty of fish. "The very sea," Byron wrote, "is found to be almost as barren as the land." Finally, somebody shot a seagull, and Captain Cheap ordered that it be divvied among the group.

The men assembled branches and struck together pieces of flint and metal from a tinderbox, struggling to ignite the damp wood. At last, a flame crackled upward, the smoke twisting in the wind. The old cook, Thomas Maclean, skinned the bird and boiled it in a large pot, sprinkling in some of their flour to make a thick soup. The steaming portions were doled out, like sacred offerings, in the few wooden bowls they had salvaged.

Byron relished his share. Yet moments later, he and his companions were all, as Byron put it, "seized with the most painful sickness at our stomachs" and "violent retchings." The flour had been contaminated. The men were now even more depleted than before, and they were discovering that the climate was marked by almost incessant tempests. A British captain who passed by the island nearly a century later noted how the fierce squalls beat down from the ever-present clouds that engulfed the surrounding lonely heights, and called it a place where "the soul of man dies in him."

As hungry as Byron and his companions were, they were afraid to wander far—their fears heightened by their deep-seated prejudices. "Being strongly prepossessed that the savages were retired but some little distance from us, and waited to see us divided, our parties did not make... any great excursions," Byron noted.

The castaways mostly stayed along the shore, which was cordoned off by the sodden grasslands and by the steep hills covered in dense, gnarly woods. Looming to the southwest was a small mountain, and to the north and east there were more daunting peaks, including one that rose about two thousand feet, with a flat top and vapors rising from it like a smoky volcano.

The men scavenged the beach for mussels and snails. Refuse from the wreck had begun to wash ashore: chunks of the decks, the stump of the mainmast, a chain pump, a gun carriage, and a bell. Byron picked through the litter, looking for anything useful. Several corpses had been disgorged from the wreck, and he recoiled at these "hideous spectacles." But lying among them, he discovered, was something that suddenly seemed more valuable than the galleon itself: a wooden cask filled with salted beef.

On May 17, three days after the wreck, the gunner, John Bulkeley, savored a few scraps of meat. In his journal, he noted that it would soon be the Pentecost—the seventh Sunday after Easter, when Christians commemorate the moment that the Holy Spirit appeared during a harvest feast. As the Scripture puts it, on that day "whoever calls on the name of the Lord shall be saved."

Like the majority of the castaways, Bulkeley had no shelter—he was eating, sleeping, and squatting outside. "It rained so hard that it had almost cost us our lives," he wrote. Byron, meanwhile, fretted that it would be "impossible for us to subsist" much longer without shelter. The temperature hovered around freezing, and the blistering ocean winds and the constant dampness made it the kind of cold that got under one's clothing, turning lips blue and causing teeth to chatter. The kind of cold that killed.

Bulkeley had an idea. He enlisted Cummins and several of the stoutest seamen to help him drag the cutter up the shore, flip it over, and prop it up with the keel pointing upward—the goal, Bulkeley wrote, was "to contrive something like a house."

He and his friends crowded into the dry sanctuary. Spotting Byron wandering aimlessly about, Bulkeley welcomed him in. As the gunner gathered the men together, assisting them, they were grateful. He had made a fire—that spark of civilization—and they huddled around the flames, trying to warm themselves. Byron, in his journal, described removing his wet clothing, wringing it out and beating it free of lice, then putting everything back on.

The men pondered their situation. Though Cheap had punished the renegades, they remained a source of turbulence, especially Mitchell. And throughout the company Bulkeley heard growing "murmurings and discontent" about the captain. They blamed him for their misery and wondered what he was doing to rescue them.

Without Commodore Anson to guide them, Bulkeley wrote, "things began to have a new *face*." There was a "general disorder and confusion among the people, who were now no longer implicitly obedient." In the British Navy, volunteer and pressed seamen stopped being paid after their ship was decommissioned, and, as two of the castaways argued, the loss of the *Wager* meant that for most of them, their earnings had likely ceased: they were suffering for nothing. Weren't they therefore entitled to be "their own masters, and no longer subjected to command"?

Bulkeley, in his journal, recorded some of the complaints about Cheap. If only the captain had conferred with his officers at sea, he wrote, "we might probably have escaped our present unhappy condition." Yet Bulkeley was careful not to openly side with the agitators, noting that he'd "always acted in obedience to command." Many of the disaffected still gravitated toward him. He'd proven his abilities on the voyage (had he not beseeched the captain to turn around?), and he now seemed to be the heartiest among them. He had even provided them shelter. In his journal, Bulkeley jotted a line from the poet John Dryden:

Presence of mind, and courage in distress,
Are more than armies to procure success.

Bulkeley knew that none of them would survive much longer without additional sources of food. He tried to pinpoint the party's location by mapping the stars and dead reckoning. He figured that they were stranded off the Chilean coast of Patagonia, at around 47 degrees south and 81:40 degrees west. But he had no sense of the island. Was the rest of it as inimical to human life? Given that mountains obscured what lay to the east, some of the castaways wondered if they might actually be on the mainland. This was farfetched. But that it was a question at all underscored that they were as starved for knowledge as they were for food. They required both if Bulkeley was ever to find a way back to his wife and five children.

The storm momentarily waned, and Bulkeley glimpsed the alien sun. Loading his musket, he set out with a party to explore. Byron went with another armed group, insisting that they had no choice but to determine if there was any food beyond the shoreline.

The ground was boggy, and their feet sank as they slogged through the grasslands and up the wooded hillsides. They scrambled around decaying trunks that had been uprooted by the winds, and the trees, both living and dead, were so densely packed together that it was like marching through hedges. Roots and creepers entangled the men's limbs; thorns tore their skin.

Byron, making a passage with bare hands, soon became exhausted, though he still marveled at the unusual plant life. "The wood here," he wrote, "is chiefly of the aromatic kind: the iron wood, a wood of a very deep red hue, and another, of an exceeding bright yellow." He did not see many birds inland. There were some woodcocks and hummingbirds, some thorn-tailed rayaditos and what he described as a "large kind of robin red-breasted," which was a long-tailed meadowlark. Besides seabirds and vultures, he lamented, these appeared to be "the only feathered inhabitants." (The British captain who surveyed the island nearly a century later wrote, "As if to complete the dreariness and utter desolation of the scene, even the birds seemed to shun its neighborhood.")

Once, when Byron was apart from his companions, he spotted a vulture sitting atop a hill, its head bald and obscene. Byron crept toward it, trying not to make a sound—to rustle the leaves or crack the brambles underfoot. He was aiming his musket when he suddenly heard a loud growling nearby. And then again, a totally unfamiliar sound. He bolted. "The woods were so gloomy I could see nothing," he noted, "but as I retired this noise followed me close." Clutching his musket, he stumbled through the clawing branches until he reached the rest of his party. Some of the men claimed that they had not only heard the growling but had glimpsed a "very large beast." Perhaps it was merely a figment of their imaginations—as their minds, like their bodies, unraveled from hunger. Or perhaps, as Byron and many of the seamen now believed, a beast was out there, stalking them.

After a while, the castaways gave up trying to cross the island—it was too impenetrable. The only nourishment they had gathered was a couple of woodcocks, which they'd shot, and some wild celery. "As for food this island produces none," Bulkeley concluded. Byron thought that the environment was "scarce to be paralleled in any part of the globe, in that it affords neither fruits, grain, nor even roots for the sustenance of man."

Byron and a few companions climbed the small mountain overlooking their encampment, hoping to at least get a better sense of where they were situated. The mountain was so steep that they had to cut steps into its side. When Byron reached the summit, breathing in the thin air, the view was breathtaking. There was no doubt that they were on an island. It extended about two miles from the southwest to northeast, and nearly four miles from the southeast to the northwest, where the encampment had been set up.

In every direction Byron looked, the wilderness spanned into more wilderness: remote, impassable, and chillingly beautiful. To the south, he saw another seemingly desolate island, and to the east, in the far distance, he could make out a series of icebound peaks—the Andes on the mainland. Surveying the island where the *Wager* had run aground, he noticed that it was battered on all sides by a wild, frothing sea—"a scene," as he put it, "of such dismal breakers as would discourage the most daring from making attempts in small boats." There seemed to be no escape.

CHAPTER 10

Our New Town

CAPTAIN DAVID CHEAP EMERGED from the native dwelling carrying a pistol. The men continued to look at him doubtfully, as if they had found out some secret about him. After less than a week on the island, he was in danger of losing their trust as they realized the full extent of their predicament. Not only were the three boats unable to weather a long journey; they were too small to carry most of the castaways. And even if they located tools and materials to build a larger vessel, it would take them months to complete the task. They were stuck here for the foreseeable future, with winter approaching, and they were already showing signs of physical and psychological deterioration.

Cheap knew that unity was paramount to their survival, intuiting a principle that science would later demonstrate. In 1945, in one of the most comprehensive modern studies of human deprivation, known as the Minnesota Starvation Experiment, scientists assessed the effects of hunger on a group of individuals. During a six-month period, thirty-six male volunteers—all were single, fit pacifists who had shown an ability to get along with others—had their calorie intake cut in half. The men lost their strength and stamina—each shedding roughly a quarter of his body weight—and they became irritable, depressed, and unable to concentrate. Many of the volunteers had hoped that self-abnegation would lead them, like monks, to a deeper spirituality, but instead they began conniving, stealing food, and coming to blows. "How many people have I hurt with my indifference, my grouchiness, my overbearing perversion for food?" one subject wrote. Another subject shouted, "I'm going to kill myself," then turned on one of the scientists and said, "I'm going to kill *you*." This person also fantasized about cannibalism and had to be removed from the experiment. A report summarizing the results of the study noted that the volunteers were shocked at "how thin their moral and social veneers seemed to be."

The castaways on Wager Island, already depleted from the voyage, were receiving far less caloric intake than those in the experiment did, and they were under far greater distress: nothing about their environment was controlled. Captain Cheap, ill and hobbling, had to cope with his own torments. Yet he domineered. He hated consulting with other officers, and there was no time to waste. And he began to forge a plan to carve out an outpost in this wilderness, planting the seed of the British Empire. To prevent them from falling into a Hobbesian state with "every man against every man," Cheap believed the castaways needed binding rules and rigid structures—and their commander.

Cheap summoned everyone and reviewed the Articles of War, reminding them that the rules still applied on land, particularly those prohibiting any "mutinous assemblies... practices, designs"—on "pain of death." The men all needed to pull together, each fulfilling his designated tasks with steadiness and courage; they were still part of that human machinery moving with precision to the captain's will.

Given the potential threats on the island and the lack of food, Cheap decided that his men must salvage the wreckage of the *Wager*, where a few segments of the quarterdeck and forecastle were still above water. "My first care was to securing a good quantity of arms, ammunition and some provisions," he wrote in a report.

He began to put together an excavation team. For this hazardous mission, he chose the gunner, John Bulkeley, though he considered him to be an argumentative sailor, a so-called sea lawyer who was always ready to insist that he knew better than his superiors. Ever since the wreck, Bulkeley seemed to carry himself with smug independence, building his own great cabin and holding forth to the other men. But, unlike Lieutenant Baynes, Bulkeley was a ferocious worker—a survivor—and other members of the excavation team would perform better with him in charge. Cheap also sent along the midshipman John Byron, who had faithfully served him during the voyage and who had helped him escape the sinking ship.

As Cheap looked on, Bulkeley, Byron, and the small team of recruits set off in a boat; the welfare of the entire group was now in their hands. As they rowed alongside the fragments of the *Wager*, the waves thrashed them. Once their boat was fastened to the man-of-war, they slithered onto the wreckage, crawling along the caved-in deck and cracked beams, which continued to break apart even as the men were perched on top of them.

As the explorers inched along the sunken ruins, they saw, down in the water, the corpses of their compatriots floating between the decks; one misstep, and they would join them. "The difficulties we had to encounter in these visits to the wreck cannot be easily described," Byron wrote.

They detected some barrels amid the debris and lassoed and transferred them to their boat. "Found several casks of wine and brandy," Bulkeley noted excitedly. At one point, he reached the captain's storeroom and pried open the door: "Got out several casks of rum and wine, and brought them ashore."

Cheap soon dispatched more parties to help with the excavation. "By the Captain's orders we were every day working on the wreck, except when the weather would not permit us," Midshipman Campbell wrote. All three boats were deployed. Cheap knew that the castaways had to salvage as much as possible before the wreck submerged entirely.

They tried to bore deeper into the hull, into the flooded chambers. The seeping water pooled around them as they burrowed through layers of debris, like shipworms eating through a hull. Hours of labor often turned up little of value. At last, the men broke into part of the hold, extracting ten barrels of flour, a cask of peas, several casks of beef and pork, a container of oatmeal, and more casks of brandy and wine. They also retrieved canvas, carpentry tools, and nails—which, Campbell noted, "in our situation were of infinite service." And there was still more: several chests of wax candles, along with bales of cloth, stockings, shoes, and several clocks.

Meanwhile, the hull had further come apart—"blown up," as Bulkeley put it. And as the wreckage became increasingly dangerous to climb on, with little more than a few rotted planks poking out of the sea, the men devised a new strategy: they fastened hooks to long wooden sticks and, reaching over the gunwale, tried to blindly fish out additional supplies.

On shore, Cheap had erected a tent by his dwelling, which stored all the provisions. As he had on the *Wager*, he relied on the strict hierarchy of officers and petty officers to enforce his edicts. But, amid the constant threat of rebelliousness, he primarily trusted an inner circle of allies—a structure within a structure—that included the marine lieutenant, Hamilton; the surgeon, Elliot; and the purser, Harvey.

Cheap also secured all the guns and ammunition in the store tent; no one was allowed access without his permission. The captain always carried a pistol, and he authorized Hamilton, Elliot, and Harvey to do so as well. With their guns gleaming, they met the transport boats as they came ashore, making sure that everything was properly transferred to the tent and registered in the purser's accounts. There would be no thievery—another Thou Shalt Not in the Articles of War.

Cheap found that, at times, Bulkeley bristled at all the rules and regulations. On nights when the moon was out, the gunner sought to continue mining the wreck with his friends, but Cheap forbade it, because of the risk of stealing. Bulkeley complained in his journal of Cheap and his inner circle, "They were so cautious of anything being embezzled that they would not suffer the boats to go off and work by night.... By this we omitted several opportunities of getting out provisions, and other useful things, which we shall shortly stand in great need of."

Despite such tensions, after a week on the island there was generally a new sense of purpose. To conserve rations, Cheap doled them out sparingly—with what Byron called "the most frugal economy." On those fortunate days when Cheap could offer the castaways meat, a slice ordinarily for one person was divided among three. Even so, this was more sustenance than the men had enjoyed since being orphaned on the island. "Our stomachs are become nice and dainty," Bulkeley wrote. Periodically, Cheap was able to further cheer the group with servings of wine or brandy.

Though the carpenter's mate Mitchell and his companions remained fractious, the open rebelliousness had quieted; even the boatswain, King, had begun keeping his distance from them. Cheap, whose insecurities could lead to sudden eruptions, also seemed calmer. And he and his men soon received an inexplicable blessing: their scurvy began to be cured, unbeknownst to them, by the island's wild celery.

Campbell wrote that, all this time, Cheap had "expressed the greatest concern for the safety of the people," adding, "If it had not been for the Captain, many would have perished."

To Byron, the castaways were all like Robinson Crusoe, ingeniously eking out an existence. One day they discovered a new source of nourishment: a long, narrow form of seaweed, which they scraped from the rocks. When boiled in water for about two hours, it made what Bulkeley deemed "a good and wholesome food." Other times Byron and his companions would mix the seaweed with flour and fry it with the tallow from candles; they called the crispy concoction "slaugh cakes." Campbell noted, "I had the honour to sup" with Cheap one night, adding, "We had a slaugh cake of his making, the best I ever eat on the island." (Campbell was still startled by the sight of his commander being reduced to such fare: "This poor stuff even the Captain was forced to content himself with!")

Though the castaways were desperate to hunt the black-necked cormorants and the white-chinned petrels and the other aquatic birds that perched tantalizingly on the rocks out at sea, they had no way to reach them, because the boats were occupied mining the wreck. Even the men who could swim were deterred by the surf and the water temperature, which at that time of year was often in the forties. If they dove in anyway, they would soon suffer from hypothermia, and given their thin bodies, they could die within an hour. Some of the castaways, refusing to give up the bird hunt, scrounged whatever materials they could find and pieced together makeshift miniature rafts. These included, Bulkeley wrote, "punts, cask-boats, leather-boats, and the like."

A thirty-year-old seaman named Richard Phipps improvised a raft by cracking open a large barrel, then taking part of the wooden shell and lashing it with rope to a pair of logs. Though a poor swimmer, he bravely set out, as Byron put it, "in quest of adventures in this extraordinary and original piece of embarkation." He carried a shotgun, with Cheap's permission, and whenever he spied a bird, he steadied himself as well as he could amid the waves, held his breath, and fired. After some success, he began to venture farther along the coast, mapping out new realms.

One night he failed to return. After he didn't come back the next day as well, Byron and the rest of the castaways mourned the loss of one more companion.

The following day, another seaman, undaunted, headed out on his own raft to hunt. As he approached a rocky islet, he spotted a large animal. He edged closer, gun ready. It was Phipps! His craft had been capsized by a wave, and he'd just managed to scramble onto the rock, where he'd been stranded, shivering and hungry—the castaway of castaways.

After Phipps was brought back to the encampment, he immediately began building a new, sturdier craft. This time he took an oxhide, which had been used on the *Wager* to sift gunpowder, and wrapped it around several bent wooden poles, forming a suitable canoe. And off he went again.

Byron and two friends designed their own precarious craft—a flat-bottomed raft, which they propelled with a pole. When they weren't mining the wreck, they went on excursions. Byron made a study of the seabirds that he saw, including the steamer duck, which had short wings and big webbed feet, and made a snoring sound when it cleaned its feathers at night. He considered this duck an avian equivalent of a racehorse, because of "the velocity with which it moved across the surface of the water, in a sort of half flying, half running motion."

Once, while Byron and his two friends were on a long journey on their raft, they were caught in a squall. They took refuge on a protruding rock, but while pulling their vessel out of the water they lost hold of it. Byron could not swim well, and he watched their lifeline drifting away. But one of the other men dove into the water and retrieved it; there were still acts of gallantry.

The castaways never caught many birds on these voyages, but they relished the few they did catch, and Byron marveled at the fact that their proud navy was patrolling the coastal waters.

John Bulkeley was on a mission. With the carpenter, Cummins, and several other stout friends, he began collecting branches; at a flat spot in the encampment, the men hammered them into an extended skeletal frame. Then they picked leaves and reeds from the forest and used them to cover the exterior with thatch, further insulating the walls with bits of camlet wool taken from the wreck. Using strips of canvas sails as curtains, they divided the space into fourteen quarters—or "cabins," as Bulkeley called them. And voilà! they had built a dwelling, one that dwarfed the captain's. "This is a rich house, and, in some parts of the world, would purchase a pretty estate,"

Bulkeley wrote. "Considering where we are, we cannot desire a better habitation."

Inside, wooden planks served as tables, and barrels were used as chairs. Bulkeley had private sleeping quarters, along with a place by the firelight to read his cherished book, *The Christian's Pattern: or, A Treatise of the Imitation of Jesus Christ*, which he'd rescued from the ship. "Providence made it the means of comforting me," he noted. He also now had a dry refuge where he could write regularly in his journal—a ritual that kept his mind alert and preserved some part of his former self from the ravaging world. Moreover, he had discovered Master Clark's logbook, which had been torn to pieces—yet another sign that someone had been determined to expunge evidence of any human errors that might have contributed to the wreck. Bulkeley vowed to be exceedingly "careful in writing each day's transaction," in order to ensure a "faithful relation of facts."

Other castaways, meanwhile, were constructing their own "irregular habitations," as Byron called them. There were tents and lean-tos and thatch-covered huts, though none as large as Bulkeley's.

Perhaps out of adherence to longstanding class and social hierarchies, or perhaps simply from a desire for familiar order, the men segregated on the island much the way they had on the ship. Cheap now had his shelter to himself, where he ate with his closest allies and where he was attended to by his steward, Plastow. Bulkeley, for his part, shared his house largely with Cummins and other warrant officers.

Byron lived in a shelter with his fellow midshipmen, crowded together with Cozens, Campbell, and Isaac Morris, as if they were back in the oaken vault on the *Wager*'s orlop deck. The captain of the marines, Robert Pemberton, occupied a habitation next to the tents of the other Army forces. And the seamen, including John Jones and John Duck, broke off into their own communal shelters. The carpenter's mate Mitchell and his band of desperados also stuck together.

The area no longer resembled a campsite. It formed, Byron noted, "a kind of village," with a street running through it. Bulkeley wrote proudly, "Observing our new town, we find there are no less than eighteen houses in it."

There were other signs of transformation. In one tent, the group had set up a makeshift hospital, where the ailing could be looked after by the surgeon and his mate. To collect drinking water, they caught rain with empty barrels. Some of the survivors cut strips of cloth salvaged from the *Wager* and stitched them into their loose garments. Fires burned constantly—not only for warmth and cooking but also for the slim possibility that the smoke might be detected by a passing ship. And the *Wager*'s bell that had washed ashore was rung the way it had been on the ship—to signal a meal or a gathering.

At night, some men would sit around a blaze, listening to the old salts spin their yarns of the world that once was. John Jones confessed that when he had confidently beseeched the crew to save the *Wager* before it struck, he'd never thought that any of them would actually survive. Perhaps they were proof of a miracle.

Others read the few books that they had salvaged. Captain Cheap had a battered copy of Sir John Narborough's account of his British expedition to Patagonia between 1669 and 1671, and Byron borrowed it, escaping into an adventure still rife with hope and excitement.

The castaways gave names to the places around them, making them their own. They christened the body of water in front of their beach Cheap's Bay. The summit overlooking their village—the one that Byron had climbed—was dubbed Mount Misery, and the largest mountain later became known as Mount Anson. And they named their new home after their old one: Wager Island.

After only a few weeks, most of their beach had been picked clean of shellfish, and the wreck was offering fewer and fewer provisions. Hunger began to gnaw at the men again, until their journals became an endless litany about it: "Hunting all day in quest of food . . . nightly task of roving after food . . . quite exhausted for want of food... not tasted a bit of bread, or any wholesome diet, for such a long time... the calls of hunger..."

Byron realized that, unlike the solitary castaway Alexander Selkirk, who had inspired *Robinson Crusoe,* he now had to cope with the most unpredictable and volatile creatures in all of nature: desperate humans. "Ill humour and discontent, from the difficulties we laboured under in procuring subsistence, and the little prospect there was of any amendment in our condition, was now breaking out apace," Byron wrote.

Mitchell and his gang roved about the island with their long beards and hollowed eyes, demanding more liquor and threatening those who opposed them. Even Byron's friend Cozens had somehow plied himself with extra wine and was getting wildly drunk.

Late one evening, someone sneaked into the supply tent next to Captain Cheap's dwelling. "The store tent was broke open, and robbed of a great deal of flour," Bulkeley wrote. The burglary threatened the very survival of the group. Byron called it a "most heinous crime."

Another day, while Mitchell and a fellow seaman were out searching the *Wager,* Byron and a party went out to join them. When they arrived, they noticed that the seaman who had been with Mitchell was lying on the half-submerged deck. His body was still, his expression unmoving. He was dead, and there were strange marks around his neck. Though Byron couldn't prove it, he suspected that Mitchell had strangled him so that he could keep all the spoils that they had salvaged from the wreck.

CHAPTER 11

Nomads of the Sea

SNOW BEGAN TO FALL, swirling with the winds and piling in great drifts on Mount Misery and across the shore. Everything seemed whited out, as if being erased. John Bulkeley wrote in his journal, "It freezes very hard, and we find it extremely cold."

Winter had arrived quickly, but that was not what most preoccupied the survivors. Before the blizzard, while Bulkeley was searching the wreck with Byron and Campbell, three slender canoes had appeared out of the mist. Unlike the castaways' rickety rafts, these were sturdy and strong, made from overlapping sheaths of bark meshed together with whale tendons and curved elegantly upward at the bow and the stern. Onboard were several men with bare chests and long black hair, carrying lances and slingshots. It was raining and blowing hard from the north, and Byron, freezing, was struck by their nakedness. "Their clothing was nothing but a bit of some beast's skin about their waists, and something woven from feathers over the shoulders," he wrote.

A fire was somehow kept going inside each canoe, and the paddlers seemed unfazed by the cold as they maneuvered expertly through the breakers. They were accompanied by several dogs—"cur-like looking" animals, Byron wrote—which surveyed the sea like fierce lookouts.

Byron and his companions stared at the men they deemed "savages." The men stared back at the white, skinny, hairy trespassers. "It was evident from their great surprise," Byron wrote, "and every part of their behavior, as well as their not having one thing in their possession which could be derived from white people, that they had never seen such."

They were a party of Kawésqar (Ka-WES-kar), which means "people who wear skins." Along with several other indigenous groups, the Kawésqar had settled in Patagonia and Tierra del Fuego thousands of years earlier. (Archeological evidence indicates that the first humans in the region arrived about twelve thousand years ago, toward the end of the Ice Age.) The Kawésqar had a population of a few thousand, and their territory spanned hundreds of miles along the coastline of southern Chile, stretching from the Golfo de Penas down to the Strait of Magellan. They generally traveled in small, familial groups. Given the impassable terrain, they spent much of their time in canoes and survived almost exclusively off marine resources. They have been called the nomads of the sea.

Over the centuries, they had adapted to the harsh environment. They knew virtually every indentation of the coastline, carrying mental maps of the labyrinthine channels and coves and fiords. They knew the storm-protected shelters; the crystal mountain streams suitable for drinking; the reefs laden with edible sea urchins and snails and blue mussels; the inlets where fish gathered in schools; and the best spots, depending on the season and the weather conditions, for hunting seals and otters and sea lions and cormorants and flightless steam ducks. The Kawésqar could identify, from circling vultures or the fetid scent, the location of a beached or wounded whale, which provided endless bounty: flesh to eat, blubber for extracting oil, and ribs and tendons for building canoes.

It was rare for the Kawésqar to stay in one place for more than a few days, as they were careful not to exhaust an area's food resources. And they were skilled navigators, especially the women, who typically steered and paddled the canoes. These long vessels were only about a meter wide, but each one had room to transport a family and its prized dogs, which served as night guards, hunting companions, and heat-bearing pets. Because the hulls had shallow bottoms, they were able to skirt over reefs and penetrate rocky channels; for ballast, their wooden floors were often covered with stonelike clay. By hugging the shoreline and reading the sky for sudden squalls, the Kawésqar journeyed through the Furious Fifties and seas that wrecked massive ships like the *Wager*. (The Yaghan, a seafaring people whose territory was farther south, faced even Cape Horn storms in their canoes.)

Though the Kawésqar and other canoe people lacked metal, they crafted an array of implements from natural materials. Whale bones were honed into chisels and barbed tips for harpoons and spears; dolphins' jawbones made fine combs. The skin and sinewy tendons from seals and whales offered string for bows, slingshots, and fishing nets. Seal bladders served as pouches. Plants were woven into baskets. Bark was carved into containers—and used as torches. Shells became everything from scoops to knives sharp enough to cut through bone. And the hides from seals and sea lions provided loincloths and shoulder capes.

European explorers, baffled by how anyone could survive in the region—and seeking to justify their brutal assaults on indigenous groups—often labeled the Kawésqar and other canoe people as "cannibals," but there is no credible evidence of this. The inhabitants had devised plenty of ways to find sustenance from the sea. The women, who did most of the fishing, tied limpets to ropy sinews and dropped them in the water, waiting to jerk a prize upward and grab it with one hand. The men, responsible for hunting, lured sea lions by singing softly or slapping the water, then harpooned them when they rose to investigate. Hunters set snares for geese that wandered on the grasslands at dusk, and they used slingshots to pick off cormorants. At night, the Kawésqar waved torches at nesting birds to blind them before clubbing them.

Moreover, they coped with the climate without wearing bulky clothing. To keep warm, they oiled their skin with insulating seal blubber. And in this land of fire they always kept a blaze going, using it not only for heat but also to roast meat, make implements, and send smoke signals. Logs were obtained from the myrtle tree, which would burn even when damp; baby bird feathers and insect nests provided highly flammable tinder. If a fire did go out, it was reignited by striking flint with the mineral pyrite, which contains sulfuric gases. In canoes, the fires were burned on sand or clay hearths, and the children were often responsible for stoking them.

The Kawésqar were so well adapted to the cold that centuries later NASA, hoping to figure out ways for astronauts to survive on a frozen planet, sent scientists to the region to learn their methods. One anthropologist described how the local inhabitants sustained themselves by moving from camp to camp: "Home could be a pebble beach, a pleasant stretch of sand, familiar rocks and islets, some during the winter months, others through the long summer days. Home was also the canoe... with its fireplace, potable water, a dog or two, domestic and hunting equipment, almost everything essential.... Whatever food or material they needed was in the water or along the shore."

Byron, Bulkeley, and Campbell waved their hats at the paddlers, beckoning them closer. Anson's expedition had been given a condescending manifesto from the King of England to present to any indigenous nations encountered during the voyage, offering to rescue them from their purportedly depraved conditions and to help them set up a government so that they could be a "happy people." Yet the castaways realized that the very people the English deemed "savages" might hold the key to their salvation.

The Kawésqar were hesitant to approach. They might have had little contact with Europeans, but no doubt they were aware of Spain's brutal conquest of other indigenous groups to the north—and had heard tales about the murderousness of pale boat people. Magellan and his band of conquistadores, the first Europeans to reach Patagonia, had lured two young inhabitants from one of the indigenous communities—the so-called giants—onto their ship with presents, then shackled them in irons. "When they saw the bolt across the fetters being struck with a hammer to rivet it and prevent them from being opened, these giants were afraid," Magellan's chronicler wrote. The Spanish boasted that they converted one of them to Christianity and renamed him Paul, as if they were somehow redeemers. Yet both hostages soon died of sickness. Later, in the nineteenth century, several Kawésqar were abducted by a German merchant and exhibited at a zoo in Paris as "savages in a natural state," drawing half a million spectators.

Byron and his companions tried to convince the Kawésqar that they meant no harm, displaying what Byron called "signs of friendship." As the rain perforated the sea, the paddlers drifted closer, the dogs growling, the wind thrumming. Both parties tried to communicate, but neither understood the other. "They uttered no word of any language we had ever heard," Byron recalled.

The three Englishmen held up bales of cloth that had been retrieved from the wreck, and offered them as gifts. The Kawésqar took them and were persuaded to come ashore. They hauled their canoes up the beach and followed Byron and Campbell through the little village of bizarre shelters, watching and being watched. Then they were led to Captain Cheap, who was evidently living in their dwelling.

Cheap greeted the strangers ceremoniously. They represented his best, and perhaps only, hope of finding food for his men, and they would undoubtedly have crucial intelligence on the location of hostile Spanish settlements and on the safest sea routes for escaping the island. Cheap presented each of the men with a sailor's hat and a red soldier's coat. Though they showed little interest in wearing such items, removing them whenever someone placed them on their bodies, they valued the color red. (The Kawésqar often painted their skin with red pigment made from burnt soil.) Captain Cheap also gave them a mirror. "They were strangely affected with the novelty," Byron wrote. "The beholder could not conceive it to be his own face that was represented, but that of some other behind it, which he therefore went round to the back of the glass to find out." Campbell noted that the Kawésqar were "extremely courteous in their behavior," and that Captain Cheap "treated them with great civility."

After a while, the Kawésqar departed in their canoes, the blue smoke from their fires marking their passage across the sea before they vanished. Cheap did not know if he would see them again. But two days later they returned, this time carrying with them a surprising amount of food, including three sheep.

They had obviously gone to great lengths to get hold of the sheep. The Kawésqar, who were not known to consume mutton, had likely obtained the animals by trading with another indigenous group that was in contact with the Spanish several hundred miles to the north. In addition, the Kawésqar brought the castaways what Bulkeley described as "the largest and best mussels I ever saw, or tasted." The famished Englishmen were extremely grateful. Campbell wrote that these people served as a "good example to many well-educated Christians!"

The Kawésqar left once more, but soon came back again with their wives and children, along with other families. There were some fifty people in total—the shipwreck being one of those attractions, like a beached whale, that drew disparate Kawésqar parties together. They seemed "much reconciled to our company," Byron wrote, and "we found that their intention was to settle among us." With fascination, he watched as they began to build dwellings, which they called *at*, by collecting tall branches and staking them into the ground in an oval. "They bend the extremities of these branches," Byron wrote, "so as to meet in a centre at top, where they bind them by a kind of woodbine, called supple-jack, which they split by holding it in their teeth. This frame, or skeleton of a hut, is made tight against the weather with a covering of boughs and bark." The Kawésqar had brought this bark with them in their canoes, having stripped it from their previous dwellings. Each shelter usually had two low entranceways, which were shielded by curtains of fern fronds. Inside, in the middle of the floor, there was a space for a hearth, and the damp ground around it was covered with ferns and branches for sitting and sleeping on. All this construction, Byron noted, was done with great quickness—it was yet another way the Kawésqar protected themselves from the elements.

When one of the ailing Englishmen died, the Kawésqar gathered with the castaways around the body. "The Indians are very watchful of the dead, sitting continually near the... corpse, and carefully covering him," Bulkeley wrote. "Every moment looking on the face of the deceased with abundance of gravity." As the body was being lowered into the earth, the Englishmen murmured prayers, and the Kawésqar stood solemnly. "Seeing the people with their hats off during the service," Bulkeley wrote, "they were very attentive and observant, and continued so till the burial was over."

Aware of how helpless the Englishmen were, the Kawésqar would regularly venture out to sea and then magically return with nourishment for them. Byron saw one woman depart with a companion in a canoe and, once offshore, grip a basket between her teeth and leap into the freezing water. "Diving to the bottom," Byron wrote, she "continued under water an amazing time." When she emerged, her basket was filled with sea urchins—a strange shellfish, Byron wrote, "from which several prickles project in all directions"; each urchin contained four or five yolks "resembling the inner divisions of an orange, which are of a very nutritive quality, and excellent flavor." After the woman deposited the urchins in the boat, she sucked in her breath and went down for more.

Bulkeley observed that some Kawésqar women dove deeper than thirty feet. "Their agility in diving, and their continuance under water for so long a time as they generally do, will be thought impossible by persons who have not been eye-witnesses," he wrote. Byron thought that "it seems as if Providence had endowed this people with a kind of amphibious nature."

The Kawésqar also managed to locate fish in a lagoon, driving them into nets with the help of their dogs, which Byron described as "very sagacious and easily trained." Bulkeley wrote, "This method of catching fish is, I believe, unknown anywhere else, and was very surprising."

The Kawésqar had provided Cheap with a lifeline. But after only a few days, the carpenter's mate Mitchell and other sailors began to run amok again. Defying Cheap's orders, they were stealing liquor and carousing and absconding with weapons from the wreck, rather than depositing them in the store tent. Byron noted that these men—"now subject to little or no control"—tried to "seduce" the Kawésqar women, which "gave the Indians such offense."

Word spread throughout the encampment that Mitchell and his marauders were conspiring to steal the Kawésqar's canoes and flee the island. Cheap dispatched Byron and other allies to foil the plot by guarding the canoes. But the Kawésqar had witnessed the insidious tensions mounting among the castaways—these men who allowed their hair to grow on their faces, who had no clue how to hunt or fish, who wore constrictive clothing that prevented a fire's heat from warming their skin, and who seemed on the brink of mayhem.

One morning when Cheap awoke, he discovered that all the Kawésqar had gone. They'd stripped the bark from their shelters and slipped away in their canoes, taking with them the secrets of their civilization. "Could we have entertained them as we ought," Byron lamented, "they would have been of great assistance to us." Given that the castaways' behavior had prompted this abrupt departure, he added, they did not expect to ever see the Kawésqar again.

CHAPTER 12

The Lord of Mount Misery

BYRON FOUND A DOG in the woods. The Kawésqar had left it behind, perhaps in their haste to get away. The dog came toward Byron and trailed him all the way back to camp, and at night it lay beside him, warming his body. During the day, it accompanied Byron wherever he went. "This creature grew so fond of me and faithful that he would suffer nobody to come near... without biting them," he wrote.

Byron was relieved to have a true companion. Since the departure of the Kawésqar, the outpost had spiraled back into chaos. The provisions were diminishing, and Captain Cheap faced an unbearable conundrum: if he continued distributing the same daily rations, he would avoid angering his men in the short term, but the food would run out sooner—and everyone would starve. So he chose to cut back on their miserably meager meals, provoking the seamen in their "tenderest point." Bulkeley noted in his journal that they switched to a "shorter allowance of flour, one pound for three men per diem." Days later, this amount was further reduced.

Bulkeley, hoping to get some nourishment, went with a party to the lagoon where the Kawésqar had caught fish. But the castaways discovered nothing on their own. "Our living now is very hard," Bulkeley wrote. "Shellfish are very scarce, and difficult to be had."

That June, with winter upon them, there were fewer hours of daylight, and the temperature was consistently below freezing. Rain often turned to snow or sleet. The hail, Bulkeley wrote, "beat with such violence against a man's face that he can hardly withstand it." Despite the gunner's stoicism, he complained that surely no one "ever met with such weather as we have," noting that conditions "are so extremely severe that a man will pause some time whether he shall stay in his tent and starve, or go out in quest of food."

One day Byron was in his shelter, trying to stay warm, when the dog, huddled beside him, began to growl. Byron looked up and saw a party of wild-eyed seamen in the doorway. They needed his dog, they said.

What for? Byron demanded.

They said that if they didn't eat it they'd starve.

Byron pleaded with them not to take the dog. But they dragged it, yelping, out of the shelter.

Soon Byron could no longer hear the dog barking. The men had slaughtered it—Byron didn't record if it was done by gunshot or by hand, as though he were unable to dwell on the killing. The animal was roasted over a fire while the ravenous men in the company gathered around the flames, awaiting their share. Byron remained by himself, distraught. But eventually he went over and watched the men in the smoky firelight devouring the meat and viscera. Under the circumstances, the gunner, Bulkeley, wrote, "we thought no English mutton preferable to it."

Byron finally reached out and took his portion. Later he found some of the discarded paws and pieces of skin, and he ate them, too. "The pressing calls of hunger drove our men to their wits' end," he confessed.

The poet Lord Byron, drawing on his grandfather's description, wrote in *Don Juan*:

> *What could they do? and hunger's rage grew wild:*
> *So Juan's spaniel, spite of his entreating,*
> *Was kill'd, and portion'd out for present eating.*

After less than a month on the island, John Bulkeley was watching the company fracture into warring parties. First, Mitchell and his band of nine outlaws deserted the main group and set up their own base, a few miles away, scouring for their own sources of food. They were known as the seceders, and it was perhaps best for everyone else that they had left the encampment. But they were armed and, as Campbell put it, "rambled wither they pleased." It was feared that such men, while flitting through the woods, might decide to raid the main settlement, making off with the transport boats or provisions.

One of the seamen at the encampment disappeared while foraging on Mount Misery, and a search party discovered his body stuffed in the bushes. The victim, Byron wrote, had been "stabbed in several places, and shockingly mangled"; his few supplies had evidently been taken. Byron suspected that Mitchell had committed "no less than two murders since the loss of our ship." The discovery of the body—and the discovery that some crewmen were willing to kill to survive—shook the search party. The seamen had always made sure to bury their fallen companions; as Byron wrote, it was a common belief that "the spirits of the dead were not at rest till their bodies were interred; and that they did not cease to haunt and trouble those who had neglected this duty to the departed." But now the men retreated hastily, leaving the half-frozen corpse on the ground.

Rifts were also growing among the men at the settlement. Many of them—including the boatswain, John King—had become brazenly vocal in their disdain for Captain Cheap. To them, he was stubborn, he was vainglorious, and he'd led them into this hellfire and was now incapable of getting them out. Why should he be the one to determine what tasks they performed and what amount of food they were allotted? What gave him the right to rule with absolute power when there was no ship, no Admiralty, no government at all? Midshipman Campbell, who remained loyal to Cheap, lamented that many men were "continually exclaiming against the Captain, and threatening the petty officers that stood by him."

Cheap had expected to be able to rely on the marine captain,

Robert Pemberton, and his soldiers to help suppress any unrest among the company. But Pemberton had broken away with his armed soldiers to form their own faction, though they continued to reside at the outpost. Because these marines were technically part of the Army, and because they were now back on land, Pemberton asserted his sole authority over them. In his hut, he had constructed a wooden chair, and he would sit majestically on it, surrounded by his soldiers. Above his shelter, he flew a tattered flag, marking his territory.

Campbell noted that the *Wager*'s company was sinking into a "state of anarchy," with various competing chiefs. There was so much animosity, so much internecine fury, that it was "absolutely uncertain what might be the consequence."

Byron, seeking to avoid what he called the cabals, moved to the edge of the village, alone. "Liking none of their parties, I built a little hut just big enough for myself," he wrote.

The shipwreck had laid waste to the old hierarchies: every man had now been dealt the same miserable hand. Bulkeley observed that such conditions—cold, hunger, disarray—could "really make a man weary of life." But amid this leveling and squalor, this democracy of suffering, Bulkeley seemed to thrive. He maintained his fine shelter and thinned out the vegetation surrounding it. And whereas many in the company seemed merely to be waiting for death, for eternal peace, he continued to forage fanatically: hunting birds, scraping seaweed off rocks, extracting what supplies he could from the wreckage. Any food that he obtained had to be placed in the communal store tent, but he was able to collect other prized materials for himself: planks, tools, shoes, strips of cloth. Money was worthless on the island, but, like a town merchant, he could barter these items for other necessities, as well as dole out favors. He also established a secret stash of guns and ammunition.

Each morning, Bulkeley would emerge warily from his estate. He believed that he must be careful, as *The Christian's Pattern* book said, "lest he be deceived by the devil, who never sleepeth but goeth about seeking whom he may devour."

He noticed that more and more of "the people," as he referred to the castaways, were flocking to his house, and in particular to *him*, John Bulkeley, to figure out what the party should do next. One day Pemberton, the marine captain, pulled Bulkeley and his friend Cummins aside, and they all conferred in Pemberton's dwelling. After ensuring that no one could overhear, Pemberton confided that he considered Lieutenant Baynes, the second-in-command, a *nothing*. What's more, he viewed Captain Cheap "in the same light." His allegiance now seemed to lie with Bulkeley, that instinctive leader.

At the moment, Captain Cheap was most worried about the thieves. Like insidious rats, they kept sneaking into the store tent at night and absconding with precious nuggets of food. With the company on the brink of mass starvation, the robberies—what Bulkeley called these "villainous practices"—enraged the rest of the castaways. Shipmates and messmates began to look at one another with growing suspicion: Who among them was stealing from their last remaining food?

The only type of commander whom seamen despised as much as a tyrant was one who could not maintain order, and who failed to uphold an unspoken promise—that in exchange for the men's loyalty, he would protect their well-being. Many of the castaways now despised Cheap for not safeguarding their supplies and catching the culprits. Some were clamoring for the food to be moved to Bulkeley's shelter, insisting that he could better look after it.

Bulkeley had not made such a demand, but he approached Cheap, seeking to "consult" about the robberies. He spoke as if he represented the people.

Cheap believed that if he did not quell the disorder, it would destroy the outpost. And so he issued a proclamation: all his officers and the marines must take turns guarding the store tent. Cheap required Bulkeley to take one of the night watches and stand alone in the damp cold for hours—a reminder of his lower rank. "Strict orders were given," Bulkeley wrote, to keep a "watchful eye." Byron had to routinely serve on lookout as well. After being "fatigued with hunting all day in quest of food," he noted, it was hard to "defend this tent from invasion by night."

One evening, while Byron was on duty, he heard something stirring. He still feared that a monstrous creature roamed the island after dark. On one occasion, he'd noted in his account, a seaman had claimed that, while sleeping, he had been "disturbed by the blowing of some animal at his face, and upon opening his eyes, was not a little astonished to see, by the glimmer of the fire, a large beast standing over him." The seaman had relayed the story of his narrow escape with "horror in his countenance." The excitable Byron later thought that he had detected a strange impression in the sandy ground: it was "deep and plain, of a large round foot well furnished with claws."

Byron now scoured the dark. There was nothing to be seen, but he heard the sound, insistent and wild. It was coming from inside the tent. Byron drew his gun and went in. There, before him, were the gleaming eyes of one of his fellow companions. The man had slithered under the tent and was in the process of pilfering food. Byron pointed his pistol at the man's breast, then with a rope secured the thief's hands to a post and went to alert the captain.

Cheap placed the man under confinement, hoping to deter further incidents. Not long after, the armed purser, Thomas Harvey, was out for a walk when he spotted a figure crawling through the bushes by the supply tent. "Who goes there?" It was a marine named Rowland Crusset. Harvey seized and searched him. He was found to be carrying, Bulkeley recorded, "upwards of a day's flour for ninety souls, with one piece of beef under his coat," and he had stashed three more slabs of beef in the bushes.

Another marine, Thomas Smith, who was Crusset's messmate, had been guarding the store tent at the time and was arrested as an accomplice.

News of the arrests hummed through the settlement, agitating the listless inhabitants into a vigilante frenzy. Cheap told Bulkeley and several other officers, "I really think that for robbing the store tent—which, in our present circumstances, is starving the whole body of people—the prisoners deserve death." No one disagreed. "This was not only the Captain's opinion but indeed the sentiments of every person present," Bulkeley noted.

Ultimately, though, Cheap decided that the accused men must be "governed by the rules of the Navy, and to stand or fall by them." And based on these regulations, he resolved that they would be hauled before a court-martial: if there was crime on Wager Island, there would be a trial.

Even in the midst of the vast wilderness—far from England and the prying eyes of the Admiralty—Cheap and many of the castaways clung to Britain's naval codes. They hastily arranged a public trial with several officers appointed to serve as judges. According to naval regulations, they were supposed to be impartial, though in this case no one could have been unaffected by the alleged crimes. The judges, in their tattered clothing, were sworn in and the defendants brought out. As the wind blew against their bodies, the charges were recited aloud. Witnesses—who swore to tell "the truth, the whole truth and nothing but the truth"—were called. The accused men's only defense seemed to be that they would have done anything, no matter how cruel or cunning, to avoid starvation. None of the proceedings lasted long: all three defendants were found guilty.

In reviewing the Articles of War, it was determined that the "crime did not touch life," and thus did not merit the death penalty. Instead, each guilty man was condemned to be given six hundred lashes—an amount so extreme that it would have to be administered in increments of two hundred, over three days. Otherwise, it would be lethal. A sailor in the Navy who was once about to be flogged severely remarked, "I am sure I cannot go through the torture; I would rather have been sentenced to be shot or hung at the yardarm."

Yet many of the castaways thought that six hundred lashings were insufficient. They wanted the ultimate punishment: death.

Bulkeley then spoke up, and proposed what he called "a way next to death"—one that would "strike a terror in all for the future." After the guilty men had been flogged, he suggested, they should be banished to a rocky islet off the coast, which contained at least some mussels, snails, and fresh water, and be left there until the company had means of returning to England.

Captain Cheap seized on the idea. Surely, after such a severe punishment, no one else would dare to defy his orders and put his own needs above those of the company.

Cheap gave the command for "all hands to witness punishment," and the castaways gathered in a hailstorm as one of the prisoners, Crusset, was led outside by sentries. The men had traveled halfway around the world with the condemned marine—sharing watches, battling hurricanes, surviving a wreck. Now they looked on as their companion's wrists were bound to a tree. The feuding company was momentarily united by a common hatred.

Crusset's shirt had been stripped off, exposing his back; stones of ice struck him first. Then one of the men seized the whip and with all his might began to thrash Crusset. The whip slashed his skin. One witness to a flogging noted that, after two dozen lashings, the "lacerated back looks inhuman; it resembles roasted meat burnt nearly black before a scorching fire; yet still the lashes fall."

The man tasked with administering the flogging whipped Crusset until he was too exhausted to whip anymore. Then a fresh inflictor took over. "When a poor fellow is being punished, his agonizing cries pierce you to the soul," another witness to a flogging recalled.

Crusset received fifty lashes, then another fifty, and another. After taking his total of two hundred lashes for the day, he was untied and helped away. The next day the beating resumed. The other guilty parties were similarly whipped. Some of the marines grew so horrified by the sight of their anguished comrades that, in at least one case, they balked at carrying out the third installment. Afterward the prisoners were rowed out in a transport boat and deposited on the islet, where they were left half conscious and bleeding.

Cheap believed that he had quelled any further insubordination among the men. "I endeavoured... to bring them to reason and a sense of their duty," he insisted in a report. But before long it was discovered that four bottles of brandy and four bags of flour had disappeared from the store tent; privation was a greater threat than any punishment Cheap could inflict.

A mob of castaways stormed some of the shelters, searching for the missing food. As these men rummaged through the tents of several marines, turning them inside out, they discovered the stolen bottles and bags. Nine marines were charged with the crime, but five managed to escape, joining the band of seceders. The four others were tried, convicted, whipped, and exiled.

The robberies continued; the beatings escalated. After another person was repeatedly whipped, Cheap ordered Byron and several men to row the thief out to the islet. The man seemed near death. Byron recalled, "We, in compassion, and contrary to order, patched him up a bit of a hut, and kindled him a fire, and then left the poor wretch to shift for himself." A few days later, Byron went with some companions to sneak the man some nibbles of food, only to find him "dead and stiff."

CHAPTER 13

Extremities

CAPTAIN CHEAP SAW A long white trail, like sprinkled flour, snaking toward his dwelling. He examined it more closely. It was gunpowder. Had it been accidentally spilled there or was it part of some plot? Midshipman Byron said that he'd heard from someone else that Mitchell and his band of separatists had slipped into the camp to "perpetuate their wicked design of blowing up their commander, when they were with difficulty dissuaded from it by one who had some bowels and remorse of conscience left in him."

It was hard for Cheap to know what to believe. Facts, too, can become casualties in a warring society. There were rumors and counterrumors, some perhaps intentionally promulgated to create greater confusion, to further undermine him. He was no longer sure whom he could trust. Even among the officers, he detected signs of disloyalty. The head of the marines, Pemberton, had lost, in Cheap's words, "all sense of honour or the interest of his country." The wishy-washy Lieutenant Baynes appeared to shift allegiances with the latest breeze, and the boatswain, King, incited so many quarrels that his own companions had booted him from their shelter. Then there was John Bulkeley, the seeming worm in the apple. Cheap had probed him regarding his loyalties, and Bulkeley had assured him that he and "the people"—there was that phrase again—"never would engage in any mutiny against him." But the gunner was constantly holding meetings in his makeshift hotel and forming alliances, building his little empire, as if he were the monarch of the island.

As Cheap listened to the tumult of shrieking winds, cracking thunder, drumming hail, and roaring surf, he paced with his cane. When Anson had given him his captaincy, it was more than a promotion: it brought a measure of the respect and honor that Cheap had long coveted. And it meant that he had a chance to burnish himself in glory, as a leader of men. All of that was now being undermined, along with the outpost. And he was being tormented—by hunger and seemingly by his own thoughts, obsessing feverishly over, as he put it, "the repeated troubles and vexations that I met with." Byron observed that Cheap was "jealous to the last degree" of his power as captain—power that he saw "daily declining, and ready to be trampled upon."

On June 7, nearly a month after the *Wager* had run aground, he gave a simple order to Midshipman Henry Cozens to roll a cask of peas salvaged from the wreck up the beach and into the store tent. Cozens, appearing unsteady from liquor, insisted that the cask was too heavy, and began to turn away. A midshipman refusing his captain!

Cheap shouted that Cozens was drunk.

"With what should I get drunk, unless it be with water?" Cozens replied.

"You scoundrel! Get more hands and roll the cask up."

Cozens made a half-hearted gesture of calling for others, but no one came, and Cheap smacked him with his cane. Then Cheap ordered Cozens seized and imprisoned in a tent, under the guard of a sentinel. "This day Mr. Henry Cozens, midshipman, was confined by the Captain," Bulkeley recorded in his journal. "The fault alleged against him was drunkenness."

That evening, Cheap checked on his prisoner. Cozens hurled a torrent of curses at him, the insults ringing through the camp. Cozens shouted that Cheap was even worse than George Shelvocke, an infamous British buccaneer who, two decades earlier, had wrecked his ship, the *Speedwell*, on one of the Juan Fernández Islands. After returning to England, Shelvocke was accused of deliberately sinking the ship to defraud his investors. "Though Shelvocke was a rogue, he was not a fool," Cozens said to Cheap. "And, by God, you are both."

In a fury, Cheap raised his cane to beat Cozens—beat him into submission—but he was restrained by the sentinel, who insisted that the captain should "strike no prisoner of his." Cheap quickly recovered himself, and in a surprising act he released Cozens from confinement.

But some of the men gave the midshipman more liquor, and he began to cause another ruckus, this time quarreling with the captain's close ally the purser, Thomas Harvey. When sober, Cozens was always congenial, and Byron believed that some of the cabalists had fed his friend liquor to turn him into their own destructive agent.

A few days later, the rain fell especially hard, the water dripping from leaves and streaming down the sides of Mount Misery. Cozens was in line awaiting his share of the rations, which the purser, Harvey, distributed from the store tent, when he heard a rumor: Cheap had decided to cut his amount of wine. In an instant, Cozens stampeded toward Harvey to demand his share. The purser, still simmering from their earlier dispute, drew his flintlock pistol with its roughly foot-long barrel. Cozens continued advancing. Harvey cocked the hammer and took aim, calling Cozens a dog and accusing him of intending to commit mutiny. A seaman standing beside Harvey interceded and knocked the barrel upward just as Harvey pulled the trigger. The bullet soared past Cozens.

Hearing the shot and the shouting about mutiny, Cheap burst out of his dwelling. His eyes were ablaze, his pistol already in hand. Squinting in the rain, he looked around for Cozens, whom he was certain had fired the bullet, and shouted, "Where's that villain?"

There was no reply, but he spied Cozens amid the growing crowd. Cheap walked over and, with neither questions nor ceremony, placed the cool tip of the barrel against Cozens's left cheek. Then, as he would later describe it, he "proceeded to extremities."

CHAPTER 14

Affections of the People

AT THE SOUND OF the blast, John Byron ran from his hut and saw Cozens on the ground, "weltering in his blood." Captain Cheap had shot him in the head.

Many of the men stood back, afraid of Cheap's rage, but Byron went over and knelt by his messmate's side as the rain washed over him. Cozens was still breathing. He opened his mouth to say something, but no words came out. Then he "took me by the hand," Byron recalled, "shaking his head, as if he meant to take leave of us."

The crowd was becoming uneasy. Bulkeley observed that Cozens's "notorious disrespectful words to the Captain might probably make the Captain suspect his design was mutiny," but it was clear that Cozens had no weapon. Byron thought that however wrong Cozens's actions had been, Cheap's response was inexcusable.

The onlookers continued to stir as Cozens lay before them, barely alive. "The unhappy victim . . . seemed to absorb their whole attention," Byron recalled. "The eyes of all were fixed upon him; and visible marks of the deepest concern appeared in the countenances of the spectators."

Amid the rising clamor, Cheap ordered the men to stand in assembly. Bulkeley wondered if he and his men should get their weapons. "But, on consideration, I thought better to go without arms," he recalled.

Cheap's once-solid frame had been eaten away by hunger. Yet, as he faced the line of men, he held his ground, gripping his pistol.

He was flanked by his allies, including the surgeon, Elliot, and the marine lieutenant, Hamilton. After Bulkeley indicated that his own men were unarmed, Cheap lay down his gun in the mud and said, "I see you are, and have only sent for you to let you all know I am still your Commander, so let every man go to his tent."

There was a moment of uncertainty as the sea broke against the shore. Bulkeley and his men knew that if they refused to comply, they would be taking the first step toward overthrowing their appointed captain and upending the rules of the Navy—the rules that they had lived by. Cheap's rash shooting of Cozens, Byron noted, had nearly provoked "open sedition and revolt." But eventually Bulkeley retreated, and the rest of the castaways followed suit. Byron, who went to his hut alone, observed that the company's resentment seemed "smothered for the present."

Finally, Captain Cheap ordered that Cozens be taken to the sick tent.

Bulkeley visited Cozens there. He was being treated by a young man named Robert—the surgeon's mate. Robert inspected the wound, which was hemorrhaging blood. The first textbook on medicine for sea surgeons warned that gunshot injuries "are always compound, never simple, and are the more difficult of cure." Robert tried to trace the path of the bullet. It had entered Cozens's left cheek, shattering his upper jaw, but there was no exit wound. The ball was still lodged inside Cozens's head, about three inches below his right eye. Robert used bandages to try to stanch the bleeding, but if Cozens were to have a chance of surviving, the bullet would need to be surgically removed.

The operation was scheduled for the following day. When the time came, though, the chief surgeon, Elliot, did not appear. Some attributed his absence to a previous fight between him and Cozens. The carpenter, Cummins, said he had heard that Elliot had intended

John Byron was a sixteen-year-old midshipman on the *Wager.*

An eighteenth-century painting of a British press gang

David Cheap, the *Centurion*'s first lieutenant, dreamed of becoming a captain.

An eighteenth-century painting of the Deptford dockyard, where the *Wager* was launched

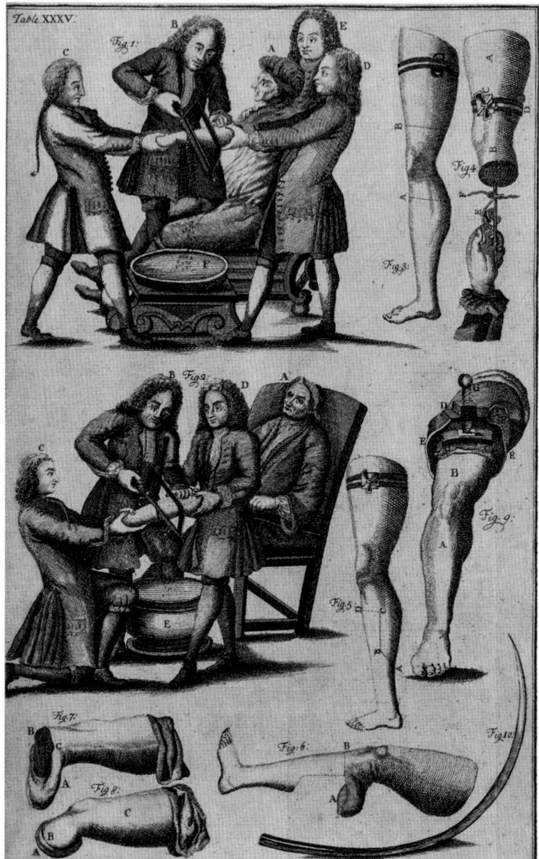

Life on a man-of-war:
(above) the lethal machinery on
a gun deck; (left) a 1742 medical
diagram for how to amputate limbs

OPPOSITE: A burial at sea

OPPOSITE A logbook from the *Centurion*, with entries detailing horrific disease and storms

(Above) An albatross off Cape Horn

(Left) A *Centurion* officer sketched the squadron arriving in St. Catherine, Brazil, in December 1740. The *Wager* is the second ship from left.

The *Wager* before it wrecked—painted by
Charles Brooking, c. 1744

to come but Captain Cheap had intervened. Midshipman Campbell said that he was unaware of the captain ever doing such a thing, suggesting perhaps that conflict was being stoked by disinformation—just as the rumor about Cozens's wine rations being cut had been false. Despite Campbell's insistence that Cheap was being maligned, the allegation that the captain had prevented the surgeon from treating Cozens spread among the company. "This was looked on as an act of inhumanity in the Captain," Bulkeley wrote in his journal, "and contributed very much to his losing the affections of the people." Bulkeley added that it would've been more honorable for Cheap to have killed Cozens with a second bullet, instead of denying him relief.

Ultimately, Robert attempted the operation on his own. The medical textbook advised that a surgeon's first duty was to God—"who seeth not as men see" and who "will direct our ways aright." Robert opened the medical chest, which contained such metal instruments as incision knives, forceps, bone saws, and a cauterizing iron. None of these were sterilized, and the surgery, without anesthesia, was just as likely to kill Cozens as to save him. Somehow, Cozens survived the procedure. A sliver of the bullet had broken off, but Robert was able to reach the main piece and extract it.

Cozens was conscious, but he was still in danger of dying from loss of blood, and there was also the risk of gangrene. He wanted to be moved to Bulkeley's house to be among friends. When Bulkeley asked Cheap for his permission to do so, the captain refused, insisting that Cozens had mutinous intentions, which threatened their outpost. "If he lives," Cheap said, "I will carry him a prisoner to the Commodore, and hang him."

On June 17, a week after the shooting, Robert performed a second operation on Cozens, in an effort to remove the remaining bullet fragment and a part of his splintered jawbone. The surgeon's mate completed the procedure, but Cozens seemed to be fading. In such cases, the textbook advised, surgeons should not despair—"for God is merciful." Cozens asked Robert for one last favor: to deliver to

Bulkeley a small package containing the extracted bullet and piece of bone. Cozens wanted the evidence preserved. Robert agreed, and Bulkeley placed the disconcerting package in his shelter.

On June 24, Bulkeley wrote in his diary, "Departed this life Mr. Henry Cozens, Midshipman, after languishing fourteen days." Cozens might have unraveled on the island, yet, as Byron wrote, he remained "greatly beloved," and most of the castaways were "extremely affected at this catastrophe."

Cold, filthy, ragged, they trudged outside and dug a hole in the mud; surrounding it were the unmarked graves of the men and boys who had, as Bulkeley's journal put it, perished in "sundry ways since the ship first struck." Cozens's stiffening body was carried out from the sick tent and laid in the ground. There was no auction of his possessions to raise funds for his family back home: he had virtually no items and the men had no money. But the congregants took care to spread dirt over the body so that the vultures wouldn't peck at it. "We buried him in as decent a manner as time, place, and circumstances would allow," Bulkeley recalled.

They had been trapped on the island for forty-one days.

CHAPTER 15

The Ark

THE MEN SAW A sudden glimmer of salvation. The carpenter, Cummins, came up with a novel idea: if they could rescue the longboat that had been submerged with the wreck, they just might be able to remake it into an ark—one that could carry them off the island. In the days immediately after Cozens's death, Captain Cheap had secluded himself in his hut, brooding, rationalizing, despairing. Would the Admiralty deem his shooting justifiable—or would he be hanged for murder? Bulkeley observed that the captain had grown more and more agitated, losing not only "the love of the men" but also "any composure of mind."

Now Cheap began to frenetically pursue Cummins's plan. The first step was to cut away the longboat, which was entangled in debris. The only way to free it was to bore a hole in the side of the *Wager*. The task was hard and perilous, but the men did it, and the boat was soon heaved ashore. Cracked, waterlogged, and too cramped to hold but a fraction of the party, the vessel did not seem as if it could carry the castaways even around the island. Yet it contained the kernel of a dream.

Cummins oversaw the engineering and remodeling of the craft. To fit more people in it, the thirty-six-foot hull would have to be extended at least another twelve feet. Many of the existing planks had rotted and would have to be replaced. And the boat would need to be transformed into a two-masted vessel so that it could power through the tremendous seas.

Cummins estimated that the construction would take them several months, and that was assuming they could gather enough materials, not to mention stay alive that long. Everyone would have to lend a hand. Cummins also required another skilled craftsman, but his two carpenter's mates, James Mitchell and William Oram, were both among the seceders. Although the madman Mitchell was no option, Cheap decided to send a small party on a covert mission to try to persuade Oram to defect from the defectors. There was no telling how Mitchell might respond if he were to learn of the overture, and Cheap was able to recruit only two men for the dangerous assignment. One was Bulkeley.

As Bulkeley and his companion trekked across the island, humping with their heavy muskets over mountains and through lacerating thickets, they took care to remain undetected. "In this affair I was obliged to act very secretly," Bulkeley wrote.

When they reached the separatists' camp, a few miles away, they waited until Oram appeared to be alone, then approached him. Bulkeley murmured that Captain Cheap had a proposition for him. Oram, who was twenty-eight, was facing a near-certain death sentence: he'd either starve with the other seceders or be executed for sedition. But if he returned to the main settlement and assisted with modifying the longboat, he'd receive a full pardon from the captain and might see his homeland again. Oram agreed to come back with them.

By the middle of July, two months after being shipwrecked and three weeks after the death of Cozens, Cheap observed Bulkeley, Byron, and the rest of the company working busily—eagerly—on the ark. Byron noted that nothing seemed "so necessary towards the advancing our delivery from this desolate place."

First, the longboat had to be rested on thick blocks of wood, so that the hull was elevated from the ground. Next, Cummins sawed the boat in half. Then the real trick began: somehow stitching these pieces not only back together again but also in an entirely new form, one that was longer, wider, and stronger.

Through rain and sleet, gales and lightning, Cummins—whom Bulkeley described as indefatigable—honed the design with his smattering of tools, including a saw, a hammer, and an adze, which resembled an ax. He sent the men to scour the forest for durable wood that had a natural bend. Once he had determined the boat's overall shape, he began to place the pieces of wood into a riblike frame above the keel. A different sort of timber—long, thick, and straight—was required for planks, which had to be cut to precise measurements and then fastened at right angles to the curved frame. With metal nails in short supply, some of the castaways combed the drowned wreckage for additional ones. When these ran out, the carpenter and his mate hewed bolts from wood. The men also scraped together other essential materials: canvas for the sails, ropes for the rigging, candle wax for caulking.

The men toiled even as many of them confronted the debilitating effects of malnourishment: their bodies thinned to the bone, their eyes bulging, their strawlike hair falling out. Bulkeley said of the castaways, "They are in great pain, and can scarce see to walk." Yet they were compelled onward by that mysterious narcotic: hope.

One day Cheap heard a panicked cry ring through the settlement. A rogue wave was surging up the beach, sweeping past the tideline and plucking at the boat's skeletal frame. The men raced over and managed to heave the frame farther up the shore before the sea swallowed it. The work went on.

Cheap's plan, meanwhile, was taking on new, hidden dimensions. Poring over charts, he began to believe that there was a way to not only preserve their lives but also fulfill their original military mission. He calculated that the nearest Spanish settlement was on the island of Chiloé, which was off the Chilean coast and some 350 miles north of their present location. Cheap was sure that the company could sail there using the ark along with the three smaller transport boats—the yawl, the cutter, and the barge. Once they arrived in Chiloé—and, to him, this was the magnificent part—they could mount a daring attack on an unsuspecting Spanish trading ship; and, having taken this vessel and its stores of food, sail to the rendezvous point and search for Commodore Anson and any surviving members of the squadron. Then they'd proceed on the quest for the galleon.

The risks were daunting, and Cheap, aware that he would have to persuade the men of his plan, did not immediately share these details with them. But as he later put it, "We need not fear taking prizes, and may have a chance to see the Commodore." There was still, he believed, a possibility of glory—and redemption.

On July 30, Bulkeley stopped by Byron's solitary hut on the edge of the village. There he found the scrawny, grimy nobleman's son subsumed in his sea tales; he was reading Sir John Narborough's chronicle again. Bulkeley asked to borrow the book, though strictly for pragmatic reasons. Narborough had explored the Patagonian region, and Bulkeley thought that the account—essentially a detailed log—might hold critical clues for how to navigate the ark safely away from Wager Island.

Byron loaned Bulkeley the book after securing Captain Cheap's permission, since it belonged to him. Then Bulkeley took it back to his quarters and began studying the text as intently as he did *The Christian's Pattern.* Narborough had described his journey through the Strait of Magellan, that 350-mile passageway between the end of the South American mainland and Tierra del Fuego, which offered an alternative route between the Pacific and the Atlantic that avoided the Drake Passage around Cape Horn. "At any time if you have a desire to enter the Strait of Magellan" from the Pacific side, Narborough wrote, "it will be safest, in my opinion, to bear in for the land, in the latitude of 52 degrees." This opening was about four hundred miles south of Wager Island, and Bulkeley was seized by an idea. With their eventual new longboat and three small transport crafts, he thought, the castaways could cross through the strait and into the Atlantic, then head north to Brazil; its government, being neutral in the war, would surely provide them a safe haven and facilitate their passage back to England.

The total distance from Wager Island to Brazil would be nearly three thousand miles. And Bulkeley conceded that many would deem it a "mad undertaking." The strait was winding and narrow in places, and it often splintered into a bewildering maze of dead-end offshoots. Shoals and rocks cluttered the waters, and there were blinding fogs. "A man may mistake the right channel, and steer in among the broken islands and rocks, so far as to endanger his ship," Narborough warned. And though the strait was more sheltered than the Drake Passage, it was notorious for unpredictable squalls and for glacial blasts—now known as williwaws—that left ships heaped on the banks. That is why Commodore Anson, navigating a sailing fleet of large, unwieldy men-of-war by dead reckoning, had preferred to risk the violence of the open seas around Cape Horn.

However, Bulkeley observed, "desperate diseases demand desperate remedies," and he believed this route to Brazil was their only feasible option. The Drake Passage, four hundred miles farther south, was too distant, and its seas were too lethal for their small boats. As for the obstacles in the strait, Narborough had recorded a safe course. Moreover, he had reported finding sources of sustenance, to ward off starvation. Along with mussels and limpets, he wrote, "here are ducks, white and pied-brant geese, grey gulls, sea mews, sea divers, and penguins."

For Bulkeley, this route seemed to have another, deeper seduction. They would be charting their own destiny, emancipating themselves from a naval mission that had been bungled by government and military officials back home—a mission that had been doomed from the outset. The castaways would now choose to survive rather than venture north through the Pacific, where a Spanish armada would likely pulverize or capture them. "Our going through the Strait of Magellan for the coast of Brazil would be the only way to prevent our throwing ourselves into the hands of a cruel, barbarous, and insulting enemy," Bulkeley concluded. "Our longboat, when finished, can be fit for no enterprise but the preservation of life. As we cannot act offensively, we ought to have regard to our safety and liberty."

Bulkeley asked Master Clark and the other navigators to review the route that he had sketched based on Narborough's information. They, too, agreed that the plan represented their best chance to survive. Bulkeley shared his vision with the other men, who were faced with a fundamental choice. They were tired of the war—tired of death and destruction—and longed to go home, but to turn back meant they'd be abandoning their mission and possibly the rest of the squadron. And to make things worse, Captain Cheap had just announced that he expected them to do their patriotic duty and head in the opposite direction. They would find the commodore, he vowed, and never retreat.

Byron watched as the outpost, briefly united over building the ark, now split into two rival forces. On one side were Cheap and his small but loyal cadre. On the other were Bulkeley and his legions of partisans. Until then, Byron had maintained his neutral stance, but that was becoming untenable. Although the dispute centered on a simple matter of which way to go, it raised profound questions about the nature of leadership, loyalty, betrayal, courage, and patriotism. Byron, an aristocrat who aspired to rise within the naval ranks to one day captain his own ship, wrestled with these questions as he was forced to choose between his commanding officer and the charismatic gunner. Knowing the stakes of his decision, Byron was somewhat circumspect in his writings. But it is clear that he felt duty bound to Cheap, and that he viewed Bulkeley, who seemed to relish his newfound status, as someone who was undermining the captain and fueling his deep insecurities and paranoia. Moreover, Cheap, in laying out his plan, had evoked the kind of imperial heroism and sacrifice—that mythopoetic life of the sea—extolled in the romances Byron so loved.

On the other hand, Bulkeley seemed far more composed and suited to command the men in their nightmarish circumstances. Unrelenting, ingenious, and cunning, he had emerged as a leader on his own merits. By contrast, Cheap's expectation that the men would unwaveringly follow him was based solely on the chain of command. And in his desperation to maintain his authority, he had become even more fanatical. As Bulkeley observed of Cheap, "The loss of the ship was the loss of him; he knew how to govern while he was a commander on board, but when things were brought to confusion and disorder, he thought to establish his command ashore by his courage, and to suppress the least insult on his authority."

On August 3, Byron learned that Bulkeley was gathering with most of the men to discuss their next steps. Should Byron go, or stay faithful to his commander?

The following day, Cheap saw Bulkeley approaching with an entourage. When the gunner was within a few feet of him, he paused and held up a piece of paper. He said that it was a petition and began to read it aloud, as if he were on the floor of Parliament:

> WE, whose names are under-mentioned, do upon mature consideration... think it the best, surest, and most safe way for the preservation of the body of people on the spot to proceed through the Strait of Magellan for England. Dated at a desolate island on the coast of Patagonia.

Though carefully worded, the statement had an unmistakable intent. At a meeting the previous day, Bulkeley had invited the men who wanted to sign the petition. One by one, they'd done so, including the head of the marines, Pemberton, and Master Clark, who continued to protect his young son, and the ancient cook, Maclean, still clinging to life, and the seaman John Duck. Even Cheap's fierce enforcer Midshipman Campbell had added his signature. Byron had scribbled his name, too.

Now Bulkeley handed the smudged paper to Cheap, who saw the long list of squirrelly signatures at the bottom. So many of Cheap's men had backed the petition that it would be hard for him to single any one of them out—including the chief instigator, Bulkeley—for punishment.

Cheap could count on one hand the number of his men who had not defied him: the purser, Harvey; the surgeon, Elliot; the marine lieutenant, Hamilton; and the steward, Peter Plastow. And there was one other name, perhaps the most significant, missing from the document: Lieutenant Baynes. Cheap still had on his side the second-highest-ranking naval officer on the island. The top chain of command remained aligned.

He had to think about his next move. Holding the document, he dismissed the gunner and his entourage, saying that he would respond after he had considered it.

Two days later, Bulkeley and Cummins were summoned by Cheap. When they entered his dwelling, they saw that he was not alone. He had made sure that Lieutenant Baynes was sitting beside him.

After Bulkeley and Cummins had settled in, Cheap told them, "This paper has given me a great deal of uneasiness, insomuch that I have not closed my eyes till eight o'clock this morning, for thinking of it; but, I think, you have not weighed the thing rightly." He was convinced that they were seducing the men with false hopes of an easy passage home, when, in fact, the route to Brazil was more than twenty-five hundred miles longer than the one to Chiloé. If they went their way, he said, "Think on the distance to be run... with the wind always against us and where no water is to be had."

Bulkeley and Cummins stressed that they'd be able to carry a month's worth of water rations in the longboat, and could use the small transport crafts to row ashore and collect provisions. "We can have no enemies to encounter there but Indians in their canoes," Bulkeley said.

Cheap didn't budge. If they headed toward Chiloé, he said, they could seize a trading vessel loaded with provisions.

Cummins asked how they could capture a vessel without any cannons.

"What are our muskets for," Cheap replied, "but to board an enemy ship?"

Cummins warned that the longboat would never survive cannon fire. And even if they somehow didn't sink, they had virtually no chance of ever meeting up with Anson: "The commodore may have shared the same fate with ourselves—or perhaps worse."

As the acrimony grew, Cummins snapped at the captain, "Sir, 'tis all owing to *you* that we are here." And there it was—that long-festering accusation. Cummins did not let up, insisting that the captain had had no business heading toward land with the *Wager* in its condition and all the men sick.

"You do not know my orders," Cheap said. "There never were any so strict given to a commander before." He repeated that he had had no choice but to head to the rendezvous: "I was obliged."

Bulkeley responded that a captain, no matter his orders, must always use his discretion.

Surprisingly, Cheap let this comment go and turned back to the question at hand. Sounding an almost diplomatic note, he announced that he might accede to their proposal to go through the Strait of Magellan, but he needed more time to make a determination.

Bulkeley, unsure if Cheap was stonewalling, said, "The people are uneasy.... Therefore the sooner you resolve, the better."

Throughout the discussion, Baynes had remained virtually

silent, deferring to Cheap. Cheap now signaled that the meeting was over and asked Bulkeley and Cummins, "Have you any more objections to make?"

"Yes, sir, one more," Bulkeley responded. He wanted the captain's assurance that if they did set off together in the longboat, he would not do anything—come to anchor, alter their course, launch an attack—without consulting his officers.

Realizing that this would effectively dismantle his authority as captain, Cheap could no longer contain himself. He cried out that he was still their commander.

"We will support you with our lives as long as you suffer reason to rule," Bulkeley said, and then walked out with Cummins.

Everyone around John Byron seemed to be gathering weapons. Because Captain Cheap was in charge of the store tent, he had access to the largest arsenal, and he transformed his dwelling into an armed bunker. Along with guns, he kept a pair of gleaming swords. The knife-wielding marine lieutenant, Hamilton, often helped him keep watch. Cheap, realizing he was still dangerously outmanned, dispatched the purser to offer brandy to the seceders as an inducement to form an alliance, but the marauders remained a freewheeling band.

Bulkeley learned of this attempt and decried it as "bribery." Meanwhile, he was busy securing more muskets and pistols and shot from the wreck, turning his own house into an armory as well. At night, Byron could see Bulkeley's associates sneaking out to mine the wreck—casks of powder could still be salvaged, as could rusted guns. Midshipman Campbell, who remained sympathetic to Cheap, noted that Bulkeley and his men were now "all in a capacity of bidding their officers defiance."

Communication between the two factions had deteriorated to the point that Bulkeley vowed never to go near Cheap again, and although the parties' leaders were situated within yards of each other, they often sent emissaries back and forth, like diplomats of warring nations. One day Cheap had Lieutenant Baynes relay an unexpected proposition to Bulkeley: on the coming Sabbath, why not use Bulkeley's large quarters as a place of divine worship, so that all the men could pray together? It seemed like a peace offering, a show of respect to Bulkeley's piousness, and a reminder that they were all made of the same clay. But the gunner sniffed a ruse and refused the offer. "We believe religion to have the least share in this proposal," Bulkeley noted in his journal. "If our tent should be turned into a house of prayer... we may, perhaps, in the midst of our devotion, be surprised, and our arms taken from us in order to frustrate our designs."

To Byron, the two factions appeared to be plotting and counterplotting, holding clandestine meetings, binding themselves in secrets. Further raising tensions, many of Bulkeley's forces began to carry out military exercises. Pemberton lined up his emaciated marines in battle formation, while bedraggled seamen practiced loading their muskets and firing at targets in the mist. Bursts of volleys echoed across the island. Byron had not experienced any combat during the War of Jenkins' Ear; now, he realized, he might witness it among his own shipmates.

On August 25, Byron felt a terrifying rumbling. It was so powerful that his body shook and everything around him seemed to be rattling and crumbling: the walls of the huts, the branches on the trees, the ground beneath him. It was an earthquake—just an earthquake.

CHAPTER 16

My Mutineers

ON AUGUST 27, TWO days after what John Bulkeley described as the "violent shocks and tremblings of the earth," he met secretly with his most trusted confidants. Although three weeks had passed since Cheap had been given the petition, he still had not offered a final response. Bulkeley concluded that the captain had no intention of ever agreeing to the Brazil plan, because he would never countermand his original orders.

At the meeting, Bulkeley broached that forbidden subject: mutiny. A full-blown mutiny was unlike other revolts. It took place within the very forces established by the state to impose order—the military—which is why it posed such a threat to the ruling authorities and was so often brutally quashed. This was also why mutinies captured the public imagination. What was it that drove the enforcers of order to descend into disorder? Were they extreme outlaws? Or was there something rotten at the very core of the system, something that imbued their rebellion with nobility?

Bulkeley argued to the others that they would be justified in rising up. He believed that, as castaways, "the rules of the Navy are not sufficient to direct us." In this state of nature, there was no written code, no preexisting text, that could fully guide them. To survive, they needed to establish their own rules. He self-consciously invoked the rights to "life" and "liberty" that British subjects, at certain times in history, had sounded when attempting to restrain an overweening monarch. But Bulkeley, recognizing that he was part of a naval apparatus, an instrument of the state itself, made a more radical argument. He suggested that the real source of chaos on the island, the one really violating the ethos of the Navy, was Cheap himself, as if he were the true mutineer.

Yet Bulkeley knew that if he and the others were caught plotting a rebellion against Cheap, and the established military command structure, they might, like Cozens, be shot before ever leaving the island. Even if they succeeded and made it back to England, they could be court-martialed by a panel of Cheap's fellow officers and condemned to take a walk up Ladder Lane and down Hemp Street. As a historian once put it, "A mutiny is like a horrible, malignant disease and the chances that the patient will die an agonizing death are so great, that the subject cannot even be mentioned aloud."

Bulkeley had to tread carefully, shrewdly, establishing a written record justifying each of the group's actions. Ever the sea lawyer and narrator, he'd already been documenting in his journal every little event that, in his view, showed the captain to be unfit to lead. Now he needed to create an unassailable story—a timeless tale of the sea—which could withstand public scrutiny and the attrition of a legal battle.

The first step was for Bulkeley to obtain the backing of Lieutenant Baynes. It was imperative that Baynes, as the next in the line of command, at least nominally assume the title of captain. This would help prove to the Admiralty that Bulkeley was not out to wantonly destroy naval order and take power for himself. Baynes had privately admitted to Bulkeley that he thought heading through the strait was the wisest course, but he seemed afraid of the repercussions of breaking with the captain. The lieutenant understood perhaps better than most what could happen if you picked the losing side in a civil conflict: his grandfather Adam Baynes, a radical republican and member of Parliament, had aligned himself against the Royalists, and in 1666, after they regained power, they had him thrown into the Tower of London on suspicions of "treasonable practices."

Bulkeley had been steadily trying to cultivate Lieutenant Baynes to his side, and after they conferred again, Baynes finally agreed to oust Cheap, but under one condition. They would first draft a formal document expressing their reasons for sailing to Brazil and give Cheap an opportunity to sign it—a last chance to bow to the will of the people. If he agreed, he'd be allowed to remain captain, though with his powers severely curtailed. Bulkeley noted, "We imagined if Captain Cheap was restored to the absolute command he had before the loss of the *Wager* that he would proceed again upon the same principles, never on any exigency consult his officers but act arbitrarily, according to his humour and confidence of superior knowledge." Bulkeley added, "We think him a gentleman worthy to have a limited command, but too dangerous a person to be trusted with an absolute one."

If Cheap balked at these terms, they would overthrow him. The shooting of Cozens, they believed, had provided a firm basis for arresting the captain. Baynes said that every officer involved in the insurrection would be able to present this paper to "justify himself in England."

Bulkeley drew up the document on a scrap of paper. It stated that the company was plagued by robberies and internecine feuds—"which must consequently end in the destruction of the whole body." Therefore, the people had "unanimously" agreed to abandon the expedition and return to England, via the Strait of Magellan and Brazil.

The next day, Bulkeley and Baynes went with a party to confront the captain, carrying muskets and pistols. They crowded into Cheap's dwelling, where the captain was surrounded by a handful of men, all heavily armed.

Bulkeley removed the document from his pocket, unfolded it, and began to read it aloud. When he finished, he asked the captain to sign it. Cheap refused and flew into a rage, telling them that they had insulted his honor.

Bulkeley left with his party and headed straight to Pemberton's hut, where the marine captain was perched on his chair, surrounded by his soldiers. Other castaways were gathering in the hut, eager to learn what had happened. Bulkeley told them that, as he later put it, the captain, "in the most scornful manner, hath rejected everything proposed for the public good." Pemberton declared that he would stand by the people with his life, and the crowd roared, "For England!"

Cheap stepped outside his dwelling and asked what the commotion was about. Bulkeley and the other officers announced that they had agreed to remove him from power and transfer command to Lieutenant Baynes.

In a booming voice, Cheap said, "Who is he that will take the command from me?" He stared at Baynes, the wind crackling between them, and said, "Is it you?"

Baynes seemed to wither—or, as Bulkeley recounted it, "The terror of the Captain's aspect intimidated the lieutenant to that degree that he looked like a ghost."

Baynes replied simply, "No, sir."

The lieutenant had abandoned the plot—and the story. Bulkeley and his men soon retreated.

For days afterward, David Cheap could hear his enemies regrouping outside his bunker. And some of his remaining allies were abandoning him. The purser, Harvey, recognizing the new center of power, deserted Cheap. Then the captain heard a rumor that his steward, Peter Plastow, the last person he ever expected to turn, had decided to head to the strait with the gunner. Cheap sent for Plastow and asked disbelievingly whether it was true.

"Yes, sir," Plastow replied. "I will take my chance, for I want to get to England."

Cheap called him a villain—they were all villains!—and bade him to leave. Cheap was almost completely isolated, a captain without a company. He listened as the men—whom he dubbed "my mutineers"—assembled in military formations and practiced firing their weapons. Yet Cheap officially remained in power, and he knew that Bulkeley could not act without Baynes and expect to escape the noose in England.

Before long, Cheap had a message relayed to Bulkeley to come meet with him, this time alone. Though Bulkeley arrived flanked by gunmen, he entered Cheap's dwelling by himself, carrying a pistol. Cheap was sitting on his sea chest. On his right thigh rested his own pistol, cocked. Cheap stared at Bulkeley, who cocked his gun but then slowly retreated backward, step by step, later claiming that he did not want to be "compelled for my own preservation to discharge a pistol at a gentleman."

Bulkeley went outside, where a crowd was growing in size and fervor. Then Cheap did something even more startling to assert his authority: he emerged from his bunker without his weapon and faced the raging mob. "Here the Captain showed all the conduct and courage imaginable," Bulkeley admitted. "He was a single man against a multitude, all of 'em dissatisfied with him, and all of 'em in arms." And in that moment not one person—not Bulkeley, not Pemberton, not even the violent boatswain, King—dared lay a finger on their captain.

Starvation continued to ravage the company. John Byron never knew who would succumb next. Once, a companion fainted beside him. "I sat next to him when he dropped," Byron wrote, "and having a few dried shellfish (about five or six) in my pocket, from time to time put one in his mouth.... However, soon after my little supply failed, he was released by death." More than fifty castaways had perished on the island, and some of Byron's companions were so famished that they had begun to contemplate a dire remedy: eating the dead. A delirious boy had cut off a piece of a cadaver before it was buried, and had to be restrained from consuming it; and, though most of the men knew not to even mention cannibalism in their written records, Byron acknowledged that some began to butcher and eat their dead companions—what Byron referred to as the "last extremity." If the surviving castaways didn't get off the island soon, more would succumb to this blasphemy.

On October 5, after 144 days on the island, Byron gazed upon what seemed like a hunger-induced mirage. There, on the blocks where the fragments of the longboat had once been, rested a glorious hull. Ten feet wide and more than fifty feet long, with planks running from stern to bow, it had a deck where the crew could keep watch, a hold below for storage, a tiller for steering, and a bowsprit. Byron and his companions now added finishing touches, such as coating the bottom of the hull with wax and tallow to prevent leaks.

Still, how would they ever get this vessel into the sea? Weighing tons, it was too heavy for them to carry or drag along the sand, especially in their weakened condition. It was as if they had created the ark only to further torment themselves. Yet they found a solution: laying down a track of logs and letting the boat roll over them until it was launched into the sea. With salvaged ropes, they proudly hoisted the two wooden masts into the sky. And there the new longboat was—bobbing in the waves. The men christened her the *Speedwell.* (The name held special meaning: the British buccaneer Shelvocke and his men, after being marooned, had built a boat from the timber of their sunken ship, the *Speedwell*, and made it back to England.) Bulkeley proclaimed that God had given them a vessel for their deliverance.

Like the others, Byron longed to go home. He missed his sister, Isabella, with whom he was especially close. Even his older brother, the Wicked Lord, no longer seemed so bad.

But though Byron had supported Bulkeley's campaign to head back to England, he had not been involved in the plot to overthrow Cheap, and he seemed to hold on to one last boyish illusion: that all of the survivors might sail off the island together in peace.

On October 9, in the early morning hours, Bulkeley and his fellow conspirators began to quietly assemble a ragtag army of castaways—half-clothed, starved figures with glazed eyes and nested hair. Bulkeley distributed all his tools of war: muskets, bayonets, pistols, ammunition, cartridges, cutlasses, and binding ropes. The men loaded the barrels of the guns and cocked the hammers.

In the creeping dawn, the party began to cross the shambles of the imperial outpost. Mount Misery loomed above them; the sea, like the men, breathed in and out. When they reached Cheap's dwelling, they paused, listening, then one after the other burst in. Cheap had been curled on the ground asleep, thin and frail, and now he saw his men storming toward him. Before he could reach for his gun, they grabbed him and, as one officer put it, abused him "somewhat rudely." In a synchronized operation, Hamilton, who had been sleeping in a nearby dwelling, was apprehended, too.

The castaways had decided that it was too "dangerous to suffer the Captain any longer to enjoy liberty," Bulkeley wrote. And this time Lieutenant Baynes had joined the rebellion.

Cheap looked bewildered, and turning to Bulkeley and the other officers, he said, "Gentlemen, do you know what you have done?"

Bulkeley and his men explained that they were there to arrest him for the death of Cozens.

"I am your commander still," Cheap replied. "I will show you my instructions." Allowed to fumble through his things, he retrieved the letter given to him by Commodore Anson naming him the captain of His Majesty's Ship the *Wager*. He waved the sheet of paper. "Look at it. Look at it!" he told Bulkeley and the other officers. "I could not think you would serve me so."

"Sir, it is your own fault," Bulkeley said. "You have given yourself no manner of concern for the public good . . . but have acted quite the reverse, or else have been so careless and indifferent about it, as if we had no commander."

Cheap turned away from his officers and addressed the rank-and-file seamen. "Very well, gentlemen, you have caught me napping.... You are a parcel of brave fellows, but my officers are scoundrels." The intruders had bound his hands behind his back. "My lads, I do not blame you," he said again. "It is the villainy of my officers." He added that these men would eventually answer for their deeds. The implication was unmistakable: they would be hanged.

He then looked at Lieutenant Baynes and asked, "Well, sir, what do you design to do by me?" When Baynes explained that the officers planned to confine him in one of the tents, Cheap said, "I should be obliged to the gentlemen, if they would let me stay in my own." His request was denied. "Well, *Captain* Baynes!" he said contemptuously.

As Cheap—who was only half dressed but wearing his hat—was led outside into the blistering cold, he strove to maintain a dignified air. He said to the crowd of onlookers, "You must excuse my not pulling my hat off, my hands are confined."

Bulkeley couldn't help conveying, in his written account, a certain admiration for his adversary. Here Cheap was, defeated, bound, humiliated, and yet he remained composed, steady, and courageous. He had finally, like a true captain, mastered himself.

A moment later, the boatswain, King, sauntered over to Cheap, cocked his fist, and slugged him in the face. "It was your time, but now, God damn you, it is mine!" King said.

"You are a scoundrel for using a gentleman ill when he is a prisoner," Cheap said, his face streaked with blood.

He and Hamilton were placed in a makeshift prison, watched over at all times by a phalanx of six seamen and an officer. No one was allowed in without being searched. Bulkeley seemed to be taking no chances—he didn't want Cheap to break out or anyone else to break in.

As the de facto commander, Bulkeley felt the burden of being fully in charge. "We now looked on [him] as Captain," Campbell conceded. Bulkeley began making final preparations for the voyage to Brazil. He ordered the men to fill empty gunpowder barrels with rainwater for drinking, and to cut up and dress the few remaining portions of meat. Then he had their meager supplies, including some bags of flour, stored on the boats. Bulkeley also slipped his two precious possessions—his journal and the book *The Christian's Pattern*—into the hold of the *Speedwell*, where they would stay drier. Byron, still stunned by the mutiny, fretted that the longboat's food stock would last only a few days: "Our flour was to be lengthened out by a mixture of seaweed; and our other supplies depended upon the success of our guns."

Bulkeley was determined to quell the atmosphere of anarchy, and with his allies he drafted a set of rules and regulations to govern the party once it set off. They included:

- Whatever fowl, fish, or necessaries of life obtained during the passage shall be divided equally among the whole.
- Any person found guilty of stealing food shall, irrespective of rank, be cast upon the nearest shore and abandoned.
- To prevent broils, quarrels, and mutiny, any man who threatens the life of another or inflicts violence shall be left on the nearest shore and abandoned.

Bulkeley declared that these commandments were for "the good of the community," and every person who intended to embark on the voyage was required to sign the document, like a blood oath.

There was one final pressing issue: what to do with Cheap? Altogether, out of the *Wager*'s original complement of some 250 men and boys, 91 were still alive, among them the seceders. To squeeze all the passengers onto the four boats, they'd have to be packed cheek to jowl. There was no separate space for a prisoner, and Cheap would be hard to restrain, while also posing a constant threat to the new order.

According to Bulkeley, the plan was nevertheless to transport Cheap back home as a prisoner, so that the captain could stand trial for murder. But at the last moment, Cheap told Bulkeley that he'd "rather be shot than carried off a prisoner." He asked to be left on the island with anyone who wanted to stick with him and with whatever supplies could be spared. Bulkeley wrote, in his account, that he conferred with several of the men, who said, "Let him stay and be damned!"

Bulkeley and his closest fellow officers then prepared their most important document yet. This one was addressed directly to the Lord High Admiral of Great Britain. It stated that because of the difficulty of carrying Cheap as a prisoner "in so small a vessel, and for so long and tedious a passage," and because he might carry out plots "in secret as may prove destructive to the whole body," they had agreed to abandon their captain on Wager Island. It was necessary, they insisted, "in order to prevent murder."

Cheap was sure that his enemies intended to do away with him, and were using the shooting of Cozens as a pretext. Surely they knew that his version of events might get them hanged.

As Bulkeley and his men were preparing to set sail, they informed Cheap that they would give him the eighteen-foot yawl. Not only was it the smallest of the four boats; it had recently been cracked on the rocks. The yawl's hull, Cheap observed, was "all in pieces." The men also provided him, as he put it, just "a very small quantity of extraordinarily bad flour, and a few pieces of salt meat." And they offered him a compass, a couple of poor guns, a telescope, and a Bible.

Lieutenant Hamilton and the surgeon, Elliot, decided to stay with Cheap, but neither Byron nor Campbell nor anyone else from the outpost did. The seceders also planned to linger on the island—in part because there wasn't space on the boats, and in part because they'd become used to living separately. This group had suffered its own attrition, and just recently Mitchell and two of his companions had disappeared, setting off on a flimsy raft in the hope of reaching the mainland. They were never heard from again; no doubt they'd met a grisly end. Just seven seceders remained, bringing the total number who would stay on the island—including Cheap—to ten.

On October 14, 1741, five months after being shipwrecked and more than a year since departing England, Bulkeley's party began to board the three boats. They were eager to flee their imprisonment in the wild, and also, perhaps, to flee what they'd become. Yet they were also afraid to be embarking on another voyage into the unknown.

Cheap, released from his confinement, strolled down to the edge of the shore and watched as a parade of men, clad in rags, were squeezing into the three boats. He spotted his midshipmen, Byron, Campbell, and Isaac Morris. There was Master Clark, making sure that his boy was safe. There were the purser, Harvey, and the cook, Maclean, and the boatswain, King, and the seamen John Duck and John Jones. Altogether, fifty-nine bodies crammed into the longboat, twelve into the cutter, and ten into the barge. Bulkeley wrote, "We are so closely pent up for want of room that the worst jail in England is a palace to our present situation."

Several men called out to Cheap with what he described as the "utmost insolence and inhumanity." They told him that he'd never see any Englishmen again, other than the few stragglers on the island with whom he would surely die.

Bulkeley approached him, and Cheap stared at the man who had usurped him. He knew that each of them was about to face another agonizing ordeal, and perhaps he recognized a small part of himself in Bulkeley—the prideful ambition, the desperate cruelty, and the vestige of goodness. He put out his hand and wished him a safe passage. Bulkeley noted in his journal, "This was the last time I ever saw the unfortunate Captain Cheap."

At eleven in the morning, with Bulkeley in the commander's perch on the *Speedwell*, the boats shoved off into Cheap's Bay, the crews hoisting sails and driving with oars in order to overcome the crashing surf. Cheap had asked Bulkeley one favor: that if he and his party reached England to relay the entire history of what had transpired, Cheap's side included. Yet, as the boats slipped away, Cheap realized that the island would likely become the place where he and his story were lost forever.

Part Four

DELIVERANCE

CHAPTER 17

Byron's Choice

AS THE BOATS HEADED out to sea, John Byron stared at Cheap standing forlorn on the shore in the spectral mist. Byron had been led to believe that Cheap would be brought along with them on the journey, at least as a prisoner. But they had just left him there. Left him without a working boat, no doubt to perish. "I had all along been in the dark as to the turn this affair would take," Byron would write.

He had originally made a choice that he could bear: abandoning the mission to return home was a decision that might subvert his naval career, but it would save his life. Doing this to Captain Cheap was different. To play a role in totally deserting his commander—no matter how flawed and tyrannical he was—threatened the romantic image of himself that he had clung to despite the horrors of the voyage. As he continued watching Cheap in the distance, he and some of the men shouted three cheers to their old captain. And then Cheap was gone and Byron's decision seemed irreversible.

Even before the boats sailed past Wager Island, the men were struck by a squall, as if they were already being punished for their sins. Then Byron heard a loud, unnerving sound: the makeshift foresail on the vaunted new longboat had split and was flapping uncontrollably. The party was forced to seek shelter in the lagoon of another island just west of Cheap's Bay, where they could repair the sail and wait out the storm. They had traveled barely a mile.

The next day, Bulkeley asked for volunteers to take the barge back to Wager Island and retrieve a discarded canvas tent in case they later needed extra sailcloth. Byron suddenly saw an opportunity. He offered to go with the party, as did Midshipman Campbell, and that afternoon they set off with eight other men, rowing through the jarring waves. Campbell shared Byron's misgivings, and while the two young midshipmen were being tossed about and doused by spray, they began to conspire. If they wanted to escape the stain of dishonor and cowardice, Byron believed, they must retrieve Cheap. Campbell agreed, murmuring that now was the time.

Hoping to sneak away with the barge, they tried to enlist the other men onboard, who included several of Cheap's erstwhile supporters. They, too, had been shocked by the abandonment of the captain. Fearing they would be hanged if they ever made it back to England, they joined the counterplot.

As Byron rowed on with the others, he became increasingly uneasy: what if Bulkeley and his men suspected that they had no intention of returning? They might not mind the defections—it would mean fewer bodies to transport and mouths to feed—but they would be enraged over the loss of the barge, which they would want for added space and to send hunting parties onshore. As night fell, Byron and his companions anxiously plowed through the waves in the dark until they spotted campfires flickering in the distance: the outpost. Byron and his party had made it safely back to Wager Island.

Cheap was astonished by the men's arrival, and when he learned what they had resolved to do he seemed invigorated. He welcomed Byron and Campbell into his dwelling, and, along with the surgeon, Elliot, and the marine lieutenant, Hamilton, they stayed up late, chatting hopefully about their prospects now that they were free of the men behind the rebellion. There were twenty people on the island: thirteen at the main settlement, and another seven at the seceders' camp. Cheap and his party had at least one usable boat—the barge—and they could also try to repair the yawl.

When Byron awoke the next morning, though, he confronted the grim reality. He had nothing to put on but a hat, torn trousers, and the remaining threads of a waistcoat. His shoes had disintegrated, leaving him barefoot. Most distressing, he had no reserves of food—not even a slaugh cake. And the rest of the men who had returned with him also had nothing. Their scant rations had been stored on the *Speedwell* with the very people they'd just double-crossed.

Cheap shared some of his meat—it was rotten, and in any case there wasn't enough of it to sustain them for long. Byron, who had constantly been guided by the whims of superiors, finally tried to formulate a plan of his own. He decided that he must go back to the mutineers and claim the portion of food owed his party. It would be risky, perhaps even foolhardy, but what other option was there?

When Byron proposed the idea, Cheap warned that his enemies would seek vengeance and commandeer the barge, once more leaving the rest of them stranded.

Byron had thought about that. He said that he and Campbell and a small party could land the barge some distance away from the lagoon. Then, while most of them guarded the boat, he and Campbell would complete the trek to Bulkeley's party. They would be vulnerable to retaliation, but the temptation of food was too overpowering. And with Cheap's encouragement, Byron and his small party embarked that morning.

After they paddled to the other island, they hid the barge in a secluded area. Byron and Campbell bade farewell to their companions and began their arduous trek. They slogged through sticky swamps and knotted forests until, that night, they reached the edge of the black lagoon. They heard voices in the darkness. Most of the mutineers, including their leaders, Bulkeley and Baynes, were on the shore scouring for food—that perpetual quest.

Bulkeley appeared baffled by the two midshipmen's sudden appearance. Why had they arrived overland and without the barge?

Byron, summoning his courage, declared that they would not desert Cheap.

Bulkeley seemed stung by Byron's defection. He assumed that Byron had been coerced by Campbell—either that, or the aristocratic midshipman had reverted to the embedded orders of class and hierarchy. (In a veiled comment in his journal, Bulkeley wrote that "the Honourable Mr. Byron" could not quite accommodate himself to "lie forward with the men.")

When Byron and Campbell asked for their party's share of food, Bulkeley and Baynes demanded to know where the barge was. Campbell told them that they intended to keep the boat—after all, it was meant to carry ten castaways, and ten of them were now staying with Cheap. One of the mutineers snapped, "Damn you," and warned them that unless they brought back the barge they would be given nothing.

Byron made a plea directly to the rest of the men, but they told him that if he did not bring the barge the next day, they'd arm the cutter and come after him.

Byron walked away; then, distraught, he walked back and asked again. It was futile. He wondered how people could be so cruel.

As he departed, he lost his hat in a gust of wind. The seaman John Duck walked over to his old companion and generously gave him his own hat.

Byron was overcome by this flash of kindness. "John!" he exclaimed. "I thank you." But insisting that he could not leave Duck without a hat, he returned it.

Then Byron hurried away with Campbell, back to the barge and across the sea with his party, occasionally glancing behind him to see if they were being pursued by a cutter gleaming with guns.

CHAPTER 18

Port of God's Mercy

THE MOMENT THE WINDS calmed, Bulkeley, Lieutenant Baynes, and the other men on the two remaining boats shipped out. They were within striking distance of the outpost, but Bulkeley ignored pleas to launch an assault to take the barge and instead led his men in another direction—south toward the Strait of Magellan. There would be no more looking back.

As they forged onward, it became clear, even to old sea dogs like Bulkeley, that the journey in the castaway boats would be unlike anything they had ever experienced. The *Speedwell* was not that much bigger than the original longboat, which had been designed to fit twenty oarsmen and to ferry supplies over short distances. Now the *Speedwell* was jammed with enough casks of water to last them a month and with enough guns and ammunition to ward off an attack. Most of all, the boat was crammed with men—men squeezed on the bow, around the masts, by the tiller, in the hold belowdecks. The boat looked as if it had been jury-rigged with human limbs.

With fifty-nine people onboard, there was no space to lie down, and it was nearly impossible for the crew to move about to raise a sail or pull a rope. After serving several hours on watch, the men on deck would struggle to switch places with those below in the hold, which was as dank and dark as a coffin but provided a measure of protection from the elements. To urinate or defecate, a person had to lean over the side of the hull. The stench of the men's wet clothes alone,

Bulkeley wrote, "makes the air we breathe nauseous to that degree that one would think it impossible for a man to live."

Weighed down with human cargo and supplies, the hull rested so low in the sea that its stern was barely four inches above the waterline. Even small waves washed over the gunwales, soaking the men; in choppy seas the crew on deck was nearly swept overboard with every roll.

The twelve people on the cutter, including the purser, Thomas Harvey, had it worse. The boat was only twenty-five feet long, and it was even less stable in the waves, which during severe storms dwarfed its single mast. The men sat bunched together on hard, narrow planks, bouncing up and down. There was no area below where crew members could find shelter, and at night they would sometimes clamber onto the *Speedwell* to sleep, while the cutter was towed behind. At such times, the longboat was stuffed with seventy-one men.

Not only did these vessels have to traverse some of the roughest seas on earth; most of the men attempting to pull off this feat were already near death. "The greatest part of the people on board are so regardless of life that they really appear quite indifferent whether they shall live or die," Bulkeley wrote, "and it is with much entreaty that any of them can be prevailed on to come upon deck to assist for their preservation." For Bulkeley, leading the party under such circumstances was extraordinarily challenging, and the unusual power dynamics at play compounded the difficulty. Although Bulkeley was in most respects acting as the captain, Lieutenant Baynes officially remained the commanding officer.

On October 30, two weeks into the voyage, the men were caught in another squall. As the winds cannonaded across the Pacific and waves crashed over them, Bulkeley spied, along the mountainous coastline to the east, a sliver of a channel. He thought it might lead to a safe harbor, but it was surrounded by rocks, like those that had carved a hole in the *Wager.* Bulkeley often consulted with Baynes, because of their arrangement, and with the carpenter, Cummins, because of trust. Such consultations also seemed to be Bulkeley's way of underlining the difference between himself and the captain he had deposed.

Bulkeley now confronted his first major tactical decision: to remain in the open ocean or try to slip between the rocks. "Nothing but death before our eyes in keeping the sea, and the same prospect in running in with the land," he noted. As the ships tipped further and further over, he chose the channel: "The entrance is so dangerous that no mortal would attempt it, unless his case was desperate as ours."

As the men approached the chute, they heard a menacing roar—breakers smashing upon the reefs. One miscue, and they would sink. Lookouts scanned the waters for submerged rocks while crewmen worked the sails. Bulkeley, bracing himself and barking out orders, guided them through the labyrinth of rocks until they were sitting snugly in a harbor shielded by cliffs with crystalline waterfalls. The spot was so commodious, Bulkeley boasted, the whole British Navy could gather within it.

He had little time to relish his triumph. Parties were ferried ashore in the cutter to collect fresh water and any shellfish—or, as Bulkeley put it, "what Providence throws in our way." Then the men were off again, plunging back into a riotous sea.

On November 3, during a heavy rainstorm, Bulkeley signaled to the cutter's crew to stay close. Soon afterward, the cutter split its mainsail and disappeared. Bulkeley and his party tacked back and forth, searching for the other boat each time the *Speedwell* crested above the waves. Yet there was no sight of the cutter—it must have gone under with all twelve men. At last, with the *Speedwell* itself laboring ominously, Bulkeley and Baynes gave up and ducked into an inlet along the coast.

Bulkeley experienced the grief of losing men who were effectively under his command, and despite the cramped conditions inside the *Speedwell*'s berth, he retrieved his journal and carefully inscribed their names. The lost included Harvey, the purser; Richard Phipps, the ingenious builder of rafts; and William Oram, the carpenter's mate whom Bulkeley had persuaded to leave the seceders in the hope of reaching England.

Because of the *Speedwell*'s deep keel and heavy hull, it could not be brought too close to the rocky coast, and without the cutter the men had no way of sending people ashore to hunt for food. Only a few of them could swim. "We are now in a most wretched condition," Bulkeley confessed.

On November 5, they tried to head out to sea, only to be beaten back by the storm. Trapped again on the boat, and consumed by hunger, they stared agonizingly at a few mussels on the rocks. At wits' end, the boatswain, King, grabbed several oars and empty barrels, fastened them together with rope, and then lowered the bizarre-looking device into the water. It floated.

He and two other men flopped on top of the contraption and began paddling toward shore. After traveling only a few feet, a wave hoisted the barrels in the air and catapulted the men into the sea. They thrashed for their lives. Two were plucked out of the water by the crew on the *Speedwell*, but King managed to grab hold of the mangled raft and kick his way to shore. That evening, he returned with what sustenance he could, and revealed that on the beach he had seen an empty food cask, which appeared to be the kind issued by the British Navy. The castaways grew solemn, wondering whether another vessel, perhaps even Commodore Anson's flagship, the *Centurion*, had sunk like the *Wager*.

The next morning, as Bulkeley and his party resumed their voyage, they glimpsed on the barren ocean a wisp of white, dipping amid the waves and then rising again. It was the cutter's sail! The boat was intact, and there were the dozen crew members—soaked and dazed but alive. The miraculous reunion, Bulkeley wrote, gave them all "new life."

After heading into a cove and deploying the cutter to collect shellfish, they tried to get some rest. The cutter was roped to the stern of the *Speedwell*, and its crew, except for a seaman named James Stewart, crawled onto the *Speedwell* to sleep.

At two in the morning, the rope snapped, sending the cutter careening across the sea. Bulkeley and several of the men looked out in the rainswept darkness—there was Stewart on the boat, barreling toward the reefs. The men called to him, but he was too far away to hear them over the wind, and before long the cutter was gone—this time no doubt forever, shattered upon the rocks.

The men had lost not only another companion but also their means of going ashore for sustenance. Moreover, seventy castaways would now have to be packed, day and night, into the *Speedwell*. "Great uneasiness among the people, many of them despairing of a deliverance," Bulkeley wrote.

The following day, eleven of the men, including Phipps, requested to be cast out into this desolate part of the world rather than continue in the seemingly doomed *Speedwell*. Bulkeley and Baynes, ever conscious of the legal ramifications, drafted a certificate for the Lords of the Admiralty, stating that the eleven men had willingly made the decision and indemnified "all persons from ever being called to an account for putting us on shore." Bulkeley wrote in his journal that these men were leaving for "the preservation of themselves and us."

Bulkeley brought the boat as close to the shore as possible, and the eleven leapt off. He watched them swim to a lifeless patch of land—the last time they would ever be reported seen. Then he and the remaining party on the *Speedwell* sailed on.

On November 10, nearly a month after embarking from Wager Island and after traveling some four hundred miles, Bulkeley observed a string of small, barren islands. They looked, he thought, exactly like those that Sir John Narborough had described as being at the northwest mouth of the Strait of Magellan. To the south, on the opposite side of the mouth, was another bleak island, with dark, rocky, serrated mountains. Bulkeley figured that this must be Desolation Island—named by Narborough because it was "so desolate a land to behold." Bulkeley, based on these observations and on his calculations of the *Speedwell*'s latitude, was confident that they had reached the Strait of Magellan.

After he tacked the *Speedwell* to the southeast, on the verge of realizing his plan, he betrayed a feeling that he rarely acknowledged: absolute fear. "I never in my life . . . have seen such a sea as runs here," he observed. The winds were of typhoon strength, and the waters seemed at war with themselves. Buckeley believed that he was witnessing the confluence of the Pacific Ocean pouring into the strait and the Atlantic Ocean pouring out—that same spot where the British buccaneer Francis Drake had been caught in what the chaplain onboard his ship had called an "intolerable tempest." (The chaplain wrote that God had seemingly "set himself against us," and would not "withdraw his judgment till he had buried our bodies, and ships also, in the bottomless depth of the raging sea.") Waves began to swallow the *Speedwell* from stern to bow, hull to mast tops. One rolled the *Speedwell* more than twenty degrees, then fifty, then eighty, until it had broached—lying completely on its side, with its masts and sails pressed against the water. As the boat creaked and buckled and flooded, Bulkeley was sure she would never rise again. After all he had been through, all his sacrifices and sins, he now confronted the prospect of a futile death—of drowning without having seen his family again. Yet, ever so slowly, the *Speedwell* began to right itself, the sails emerging as water spilled from the deck and hold.

Each momentary reprieve seemed to intensify Bulkeley's messianic fervor. He wrote of the storm, "We prayed earnestly for its clearing up, for nothing else could save us from perishing." In what he described as a grace of light, they glimpsed a cove and tried to reach it by running a gauntlet of breakers. "We were surrounded with rocks, and so near that a man might toss a biscuit on 'em," he observed. Yet they slipped into the cove, which was as smooth as a millpond. "We call this harbour the Port of God's Mercy, esteeming our preservation this day to be a miracle," Bulkeley wrote. "The most abandoned among us no longer doubt of an Almighty Being, and have promised to reform their lives."

With each grinding day, though, the men were becoming more dispirited and unruly. They incessantly demanded extra rations, and Bulkeley and Baynes found themselves in the same unwinnable position that had confounded Cheap. "If we are not exceedingly provident in regard of serving our provisions, we must all inevitably starve," Bulkeley noted. The men who had once followed him so eagerly, so devotedly, now seemed, as he put it, "ripe for mutiny and destruction." He added, "We know not what to do to bring them under any command; they have troubled us to that degree that we are weary of our lives."

Along with Baynes and Cummins, he strained to maintain order. The signed articles governing the party sanctioned the abandonment of anyone who caused unrest. Yet Bulkeley made a very different sort of threat: if the misbehavior continued, he, along with Baynes and Cummins, would demand to be deposited onshore, leaving the others to fend for themselves on the boat. The crew knew that Bulkeley was indispensable—no one else could as monomaniacally plot their course and battle the elements—so his threat had a sobering effect. "The people have promised to be under government, and seem much easier," Bulkeley wrote. To further pacify the men, he released a bit more flour from their stores, noting that many people eat the powder "raw as soon as they are served it."

Nevertheless, they were dying. Among the casualties was a sixteen-year-old boy named George Bateman. "This poor creature starved, perished, and died a skeleton," Bulkeley wrote, adding, "There are several more in the same miserable condition, and who, without a speedy relief, must undergo the same fate."

He endeavored to comfort the ailing, but what they most wanted was nourishment. One twelve-year-old boy pleaded to a close companion for some extra flour, saying that he would otherwise not live to see Brazil, but his shipmate was unmoved. "Persons who have not experienced the hardships we have met with," Bulkeley wrote, "will wonder how people can be so inhuman to see their fellow creatures starving before their faces, and afford 'em no relief. But hunger is void of all compassion." The boy's misery ended only when "heaven sent death to his relief."

On November 24, the *Speedwell* became caught in a mystifying maze of channels and lagoons. Baynes accused Bulkeley of being mistaken about having entered the strait. Had they wasted two weeks going the wrong way? Bulkeley countered that "if ever there was such a place in the world as the Strait of Magellan, we are now in them."

But faced with growing dissent, he turned the boat around, heading back the way they had come. One marine began to go mad, laughing hysterically, until he slumped over in silence, dead. Another man died shortly after, and then another. Their bodies were tossed into the sea.

It took the surviving party close to two weeks to retrace its path, only to then realize that they had found the strait all along. Now they had to start east all over again.

Maybe Cheap was right—maybe they should have headed north.

CHAPTER 19

The Haunting

CHEAP HAD NOT GIVEN up on his plan to rejoin Commodore Anson and the squadron. He had formed an alliance with the last of the seceders—desperation can also breed unity—and the combined group, after suffering one death, numbered nineteen, including Byron, Campbell, the marine lieutenant, Hamilton, and the surgeon, Elliot. It had been two months since the others had left the island, and Cheap and the remaining men were living in the shelters at the outpost and foraging for seaweed and the occasional sea fowl.

Cheap, spared what Byron described as the "riotous applications, menaces, and disturbance of an unruly crew," seemed renewed, engaged, alive. "He now became very brisk," Campbell observed, "went about everywhere to get wood and water, made fires, and proved an excellent cook." Cheap and the rest of the men, using the skills that they'd acquired while refurbishing the longboat, were able to repair the splintered yawl and reinforce the battered barge. Meanwhile, three casks of beef had been fished out of the sunken *Wager*, and Cheap had managed to conserve some of it for the upcoming journey. "I then began to conceive great hopes," Cheap wrote in his account. Now all he and the other men needed was for the storms to let up so they could set off.

On December 15, Cheap awoke to a glimmer of light—the sun shining through the clouds. With Byron and a few others, he hiked up Mount Misery to get a clearer view of the sea. When they reached the top, he took out his telescope and scanned the horizon. Rough waves could be seen in the distance.

But the men were impatient to flee the island. Many of them, spooked by their endless bad luck, were convinced that because nobody had buried the seaman whom James Mitchell murdered on Mount Misery, his spirit was hounding them. "One night we were alarmed with a strange cry, which resembled that of a man drowning," Byron wrote. "Many of us ran out of our huts towards the place from whence the noise proceeded, which was not far off shore, where we could perceive, but not distinctly (for it was then moonlight), an appearance like that of a man swimming half out of water. The noise that this creature uttered was so unlike that of any animal they had heard before that it made a great impression upon the men; and they frequently recalled the apparition at the time of their distresses."

The castaways began to pack their few supplies into the twenty-four-foot barge and the eighteen-foot yawl. Even smaller than the cutter, these vessels were open boats with only cross planks for seats. Each had a short single mast, enabling it to be sailed, but oars had to provide much of the power. Cheap wedged himself into the barge, along with Byron and eight others. Amid the tangle of bodies and ropes and sails and casks of food and water, they each had barely a foot of room. Campbell, Hamilton, and six others were similarly crammed into the yawl, their elbows and knees jostling those of the person beside them.

Cheap glanced at the outpost, their home for the past seven months. All that remained were some scattered, windbeaten shelters—evidence of a life-and-death struggle that would soon be wiped away by the elements.

Cheap was eager to depart—as he put it, the longing filled "all my heart." At his signal, Byron and the rest of the men shoved off from Wager Island, beginning their long, daunting journey north.

They'd have to navigate nearly 100 miles through the Gulf of Pain, then proceed another 250 miles along the Pacific coastline to the island of Chiloé.

After only an hour, the rains began to beat down and the winds came out of the west, cold and hard. Avalanches of waves buried the boats, and Cheap instructed Byron and the others to impede the deluge by forming a human wall, with their backs to the sea. The waters kept coming, swamping the hulls. It was impossible for the men to bail fast enough with their hats and hands, and Cheap knew that if they didn't lighten the already overloaded boats they would sink for a second time off Wager Island. And so the men were forced to do the unthinkable: throw overboard virtually all their supplies, including the precious casks of food. The famished men looked on as their last rations were swallowed by the voracious sea.

By nightfall, Cheap and the party had found their way into a cove along the coast. They went ashore and climbed the mountainous terrain, hoping to discover a covering to sleep under, but eventually they collapsed on an open bed of rocks, staring into the rain. They dreamed of their shelters on Wager Island. "Here we have no other house than the wide world," Campbell wrote. "It froze so hard that by morning several of us were almost dead."

Cheap knew that they had to keep moving, and he hastened everyone back into the boats. They rowed hour after hour, day after day, occasionally stopping to peel seaweed off sunken rocks and make a meal of what they called "sea-tangle." When the winds shifted to the south, they sailed downwind, with the stitched-together canvases extended and the hulls riding the waves.

Nine days after leaving Wager Island, they had traveled north nearly a hundred miles. To the northwest, they could see the tip of a cape with three enormous cliffs jutting into the sea. They were almost at the end of the gulf; surely they had weathered the worst of the journey.

They paused onshore to sleep, and when they awoke the next

morning, they realized that the date was December 25. They celebrated Christmas with a feast of sea-tangle and cups of fresh streamwater—"Adam's wine," as they called it, because that was all God had given Adam to drink. Cheap toasted to the health of King George II, before they packed up and sailed on.

A few days later, they descended on the cape, the most critical point in the route. The seas converging here seethed with overpowering currents and colossal waves with frothing peaks, which Campbell referred to as the white of whites. Cheap ordered the men to lower the sails before they capsized, and they began to pull the oars with all their might.

Cheap urged them on. After hours, they came abreast of the first of the three cliffs, but they were soon driven backward by the waves and the currents. Although they tried to retreat to a nearby bay, they were so tired that they couldn't make it there before dark, and so everyone fell asleep on the boats, lying on their oars. After the sun rose, they recuperated in the bay until Cheap ordered them to try again for the cape. They must pull for their king and country. They must pull for their wives and sons and daughters and mothers and fathers and sweethearts and one another. This time, the castaways reached the second cliff, only to be hurled back and forced to retreat into the bay again.

The next morning, the conditions were so severe that Cheap knew none of the men would dare try to navigate around the cape, and so they went ashore to hunt for food. They would need their strength. One of the castaways came upon a seal, raised his musket, and shot it. The men cooked it over a wood fire, tearing off chunks of fat and chewing them. Nothing was left to waste. Byron even made shoes of the skins, wrapping them around his nearly frostbitten feet.

The men's boats were anchored just offshore, and Cheap designated two men to each vessel, to keep watch at night. It was Byron's lot to be on the barge. But he and the other men had been revived by the nourishment, and they fell asleep, in anticipation: perhaps the next day they would finally round the cape.

Something was thudding into the barge. "I was . . . awakened by the uncommon motion of the boat, and the roaring of the breakers everywhere about us," Byron wrote. "At the same time I heard a shrieking." It was as if the ghost from Wager Island had reappeared. The cries were coming from the yawl, anchored a few yards away, and Byron turned just in time to see this boat, with two men onboard, being capsized by a wave. Then it sank. One man was cast by the surf onto the beach, but the other drowned.

Byron expected his own boat to flip at any moment. With his companion, he heaved the anchor and rowed with the barge's bow pointed into the waves, trying to avoid being hit broadside and waiting for the storm to blow itself out. "Here we lay all the next day, in a great sea, not knowing what would be our fate," he wrote.

After they made it ashore, they gathered with Cheap and the other survivors. The party now numbered eighteen, and without the yawl, there was no longer room to transport them all. Three more men could fit with difficulty in the barge, but four members of the party would have to remain behind—or they would all perish.

Four marines were selected. Being soldiers, they lacked sailing skills. "The marines were fixed on, as not being of any service on board," Campbell confessed, noting, "This was a melancholy thing, but necessity compelled us." He recorded each of the marines' last names: Smith, Hobbs, Hertford, and Crosslet.

Cheap distributed to them some armaments and a frying pan. "Our hearts melted with compassion for them," Campbell wrote. As the barge sailed away, the four marines stood on the beach, gave them three cheers, and cried, "God bless the King!"

Six weeks after Cheap and his party fled Wager Island, they reached the cape for the third time. The seas were more frenzied than ever, but he beckoned the men on, and they powered past one cliff and then another. There was just the last cliff. They were almost past it. But the crew collapsed, exhausted and defeated. "Perceiving now that it was impossible for any boat to get round, the men lay upon their oars till the boat was very near the breakers," Byron wrote. "I thought it was their intention to put an end to their lives and misery at once." For a time, not a soul moved or spoke. They were almost upon the breakers, the roar of the surf deafening. "At last, Captain Cheap told them they must either perish immediately, or pull stoutly."

The men picked up the oars, exerting themselves just enough to avoid the rocks and turn the boat around. "We were now resigned to our fate," Byron wrote, having given up "all thoughts of making any further attempt to double the cape."

Many of the men attributed their failures to not having buried the seaman on Wager Island. The castaways went back to the bay, in the hope of at least finding the marines. Somehow, they resolved they would squeeze them onboard. As Campbell wrote, "We considered that if the boat sunk, we then should be free from the miserable life we led, and die all together."

Yet, except for a musket lying on the beach, there was no trace of them. They had undoubtedly perished, but where were their bodies? The castaways sought some way to commemorate the four men. "This bay we named Marine Bay," Byron wrote.

Cheap wanted to make one final attempt to round the cape. They were so close, and if they made it he was sure that his plan would succeed. But the men would no longer abide his devouring obsessions, and they decided to return to the place they had long been trying to escape: Wager Island. "We had now lost all hopes of ever revisiting our native country," Campbell wrote, and they preferred to spend their last days on the island, which had become "a kind of home."

Cheap reluctantly assented. It took them nearly two weeks to circle back to the island, and by then the entire disastrous foray had lasted two months. They'd exhausted all of their food from the journey; Byron had even eaten the rancid, foul-smelling sealskins covering his feet. He heard a few of the castaways whispering about drawing lots and "consigning one man to death for the support of the rest." This was different than when some of the men had earlier cannibalized dead bodies. This was killing a companion for food—a grisly ritual later imagined by the poet Lord Byron:

The lots were made, and marked, and mixed, and handed,
In silent horror, and their distribution
Lulled even the savage hunger which demanded,
Like the Promethean vulture, this pollution.

In the end, the castaways could not go this far. Instead, they staggered up Mount Misery and found the decayed body of their companion—the man whose spirit, they believed, had been haunting them. They dug a hole and buried him. Then they went back to the outpost and huddled together, listening to the hush of the sea.

CHAPTER 20

The Day of Our Deliverance

BULKELEY AND THE FIFTY-EIGHT other castaways on the *Speedwell* were back on course, drifting slowly through the Strait of Magellan toward the Atlantic. The *Speedwell*, in its battered, leaking condition, was unable to sail close to the wind, and Bulkeley struggled to maintain his course. "It is enough to deject any thinking man to see that the boat will not turn to windward," he wrote, adding that the vessel kept "swimming so poignant upon the sea."

Bulkeley also served as the chief navigator, and without a detailed chart of the region he had to piece together clues about the landscape from Narborough's account and match them with his own observations. At night, dizzy and haggard, he read the stars to fix the ship's latitude; during the day, he estimated its longitude through dead reckoning. He'd then compare these coordinates with those cited by Narborough—another piece of the puzzle. A typical entry in his journal read: "At eight saw two ledges of rocks, running two leagues out from a point of land which makes like an old castle."

As he and his men progressed through the strait, sometimes sailing, sometimes rowing, they floated past dusty wooded hills and blue glaciers, the Andes looming in the distance with their immortal caps of snow. As Charles Darwin later wrote, it was a coastline that made a "landsman dream for a week about shipwrecks, peril, and death." The castaways rowed past a cliff where they spotted two indigenous men with white-feathered caps lying on their bellies and peering down at them before disappearing. They went past Cape

Froward, the southernmost point of the continental mainland, where the two arms of the strait—one extending inward from the Pacific, the other reaching back from the Atlantic—conjoined.

At this junction, the passageway twisted sharply to the northeast. After following this trajectory for more than twenty miles, Bulkeley and his men came upon Port Famine—the site of another exercise in imperial hubris. In 1584, the Spanish, determined to control access to the strait, had attempted to set up a colony here with some three hundred settlers, including soldiers, Franciscan priests, women, and children. But during the freezing winter they began to run out of food. By the time another expedition visited, nearly three years later, most of the colonists had, as one witness wrote, "died like dogs in their houses," and the whole village was "tainted with the smell and the savor of the dead."

When Bulkeley and his party passed the ruins of Port Famine, on December 7, 1741, they had been gone from Wager Island for nearly two months. Without more food and fresh water, they, too, would soon perish.

Two days later, they spied a herd of guanacos along the wooded bank. Bulkeley, with the eye of a predator, described the animal—a wild cousin of the llama—as being "as large as any English deer, with a long neck; his head, mouth, and ears, resembling a sheep." The creature, he added, "has very long slender legs, and is cloven-footed like a deer, with a short bushy tail, of reddish colour." Though he noted that these animals were exceedingly "nimble, of an exquisite quick sight, very shy, and difficult to be shot," he tried to bring the *Speedwell* close enough to the coast for some of the men to wade ashore with guns. But the williwaws blowing down from the mountains forced him to bear away. The herd flitted off; the men drifted on.

As Narborough had described, the channel began to constrict. Bulkeley realized that they had entered what was known as the First Narrow. At its widest, the strait extended twenty miles, but here it tapered to just two. Navigating the narrowest point in the passageway was treacherous. The tide rose and fell some forty feet, and there were often countervailing winds and eight-knot currents. It was nighttime when the castaways began sailing through the nine-mile-long chute, and they strained to see in the dark. For hours, they maneuvered between the shrouded banks, trying to avoid the shoals and curtail the boat's constant leeward drift, until, at dawn, they emerged from the chute.

On December 11, as they rowed on, Bulkeley noticed a bluff in the distance with several majestic white cliffs. He felt a shiver of recognition. It was the Cape of Eleven Thousand Virgins, which he had passed with Anson's squadron nearly a year earlier on the way to Cape Horn. Bulkeley and his party had reached the strait's eastern mouth, and were being swept into the Atlantic. They had not only made it through the 350-mile passageway in their jury-rigged boat; they had also, thanks to a remarkable feat of navigation by Bulkeley, taken, even with their initial false start, only thirty-one days—a week faster than Ferdinand Magellan and his armada.

Still, the port of Rio Grande, which was the closest settlement in Brazil, was more than sixteen hundred miles north, and to get there they would have to traverse a coastline (now part of Argentina) under Spanish control, which meant that they would face the added danger of being captured. And except for a bit of raw flour, they were out of food.

The men decided that they had no choice but to risk landing a hunting party, and they set their course for a bay where Narborough had reported seeing a small island with seals. On December 16, they sailed into the bay, known as Port Desire. Bulkeley observed on the shore a "peaked-up rock, much like a tower, looking as though it was a work of art set up for a landmark." Seeing no sign of Spanish inhabitants, he guided his party deeper into the harbor. Soon they found the small island: lounging upon it, as if unmoved from Narborough's day, were numerous seals. Bulkeley was able to anchor close enough to the shore that he and the rest of the men, including the nonswimmers, could climb overboard with their guns, wading up to their necks in the water. As soon as they stepped onto the island, they began deliriously picking off the seals. They smoked the meat over a fire and ravaged their rations—"the people eating greedily," as Bulkeley put it.

Before long, many of the men had collapsed in sickness. Most likely, they were suffering from what is now known as refeeding syndrome, in which a starved person, after suddenly ingesting large quantities of food, can go into shock, and even die. (Scientists later noticed this syndrome when it befell prisoners released from concentration camps after World War II.) The purser, Thomas Harvey, perished after consuming several rations of seal, and at least one other castaway died shortly after tasting what he thought was his salvation.

The surviving men resumed following the coastline northward. Not long afterward, their stores of seal began to run out. Bulkeley could not stop many of them from fighting over the last rations. Soon all the food was gone anyway. "To go from hence without meat or drink is certain death," Bulkeley wrote.

Once again, they attempted to land a hunting party. But now the seas were so rough that they had to anchor at a distance from the shore. A man would have to swim through the breakers to reach the land. Most of the castaways, unable to swim and paralyzed with exhaustion, did not budge. Bulkeley, a nonswimmer as well, was required to helm the ship. But the boatswain, King, the carpenter, Cummins, and another man—propelled by courage or desperation or perhaps both—leapt into the water. Galvanized by the sight, eleven others, including John Duck, the free Black seaman, and Midshipman Isaac Morris, followed. One marine grew tired and began to flail. Morris tried to reach him, but the marine drowned within twenty feet of the beach.

The other swimmers tumbled onto the sand, and Bulkeley tossed overboard four empty casks, which the surf carried ashore. They were to be filled with fresh water. Bulkeley had lashed to these casks several guns, and some of the men took them and began to hunt. They discovered a horse branded with the letters AR. The Spanish must be near. The castaways, who were increasingly anxious, shot the horse and a few seals, butchered them, then grilled the meat. Cummins, King, and four others swam back to the boat, bringing some food and fresh water. But a squall drove the *Speedwell* out to sea, and eight men, including Duck and Morris, were left stranded on land. "We still see the people ashore, but can't get them off," Bulkeley wrote.

That night, as the boat banged in the waves, part of the rudder broke off, making it even harder to maneuver. Bulkeley discussed with Baynes, Cummins, and the others what they should do. They summed up their decision in another signed document. Dated from onboard the *Speedwell*—"on the coast of South America, in the latitude of 37:25 S. longitude from the meridian of London, 65:00 W. this 14th day of January"—it stated that after the rudder broke they "expected every minute the vessel would founder," and it was "every man's opinion that we must put to sea or perish." They placed some guns and ammunition, as well as a letter explaining their decision, in a barrel, and then tossed it overboard, letting the waves wash it ashore. They waited until Duck, Morris, and the six others had received it. When the men read the letter, they fell to their knees and watched as the *Speedwell* sailed away.

Was God seeing the things they did out here? Bulkeley still sought solace from *The Christian's Pattern*, but a passage in it warned, "Hadst thou a clear conscience, thou could not fear death. It were better to avoid sin than to flee death." Yet was it a sin to want to live?

The broken rudder made the boat wander, as if it were following its own cryptic path. Within days, the men were out of food and virtually all their water. Few stirred. Bulkeley had noted, "There are not above fifteen of us healthy (if people may be called healthy that are scarce able to crawl). I am reckoned at present one of the strongest men in the boat, yet can hardly stand on my legs ten minutes together.... We that are in the best state of health do all we can to encourage the rest."

Lieutenant Baynes, who was ill, wrote of "our poor fellows

dying daily, looking with their ghastly countenances at me to assist them, which was not in my power." On January 23, Master Thomas Clark, who had so devotedly protected his young son, died, and the following day his son died, too. Two days later, the cook, Thomas Maclean—the oldest man on the voyage, who had endured hurricanes and scurvy and shipwreck—took his last breath. He was eighty-two.

Bulkeley still jotted scratchily in his journal. If he was writing with the future in mind, then he had to believe that, somehow, his journal would one day make it back to land. But his mind was fading. Once, he thought he saw butterflies snowing from the sky.

On January 28, 1742, the boat was blown toward the shore, and Bulkeley perceived a tableau of strange shapes. Was it another mirage? He looked again. The shapes, he was sure, were wooden structures—houses—and they were situated on the edge of a major river. It had to be the port of Rio Grande on the southern border of Brazil. Bulkeley called to the other crew members, and those who were still conscious grabbed the ropes and tried to work what remained of the sails. After the castaways had spent three and a half months traversing nearly three thousand miles, they had reached the safety of Brazil.

As the *Speedwell* drifted into the port, a crowd of townspeople gathered. They gaped at the battered, waterlogged vessel with its sun-bleached, shredded sails. Then they saw the almost unrecognizable human forms strewn about the deck and piled on top of one another in the hold—half-naked figures with protruding bones, their skin peeled off from the sun, as if they had emerged from a scalding fire. Manes of salted hair fell about their chins and down their backs. Bulkeley had written in his journal, "I believe no mortals have experienced more difficulties and miseries than we have."

Many of the men could not move, but Bulkeley staggered to his feet. When he explained that they were remnants of the crew of HMS *Wager*, which had sunk eight months earlier off the coast of Chile, the onlookers were even more astounded. "They were surprised that thirty souls, the number of people now living, could be stowed in so small a vessel," Bulkeley wrote. "But that she could contain the number which first embarked with us was to them amazing and beyond all belief."

The governor of the town came to meet them, and after learning of their harrowing experiences, he crossed himself and called their arrival a miracle. He promised them everything his country had to offer. The sick were carted to a hospital, where the carpenter's mate William Oram—who had helped build the *Speedwell* and had completed the entire odyssey—soon died. The party, which had set out from Wager Island with eighty-one men, had dwindled to twenty-nine.

To Bulkeley, the fact that a single one of them had survived was proof of God, and he believed that any person who could still doubt this truth "justly deserves the wrath of an incensed deity." In his journal, he noted that the occasion of their arrival in Brazil should be known as "the day of our deliverance, and ought to be remembered accordingly."

He and some of the men were provided a warm, comfortable house in which to recuperate, and brought plates with fresh bread and grilled slabs of beef. "We think ourselves very happily fixed," Bulkeley wrote.

People from across Brazil began to travel to pay tribute to them—this band of seafarers, commanded by a gunner, who had pulled off one of the longest castaway voyages. The *Speedwell* was hauled on land and became an object of pilgrimage—"this wonder," as Bulkeley put it, that "people are continually flocking to see."

Bulkeley learned that the War of Jenkins' Ear had dragged on, and he sent off a letter to a British naval officer in Rio de Janeiro to inform him of his group's arrival. And he mentioned one other thing: that Captain Cheap had, "at his own request, tarried behind."

Part Five

JUDGMENT

CHAPTER 21

A Literary Rebellion

ONE EVENING, JOHN BULKELEY went with a companion for a walk in the Brazilian countryside, relishing his newfound freedom. When they returned to the house where they were staying, they noticed that the locks to the doors had been broken. The two men gingerly stepped inside. Objects were scattered about Bulkeley's bedroom, as if someone had been rummaging around.

Bulkeley heard a noise and turned just as two intruders leapt toward them. One struck Bulkeley, and Bulkeley struck him back. After a violent struggle, the assailants fled into the darkness. Bulkeley had recognized one of them. It was a fellow castaway who was known to do the bidding of John King—the boatswain, who, during the mutiny on Wager Island, had punched Captain Cheap in the face. The intruders had been clearly searching Bulkeley's quarters. But what could they possibly want from a gunner who was now destitute?

Bulkeley felt so uneasy that he moved with his closest companions into another lodging house in a fishing village. "Here we thought ourselves safe and secure," he observed.

A few nights later, a gang of men appeared, banging on the door. Bulkeley refused to open it, declaring that it was "an improper season of the night." But they kept on banging, threatening to break in. Bulkeley and his party ran around the lodging house, looking for weaponry, but they could find nothing to defend themselves with. And so they sneaked out the back, climbing over a wall to escape.

One member of the gang had told Bulkeley what they were after: his journal. Bulkeley had been the only person to keep a contemporaneous account on Wager Island, and King and some of his allies apparently feared what it might divulge about their roles in overthrowing Captain Cheap. The lives of the former castaways were once again at risk—only now the danger was not from the natural elements but from the stories that they would tell the Admiralty. There was still no news of Cheap and his party, and it seemed unlikely they would ever emerge to tell their side. But what if they did? And even if they never returned, someone in Bulkeley's group might offer a conflicting account—one that implicated his compatriots in order to spare himself.

As the sense of paranoia deepened, Bulkeley wrote that he'd heard King had vowed "either to compel us to deliver up the journal, or to take our lives." An official in Brazil remarked how strange it was that "people who had undergone so many hardships and difficulties could not agree lovingly together." The forces unleashed on Wager Island were like the horrors inside Pandora's box: once unlocked, they could not be contained.

Lieutenant Baynes was particularly worried as the ranking officer in the group. Bulkeley got word that the lieutenant was whispering to officials in Brazil that any blame for what had happened to Captain Cheap lay with Bulkeley and Cummins. In response, Bulkeley did what he always did: he took up his quill and scribbled a note. In a message delivered to Baynes, he accused him of spreading false and vile allegations, and observed that once they had returned to England, each of them would have to "give account of his actions, and justice take place."

In March 1742, Baynes fled on a boat for England. He wanted to arrive before the others and get his story on the record first. It took months for Bulkeley and Cummins to secure passage on another vessel, and when they stopped along the way in Portugal, they were informed by several English merchants at the port there that Baynes had already made damning accusations against them. "We were even advised by some of our friends there not to return to our country, lest we should suffer death for mutiny," Bulkeley wrote.

He told the merchants that Baynes was an unreliable source, who, tellingly, had never kept a diary on the island. Then Bulkeley revealed, like a Holy Writ, his own voluminous journal. When the merchants looked at it, Bulkeley claimed, "they found, if there was any mutiny in the case, the very person who accused us was the ringleader."

Bulkeley and Cummins proceeded on their voyage home. Bulkeley was still compulsively adding to his journal. "We were confident of our own innocence, and determined to see our country at all events," he wrote.

On January 1, 1743, their ship dropped anchor in Portsmouth. In the distance, they could observe their houses. Bulkeley had not seen his wife and five children for more than two years. "We thought of nothing but going ashore immediately to our families," Bulkeley wrote. But the Navy barred the men from leaving the ship.

Baynes had provided a written statement to the Admiralty in which he alleged that Cheap had been overthrown by a band of mutineers led by Bulkeley and Cummins, who tied up the captain and deserted him on Wager Island. The Admiralty ordered both men to be detained under guard, pending a court-martial. They were now captives in their own country.

Bulkeley called Baynes's account an "imperfect narrative," arguing that a story drawn from memory, as Baynes admitted his was, had less probative value than one written contemporaneously. And when Bulkeley was asked to furnish his own statement to the Admiralty, he decided to offer his entire journal—which, he noted, he'd risked his life to protect. Although he had composed it in the first person, he added Cummins as a coauthor, likely to lend the account greater authority and to shield his best friend from punishment.

The journal laid out, from their point of view, the events that had led to the uprising, including allegations that Captain Cheap had mentally unraveled and killed Cozens by shooting him in the head.

"If things were not carried on with that order and regularity which is strictly observed in the Navy, necessity drove us out of the common road," Bulkeley wrote. "Our case was singular: Since the loss of the ship, our chiefest concern was for the preservation of our lives and liberties." In the end, they had been given no choice but to act "according to the dictates of nature."

When Bulkeley submitted the journal, he also handed over the supporting legalistic documents that had been drafted on the island—documents that Baynes himself had conspicuously signed. The Admiralty seemed overwhelmed by the materials, and the journal on which the men's fates rested lay for some time in its offices. Finally, Bulkeley wrote, the office sent him back the journal with an order: "to make an abstract by way of narrative that it might not be too tedious for their Lordships' perusal."

Bulkeley and Cummins promptly distilled their account, turning it in with a note that said, "We have strictly complied with the desire of the unfortunate Capt. Cheap, whose last injunction was to give a faithful narrative to your Lordships."

Members of the Admiralty found themselves confounded by the competing versions of events, and decided to postpone the investigation at least until Cheap could be officially pronounced dead. Bulkeley and Cummins, meanwhile, were released after two weeks in confinement. "Our families had long given us over for lost," Bulkeley wrote, and they "looked upon us as sons, husbands, and fathers restored to them in a miraculous manner."

Yet until the judicial case was resolved, Bulkeley and his party remained in a kind of purgatory. They were denied their pay for the expedition and prevented from being employed again in His Majesty's service. "After surviving the loss of the ship, and combating with famine and innumerable difficulties, a remnant of us are returned to our native country," Bulkeley wrote. "But even here we are still unfortunate, destitute of employment, almost without support."

Bulkeley, now desperate for money, received an offer to bring a merchant ship from Plymouth to London. He sent a letter to the

Admiralty pleading to be allowed to travel for the job. Though he thought it was his duty to accept, he wrote, he would not do so without approval—"lest your Lordships should imagine I had flown from justice." He added, "I am willing and desirous of abiding by the strictest trial of my conduct in regard to Captain Cheap, and hope to live to see him face to face, but in the meantime do hope I am not to be left on the earth to perish." The Admiralty granted him permission, but he remained impoverished. And he lived with the constant fear that at any moment he and the other surviving castaways might be summoned to trial and sentenced to death.

When Bulkeley was a castaway, he had stopped waiting around for others in power to display leadership. And now, months after his return to his native island, he decided to launch another kind of rebellion—a literary one. He began plotting to publish his journal. Bulkeley would shape the public's perceptions and, just as he had on the island, rally the people to his side.

Anticipating that some would consider the journal's publication a scandal—it was common for senior officers to release narratives of their voyages, but not a mere gunner—he wrote a preface to preempt criticisms of his decision. Among other things, he argued that it would be unfair to presume that he and Cummins, given their status, could not possibly have produced such an exacting work. "We don't set up for naturalists and men of great learning," Bulkeley wrote. But he noted, "Persons with a common share of understanding are capable of committing to paper daily remarks of matters worthy their observation, especially of facts in which they themselves had so large a share. We only relate such things as could not possibly escape our knowledge, and what we actually know to be true." He also dismissed the potential complaint that he and Cummins did not have the right to divulge the secrets of what had happened to them and their crew: "It has been hinted to us, as if publishing this journal would give offence to some persons of distinction. We can't conceive how any transactions relating to the *Wager*, although made ever so public, can give offence to any great man at home. Can it be any offence to tell the world that we were shipwrecked in the *Wager*, when all people know it already?... Don't they also know that we went abroad with hopes of acquiring great riches, but are returned home as poor as beggars?" He went on, "When persons have surmounted great difficulties, it is a pleasure for them to relate their story; and if we give ourselves this satisfaction, who has any cause to be offended? Are we, who have faced death in so many shapes, to be intimidated, lest we should give offence to the—Lord knows whom?"

Bulkeley struck a similar populist tone in defending his and Cummins's conduct on the island. He wrote that many had condemned them for being "too busy and active for persons in our stations," but it was only because of their actions that anyone had made it back to England. After reading the journal, he argued, people would be able to judge for themselves whether he and Cummins deserved any punishment: "Our confining the Captain is reckoned an audacious and unprecedented action, and our not bringing him home with us, is reckoned worse; but the reader will find that necessity absolutely compelled us to act as we did."

Bulkeley acknowledged that the authors of sea narratives liked to enhance their reputations by fabricating marvelous tales. He insisted, though, that he and Cummins had "taken care to deviate from those, by having a strict regard to truth."

The account was something striking in English letters. Though hardly a work of literature, the journal was packed with more narrative and personal detail than a traditional logbook, and the story was told in a bracing new voice—that of a hard-nosed seaman. In contrast to the often flowery and convoluted prose of the time, it was written in a crisp style that reflected Bulkeley's personality and was, in many ways, distinctly modern. The gunner declared that the journal had "a plain maritime style."

By the time Bulkeley and Cummins were ready to sell their manuscript, most of the members of their party had returned to England, and there was intense public demand for any information about the shipwreck and the alleged mutiny. The two men received what they described as a considerable sum from a London bookseller to publish the journal. The amount, which was undisclosed, would not put an end to their financial insecurities; yet for men in their dire situation it represented an enormous prize. "Money is a great temptation to people in our circumstances," Bulkeley acknowledged.

Published six months after Bulkeley and Cummins had returned to England, the book was called simply *A Voyage to the South-Seas, in the Years 1740–1*. But it contained a long, tantalizing subtitle to attract readers:

> A faithful Narrative of the Loss of his Majesty's ship the *Wager* on a desolate Island in the Latitude 47 South, longitude 81:40 West: With the Proceedings and Conduct of the Officers and Crew, and the Hardships they endured in the said Island for the Space of five Months; their bold Attempt for Liberty, in Coasting the Southern Part of the vast Region of *Patagonia;* setting out with upwards of Eighty Souls in their Boats; the Loss of the Cutter; their Passage through the Streights of *Magellan;* an Account of... the incredible Hardships they frequently underwent for Want of Food of any Kind...

The book sold for three shillings and sixpence a copy, and was serialized in *The London Magazine*. Some members of the Admiralty and aristocracy expressed outrage at what they considered a two-pronged attack by a gunner and a carpenter on their commanding officer: first they had tied up Cheap, and now they were impugning him in print. One of the Lords Commissioners of the Admiralty told Bulkeley, "How dare you presume to touch a gentleman's character in so public a manner?" A naval officer told the popular weekly journal *Universal Spectator*, "We are ready enough likewise to blame the crew of the *Wager*, and defend the Captain.... We are even apt to think that if Captain Cheap comes home he will remove the censure that has been thrown upon his own obstinacy, and fix it upon the disobedience of those under him." Bulkeley acknowledged that his defiant act of publishing the journal had in some quarters only fueled calls for his execution.

But the book, later praised by one historian for carrying "a true ring of the sea in every page," went into a second printing and swayed much of the public to take the side of Bulkeley and his party. The historian noted that the "gallant pugnacity" of the book seemed to have even won "some reluctant admiration from the gold-braided gentry."

Bulkeley had feared a written rejoinder—a counter tale—but none came. He had not only published the first draft of history; he had also seemingly changed the future. He and his followers might be exiled from the Navy, and might still be poor, but they were alive and free.

As Bulkeley had learned from his voyage, a reprieve rarely lasts—it is inevitably shattered by some unforeseen event. And it was not long before excited reports began appearing in the press that Commodore George Anson, the man who had led the expedition, was blazing a trail across the Pacific.

CHAPTER 22

The Prize

ANSON STOOD ON THE quarterdeck of the *Centurion*, staring across the vast, watery expanse off the southeastern coast of China. It was April 1743, and it had been two years since he had lost sight of the *Wager*. He still did not know what had happened to the ship, only that she was gone. As for the *Pearl* and the *Severn*, he knew their officers had turned their scurvy-ridden, storm-beaten vessels back around Cape Horn—a decision that had caused the *Pearl*'s captain to see himself in "no other light than a disgrace." The *Centurion*'s schoolmaster and some others had sometimes murmured that these officers had deserted Anson, but the commodore himself had never condemned them: he'd experienced the "blind Horn's hate," and seemed to trust that the officers had retreated to avoid being completely wiped out.

Although three other ships in Anson's squadron—the *Gloucester*, the *Trial*, and the *Anna*, a small cargo ship—had miraculously made it around the Horn and joined him at the rendezvous point in the fabled Juan Fernández Islands, they, too, were now gone. The *Anna* had been devoured by the elements and scuttled for parts. Then the *Trial*, bereft of men and no longer seaworthy, was abandoned. Finally, the *Gloucester* began to leak so badly that Anson had no choice but to bury his only other vessel at sea.

Three quarters of the *Gloucester*'s roughly four hundred men had already perished, and after the remainder were transferred to the *Centurion*—most of them so sick that they had to be hoisted onboard on wooden grates—Anson had the *Gloucester*'s hull set on fire to prevent it from falling into enemy hands. He watched as its wooden world ignited, producing what one of his lieutenants, Philip Saumarez, called "as melancholy a scene as I ever observed since I have been in the Navy." The *Trial*'s former purser, Lawrence Millechamp, who was now onboard the *Centurion*, wrote of the *Gloucester*, "She burnt all night, making a most grand, horrid appearance. Her guns, which were all loaded, fired so regularly . . . that they sounded like mourning guns." The next day, as the flames reached the powder room, the hull exploded: "Thus ended the *Gloucester*, a ship justly esteemed the beauty of the English Navy."

Despite these calamities, Anson was determined to keep at least part of the expedition afloat, and to fulfill his orders to circumnavigate the globe in his sole remaining ship. Before crossing the Pacific, he'd attempted to weaken the Spanish by capturing a few of their trading vessels and by raiding a tiny colonial town in Peru. But these victories were of meager military significance, and while making its way to Asia, the party had suffered yet another scurvy outbreak—an outbreak that caused even more suffering than before, because the men knew what was coming (the aching, the swelling, the falling teeth, the madness), and because they died in such large numbers. One officer wrote that the bodies smelled "like rotten sheep," and recalled "tossing overboard six, eight, ten or twelve in a day." Anson was anguished by the death and the failure of his mission, confessing, "I should have great pain in returning to my country, after all the fatigue and hazard I have undergone in endeavouring to serve it, if I thought I had forfeited . . . the esteem of the public." His forces had withered from some 2,000 to a mere 227, and many of them were just boys. He had only a third of the complement required to properly operate a man-of-war of the *Centurion*'s size.

Despite the crew's many agonies, they had remained remarkably loyal to their commander. When they periodically grumbled, he might read aloud to them the rules and regulations, making sure that they were aware of the punishment for disobedience, but he had avoided the lash. "We had the example of a brave, humane, equal-minded, prudent commander," an officer on the *Centurion* said of Anson, adding, "His temper was so steady and unruffled that the men and officers all looked on him with wonder and delight, and could not for shame betray any great dejection under the most imminent danger."

On one occasion, after Anson had anchored the *Centurion* by an uninhabited island in the Pacific, he went ashore with many of the men. A storm whipped up and the *Centurion* vanished. Anson and his party, like their brethren on the *Wager*, found themselves castaways on a desolate island. "It is almost impossible to describe the sorrow and anguish that possessed us," Millechamp wrote. "Grief, discontent, terror and despair seemed visible in the countenances of every one of us."

Days passed, and Anson, fearing the *Centurion* had been lost forever, planned to expand a tiny transport boat that they had on the island into a vessel large enough to carry them to the nearest safe port—on the coast of China, fifteen hundred miles away. "Unless we wish to end our days here in this wild place," Anson told the men, "we must put our backs into the work before us, and each labour as much for himself as for his shipmates."

The commodore joined in the toil, putting himself, as one of the men recalled it, on the same level as "the meanest sailor in his crew." Millechamp noted that the sight of Anson, along with all the other senior officers, sharing in the hardest tasks made everyone "endeavour to excel, and indeed we soon found that our work went on with great spirit and vigour."

Three weeks after the *Centurion* went missing, it reappeared. The ship had been damaged while being swept out to sea; all this time its crew had struggled to return. After a joyous reunion, Anson pressed on with their voyage around the world.

Now, while sailing through the South China Sea, Anson summoned his men on deck and climbed onto the roof of his cabin to address them. The party had recently stopped in Canton, where they had repaired and resupplied the *Centurion* and where Anson had let it be known that he intended to return to England at last, bringing an end to their doomed endeavor. The governor of Manila, in the Philippines, had passed on to the King of Spain a report that "the English are tired of their venture, having accomplished nothing."

Peering down from the cabin roof, Anson shouted, "Gentlemen, and all of you, my gallant lads, forward, I have sent for you, now that we are once more clear of the shore... to declare to you where we are bound." He paused, then cried, "Not to England!"

Anson, that inscrutable card player, revealed that all his talk about heading home had been a ruse. He had studied the timing and patterns that the Spanish galleon historically followed on its route, and he had gathered further intelligence from sources in China. Based on all this information, he suspected that the galleon would soon be off the coast of the Philippines. And he planned to try to intercept it. After all their squandered blood, this was their chance to strike a blow against their enemy and obtain the valuable treasure said to be onboard. He dismissed the fearsome tales that the Spanish galleons had hulls so thick they were impenetrable to cannon fire. Yet he acknowledged that their adversary would be formidable. Looking at his crew, he declared that the spirit that had carried them this far, and that had helped them weather the gales of Cape Horn and the ravages of the Pacific—that "spirit in you, my lads"—would be enough to prevail. One naval historian later described Anson's gambit as "an act of desperation by a commander who faced professional ruin, a last throw by a gambler who had lost all." The crew waved their hats and gave three loud cheers, promising to share with him victory or death.

Anson turned the *Centurion* toward Samar Island, the third-largest in the Philippines, about a thousand miles to the southeast. He had the men drill constantly—firing their muskets at objects hung, like disembodied heads, from the yardarms; running cannons in and out; and practicing with cutlasses and swords in case they had to board the enemy's ship. And when all these drills were done, Anson made everyone do them again—faster. His edict was simple: prepare or perish.

On May 20, a lookout spotted Cape Espiritu Santo, the northernmost point of Samar Island. Anson immediately ordered members of the crew to furl the topgallant sails, so the ship would be harder to spy from a distance. He wanted the edge of surprise.

For weeks, under the beating sun, he and his party cruised back and forth in hopes of spotting the galleon. One officer wrote in his logbook, "Exercising our men at their quarters, in great expectation." Later, he added, "Keeping in our stations, and looking out." But after a month of exhausting drills and searching in the sultry heat, the men were losing hope of seeing their quarry. "All hands began to look very melancholy," Lieutenant Saumarez wrote in his logbook.

On June 20, the dawn broke at 5:40 a.m. As the sun crept over the sea, a lookout shouted that he'd seen something far to the southeast. Anson, on the quarterdeck, picked up his telescope and glassed the horizon. There, on the jagged edge of the sea, he spied several white specks: topgallant sails. The vessel, miles away, bore no Spanish flag, but as it came further into focus, he had no doubt that it was the galleon. And she was alone.

Ordering all hands to clear the decks for action, Anson gave chase. "Our ship immediately grew into a ferment," Millechamp noted. "Every man was ready to assist, and everyone thought the thing could not be well done without his having a hand in it. For my part I thought they would all have run mad with joy."

They knocked down cabin partitions, to make more room for the gun crews; dumped overboard any livestock that was in the way; and tossed any unnecessary timber that might shatter under fire and rain down lethal splinters. Sand was sprinkled on the decks to make them less slippery. Men working the cannons were given rammers and sponges and priming irons and horns and wads and—in case of fire—tubs of water. Down in the magazine room, the gunner and his mates distributed gunpowder to the powder monkeys, who then ran them up the ladders and through the ship, making sure not to trip and cause an explosion before the battle had begun. Lanterns were extinguished, and so was the galley stove. In the bowels of the orlop deck, George Allen, who had begun the voyage as a twenty-five-year-old surgeon's mate and through attrition became the chief surgeon, prepared with his loblolly boys for the expected casualties—building an operating table from sea chests, organizing bone saws and bandages, and laying on the floor a sail canvas that would prevent his men from slipping on blood.

The Spanish called the galleon *Our Lady of Covadonga.* The men inside it must have recognized that they were being chased. But they did not attempt to flee, perhaps because of courage, or perhaps because they did not expect the *Centurion* to be in any condition to fight. They were under the command of an experienced officer, Gerónimo Montero, who had served on the *Covadonga* for fourteen years. He had orders to defend the treasure-filled ship to the death, and if necessary to blow it up before it fell into enemy hands.

Montero turned the *Covadonga* and headed boldly toward the *Centurion.* The two vessels approached each other on a collision course. Anson peered through his telescope, trying to assess the enemy's strength. The galleon's gun deck extended 124 feet—20 feet shorter than the *Centurion*'s. And compared to the *Centurion*'s sixty cannons, many of which fired twenty-four-pound balls, the galleon had only thirty-two guns, the largest mere twelve-pounders. In terms of firepower, the *Centurion* was clearly superior.

But Montero had one crucial advantage. His ship was carrying 530 people—300 more than the *Centurion*—and the men on the *Covadonga* were generally healthy. For all of Anson's potent gunnery, he lacked sufficient hands to operate his full arsenal while maintaining enough crew to manage the ship. He decided to deploy only half the *Centurion*'s guns—those on the starboard side—which was safe to do now that he knew there was no second Spanish ship to attack his other flank.

Still, he did not have even enough crewmen to handle all the starboard guns, so rather than assign at least eight people to operate each cannon, as was customary, he designated just two. Each pair would be strictly responsible for loading and sponging the muzzle. Meanwhile, several squads, each consisting of about a dozen people, would be tasked with sprinting from gun to gun—running them forward and lighting them. Anson hoped that this approach would allow him to maintain a continuous blaze of fire. The commodore made one other tactical decision. Having noticed that the galleon's plank sidings above the gunwales were surprisingly low, which left its officers and crew exposed on deck, Anson stationed a dozen of his finest marksmen on the mast tops. Perched high above the sea, they would have a clear vantage point for picking off their enemies.

As the ships continued to converge, the dueling commanders mirrored each other's actions. After Anson's men cleared their decks, Montero's crew did the same, throwing overboard bellowing cattle and other screaming livestock; like Anson, Montero placed some of his men with small arms on the mast tops. Montero raised his crimson Spanish royal flag, emblazoned with castles and lions; then Anson hoisted his British colors.

Both commanders opened their gunports and ran out the black muzzles. Montero fired a shot, and Anson replied with his own. The blasts were meant merely to rattle the other side: given the inaccuracy of cannons, they were still too far away to truly engage.

Shortly past noon, when the two ships were about three miles apart, a storm arose. Rain rifled down and winds boomed and the sea smoked with mist—God's own battlefield. At times, Anson and his men lost sight of the galleon, though they knew it was out there, moving with all its metal. Afraid of a stealthy broadside, they scoured the sea. Then a cry went out—it was over there!—and the men glimpsed it before it vanished again. Each time the galleon emerged it was closer. Two miles away, then one, then half a mile. Anson, not wanting to engage the enemy until it was within pistol shot, ordered the men to hold their fire: every blast must count.

After the excitement of the chase, there was now an unnerving stillness. The crew knew some of them might soon be missing an arm or a leg, or worse. Saumarez, the lieutenant, noted that he hoped to "face death cheerfully" whenever duty called on him. Some of Anson's men were so anxious their stomachs cramped.

The rain stopped, and Anson and his crew could clearly see the black mouths of the galleon's cannons. The ship was less than a hundred yards away. The wind dropped, and Anson tried to maintain enough sail to maneuver but not so much as to make the ship unruly, or to give the enemy lots of large targets that, if hit, could cripple the *Centurion.*

Anson guided his ship across the galleon's wake, and then swiftly came abreast of the *Covadonga* from the leeward side, so it would be harder for Montero to escape downwind.

Fifty yards away . . . twenty-five . . .

Anson's men were silent fore and aft, awaiting the commodore's command. At one p.m., the two ships were so close their yardarms nearly touched, and Anson finally gave the signal: Fire!

The men on the mast tops began to shoot. Their muskets crackled and flashed; smoke stung their eyes. As the barrels recoiled and the *Centurion*'s masts swayed with the rolling ship, they braced themselves with ropes, to keep from plunging to an inglorious death. After discharging a musket, a shooter would grab another cartridge, bite off a wad of paper at the top, and pour a small amount of black powder into the gun's flash pan. Then he would jam the new cartridge—which contained more powder and a lead ball about the size of a marble—into the barrel, using a ramrod, and fire again. Initially, these sharpshooters targeted their counterparts in the galleon's rigging, who were trying to pick off the *Centurion*'s officers and crew.

Both sides were fighting a battle from the sky; balls whizzed through the air, ripping through sails and ropes and occasionally a chunk of flesh.

Anson and Montero had also unleashed their cannons. Whereas Montero's men were able to fire broadsides—simultaneously blasting all the cannons in a row—Anson's crew relied on his unconventional system to set off the guns in rapid succession. The moment after a squad on the *Centurion* discharged a cannon, the men ran the gun back in and closed the porthole to shield themselves from incoming fire. Then the two loaders began to swab the sizzling barrel and prepare the next round while the squad raced on to another loaded cannon—priming it and pointing it and lighting the match, then jumping out of the way before they became casualties of their own recoiling two-ton weapon. The guns rattled and roared, the breeches strained, and the decks shook. The men's ears ached from the murderous ringing, and their faces were powder blackened. "Nothing was to be seen but fire and smoke, nor heard but the thunder of the cannon, which was fired so quick that it made one continued sound," Millechamp noted.

Anson watched the unfolding battle from the quarterdeck, his sword in hand. Through the choking smoke, he detected a flickering on the galleon's stern: a stretch of netting had caught fire. The flames were spreading, creeping halfway up the mizzenmast. It threw Montero's men into a state of confusion. Yet the two vessels were close enough that the fire threatened to engulf the *Centurion*, too. Using axes, Montero's men cut away the burning mass of netting and wood until it fell into the sea.

The fighting continued, the noise so deafening that Anson conveyed his orders with hand signals. The galleon's cannons were spraying the *Centurion* with a malignant mix of nails and stones and lead balls, as well as chunks of iron linked by bits of chain—an assortment "very well contrived for death and murder," as the schoolmaster, Pascoe Thomas, put it.

The *Centurion*'s sails and shrouds had begun to shred, and several cannonballs had smashed into the hull. Whenever one hit below the waterline, the carpenter and his crew hurried to fill the hole with wooden plugs, so the sea would not swamp them. A nine-pound cast-iron ball struck one of Anson's men, Thomas Richmond, directly in the head, decapitating him. Another seaman was hit in the leg, and as his artery spouted blood, his mates carried him down to the orlop deck, where he was laid on the operating table. As the ship convulsed from the explosions, the doctor, Allen, grabbed his blades and, without anesthesia, began to cut off the man's leg. A naval surgeon described how challenging it was to operate in these conditions: "At the very instant when I was amputating the limb of one of our wounded seamen, I met with an almost continual interruption from the rest of his companions, who were in the like distressful circumstances; some pouring forth the most piercing cries to be taken care of, while others seized my arms in their earnestness of being relieved, even at the time I was passing the needle for securing the divided blood vessels by a ligature." While Allen worked, the ship shook continuously from the recoil of the large cannons. The doctor managed to saw off the leg just above the knee and to cauterize the wound with boiling tar, but the man soon died.

The battle raged on. Anson realized that the enemy's gunports were very narrow, limiting the movement of its muzzles. And so he maneuvered his ship to lie nearly perpendicular to the galleon, thereby depriving many of the enemy's guns of a clear shot. The *Covadonga*'s cannonballs began to soar wide of the *Centurion* and into the sea, where they sent up harmless waterspouts. The *Centurion*'s gunports were larger, and Anson's squads used handspikes and crowbars to point their cannons squarely at the galleon. The commodore gave the signal to fire the heaviest balls—the twenty-four-pounders—at the enemy's hull. At the same time, some of Anson's men raked the *Covadonga*'s sails and rigging with chain shot, paralyzing her on the sea. The galleon shuddered amid a pitiless storm of metallic hail.

Anson's sharpshooters in the tops had taken out their counterparts in the galleon's rigging, and they were sniping one Spaniard after another on the decks.

Montero exhorted his men to fight for their king and country, shouting that life was meaningless without honor. A musket ball glanced off his chest. He was stunned but stayed on the quarterdeck until a flying splinter speared his foot; then he was taken below, joining the mass of wounded. He left in charge the sergeant major, who was promptly shot in the thigh. The head of the soldiers onboard tried to rally the crew, but his leg was blown off. As the schoolmaster, Thomas, noted, the Spanish "being frightened by seeing abundance fall dead before them every moment…began to run from their quarters, and to tumble down the hatchways and scuttles in heaps."

After an hour and a half of unrelenting fire, the galleon lay motionless, her masts cracked, her sails in pieces, her hull rife with holes. The mythic ship was indeed mortal. On its deck, amid the strewn bodies and eddies of smoke, a man was seen staggering toward the mainmast, where the Spanish royal flag hung in tatters. Anson signaled to his crew to hold their fire. For a moment, the world fell quiet, and Anson and his party watched in exhaustion and relief as the man on the galleon began to lower the flag, signaling surrender.

Montero, who was still below and unaware of what was happening on deck, told an officer to quickly detonate the powder room and sink the ship. The officer replied, "It is too late."

Anson dispatched Lieutenant Saumarez with a party to take possession of the galleon. When Saumarez stepped onboard the *Covadonga*, he recoiled at seeing its decks "promiscuously covered with carcasses, entrails and dismembered limbs." One of Anson's men confessed that war was awful to anyone with a "humane disposition." The British had lost just three men; the Spanish had seen nearly seventy killed and more than eighty injured. Anson sent his surgeon across to help attend to their wounded, including Montero.

Saumarez and his party secured the prisoners—assuring them they would be treated well, because they had fought with honor—

then descended with lanterns into the galleon's smoky hold. Storage bags and wooden chests and other containers were stacked on top of one another, disordered from the battle; water had seeped inside from gouges in the ship's hull.

The men opened a bag but found only cheese. When a man pressed his hand deep into the soft fatty substance, though, he felt something hard: treasure. The party examined a large porcelain vase—it was filled with gold dust. Other bags were stuffed with silver coins, tens of thousands of them—no, hundreds of thousands of them! And the chests abounded with more silver, including handwrought bowls and bells and at least a ton of virgin silver. Everywhere the party discerned more riches. Jewels and money were tucked under floorboards, and in the false bottoms of sea chests. Spain's colonial plunder was now Britain's. It was the largest treasure ever seized by a British naval commander—the equivalent today of nearly $80 million. Anson and his party had captured the greatest prize of all the oceans.

A year later, on June 15, 1744, after removing the treasure and circling the globe in the *Centurion*, Anson and his men finally returned to England. The other British military offensives during the War of Jenkins' Ear had been largely grisly failures, and the conflict was at a stalemate. The taking of the galleon would not change the outcome. But here, at last, was news of a victory—"GREAT BRITAIN'S TRIUMPH," as one headline put it. Anson and his men were greeted by jubilant throngs when they arrived in London. The officers and crew led a procession with the bundles of silver and gold carted on thirty-two heavily guarded wagons. A share of the prize money was given to each seaman: about three hundred pounds, some twenty years' worth of wages. Anson, who was soon promoted to rear admiral, was awarded about ninety thousand pounds—the equivalent today of $20 million.

As a band sounded French horns and trumpets and kettle drums, the party marched over Fulham Bridge and through the city streets, past Piccadilly and St. James's. At Pall Mall, Anson stood beside the Prince and the Princess of Wales, peering out at the delirious crowds—a scene that one observer compared to the Roman games. As the historian N. A. M. Rodger has noted, "It was the treasure of the galleon, triumphantly paraded through the streets of London, which did something to restore battered national self-esteem." A sea ballad was later composed with the lines "The wagon loads of money come, / And all taken by brave Anson."

Amid all the hoopla, the scandalous *Wager* affair seemed to blissfully fade away. But almost two years later, on a March day in 1746, a boat arrived in Dover, carrying a thin, stern man with eyes fixed like bayonets. It was the long-lost Captain David Cheap, and accompanying him were the marine lieutenant, Thomas Hamilton, and the midshipman John Byron.

CHAPTER 23

Grub Street Hacks

FIVE AND A HALF years. That's how long the three men had been gone from England. Presumed dead, they had been mourned, and yet here they were, like three Lazaruses.

They began to unspool details of what had happened. Days after they had returned to Wager Island following their failed attempt to leave, and after they had buried their murdered companion, a small party of native Patagonians had appeared in two canoes. At that time, Cheap, Byron, and Hamilton were stranded with ten other castaways, including Midshipman Campbell and the surgeon, Elliot. A Patagonian man approached them and addressed them in Spanish, which Elliot could understand. The man said that his name was Martin, and that he was a member of a seafaring people known as the Chono. They lived farther north than the Kawésqar people who had visited earlier. Martin indicated that he'd been to Chiloé Island, the site of the nearest Spanish settlement, and the castaways beseeched him to help them navigate their one remaining boat—the barge—there. In exchange, they'd give him the barge when they arrived.

Martin agreed, and on March 6, 1742, they set out, along with the other Chono, hugging the coast as they rowed northward. Soon afterward, while many in the party were searching for food along the shore, six of the castaways absconded with the barge, never to be heard from again. "What could provoke the villains to so foul a deed I cannot tell, except it was their cowardice," Cheap recalled in his account. Midshipman Campbell, however, had overheard the deserters whispering about their desire to be free of their monomaniacal captain.

The Chono continued piloting the group across the Golfo de Penas toward Chiloé Island. Without the barge, they proceeded in the Chono's canoes, stopping periodically to gather food onshore. During the journey, a castaway died, leaving only "five poor souls," as one of them put it: Cheap, Byron, Campbell, Hamilton, and Elliot.

Byron had always thought that Elliot would be the most likely among them to survive, but this once indomitable man was growing weaker and weaker, until he laid down on a barren stretch of shoreline. His body was shriveled to the bone, and his voice was fading. He fumbled for his one valuable possession—his pocket watch—and offered it to Campbell. Then, Campbell noted, he "departed this miserable life." Byron, lamenting how they "scraped a hole for him in the sand," seemed burdened by the arbitrary nature of their fates. Why had so many of his companions died, and why should he live?

As the four castaways continued across the gulf, they followed their Chono guides' advice about when to row and when to rest, and how to find shelter and limpets. Even so, the castaways' accounts betrayed their inherent racism. Byron routinely referred to Patagonians as "savages," and Campbell complained, "We durst not find the least fault with their conduct, they looking upon themselves as our masters, and we finding ourselves obliged to submit to them in all things." But the castaways' feelings of superiority were upended daily. When Byron plucked some berries to eat, one of the Chono snatched them from his hand, indicating that they were poisonous. "Thus, in all probability, did these people now save my life," Byron wrote.

After traveling some seventy miles, the castaways could see to the northwest the cape of the gulf that they had previously failed to round. To their surprise, their guides didn't lead them in that direction. Instead, they hauled the canoes on land and proceeded to break the boats apart, each one separating into five distinct components, which made them easier to transport. Everyone was given a piece to lug except for Cheap. Without any more dreams to sustain him, he seemed to be disintegrating not only physically but mentally. Hoarding his small bits of food and muttering to himself, he required help walking the moment the trek started.

The castaways followed Martin and his party overland along a secret path—an eight-mile portage route through the wilderness, which allowed them to avoid the perilous seas around the cape. They trudged through a swamp, with their knees and sometimes their waists submerged. Byron realized that the theft of the barge had made things easier: there was no way they could have dragged it overland. Even without it, Byron grew exhausted, and after a few miles he collapsed under a tree, where, as he put it, he "gave way to melancholy reflections." He'd seen others finally give in to the tempting prospect of dissolving into another world. At least it would require no more labor to get there. But Byron forced himself to stand: "These reflections would answer no end."

At the end of the portage, the Chono reassembled the canoes and launched them into a channel that wound between the fractured islands off Chile. For weeks, the party edged northward, rowing from channel to channel, fiord to fiord, until one day in June 1742, the castaways glimpsed a headland in the distance. It was, Martin announced, Chiloé Island.

To get there, they still had to cross a gulf that opened onto the unobstructed Pacific, and that was so perilous it had served as a natural barrier to Spanish incursions farther south. "There ran a most dreadful hollow sea, dangerous, indeed, for any open boat," Byron noted, but "a thousand times more" for their tiny canoes. Hamilton decided to wait several days with one of the Chono before daring an attempt. But the three other castaways set out in a canoe with Martin, who constructed a small sail from bits of blankets to propel them. It began to snow, and the boat sprung a leak. Byron frantically bailed, while Cheap mumbled into the wind. They pressed on through the night, the boat teetering. But as the sun rose, the castaways made it across the passage and touched the southern tip of Chiloé. It had been three months since they had departed Wager Island and nearly a year since they had been shipwrecked. As Byron wrote, he and the other castaways with him "hardly appeared the figures of men." Cheap was in the gravest condition. "I could compare his body to nothing but an anthill, with thousands of those insects crawling over it," Byron noted. "He was now past attempting to rid himself in the least from this torment, as he had quite lost himself, not recollecting our names that were about him, or even his own. His beard was as long as a hermit's.... His legs were as big as mill-posts, though his body appeared nothing but skin and bone."

The men trudged several miles through heavy snow to an indigenous village, where the inhabitants provided them food and shelter. "They made a bed of sheepskins close to the fire for Captain Cheap, and laid him upon it," Byron wrote, "and indeed had it not been for the kind assistance he now met with, he could not have survived."

Though Byron and Campbell had grown weary of Cheap's tempestuous leadership, they clung to the notion that the captain's original plan might have succeeded had Bulkeley and his party not abandoned them. There had been no Spanish armada lurking off Chiloé, and perhaps they could have crept into a harbor undetected and seized a defenseless trading vessel—doing "considerable service to our country," as Campbell put it. Or perhaps this was a fantasy that simply made it easier to live with the choices they had made.

Hamilton soon joined the party. One night, after they had begun to recover—even Cheap had rebounded some—they feasted on fresh meat and drank liquor brewed from barley. "We all made merry," Campbell wrote, adding, "We thought ourselves once more in the land of the living." Byron, who had had two birthdays since leaving England, was now eighteen.

In a few days, they set out for another village. As they made their way, a phalanx of Spanish soldiers suddenly descended upon them. After enduring tempests, scurvy, shipwreck, abandonment, and starvation, the castaways were now captives.

"I was now reduced to the infamous necessity of surrendering myself," Cheap noted, which he called the "greatest misfortune that can befall a man." When he was initially handed a document acknowledging his submission to the Spanish Crown and told to sign it in exchange for food, he indignantly tossed it to the ground, saying, "The officers of the King of England could die of hunger, but they disdained to beg."

Yet it didn't matter that he would not sign it. There was no way out, and Cheap and the others were eventually transported in a ship to Valparaíso, a city on the Chilean mainland. They were thrown into what was called the "condemned hole," which was so dark that they were unable to see one another's faces. "There was nothing but four bare walls," Byron wrote. And a swarm of fleas. As people from the region came to catch a glimpse of the prized prisoners, the guards would take them out of the hole and parade them about, like circus animals. "The soldiers made a pretty penny, as they took money from every person for the sight," Byron noted.

Seven months after the four men were apprehended, they were moved again, this time to Santiago, where they met with the governor. He considered them prisoners of war but also gentlemen, and he treated them kindlier. He granted them parole, and as long they did not try to communicate with anyone in England, they were allowed to live outside the prison.

One evening, they were invited to dine with Don José Pizarro, the Spanish admiral who had chased Anson's squadron for months after its departure from England. Pizarro's armada, in turned out, had tried to round Cape Horn ahead of the British ships, hoping to intercept them in the Pacific; but it, too, had been almost completely wiped out by storms. One warship with five hundred men had vanished. Another, with seven hundred, had sunk. Because of delays from the weather, the three remaining warships had run out of food—sailors had started catching rats and selling them to one another for four dollars apiece. Most of the seamen had eventually starved to death. And Pizarro, after snuffing out a mutiny and executing three of the conspirators, had ordered his few surviving men to turn back. It was hard to say whether Anson's or Pizarro's fleet had suffered the more devastating loss.

Though Cheap and the others were no longer imprisoned, they couldn't leave Chile, and their lives moved glacially. "Every day here seems to me an age," Cheap lamented. Finally, two and a half years after they had been captured, they were told that they could go home: although the War of Jenkins' Ear was never formally resolved, major offensives between Britain and Spain had ceased, and the countries had reached an agreement to exchange any prisoners. Cheap embarked on a ship with Byron and Hamilton, whom he referred to as "my two faithful companions and fellow sufferers." Campbell, however, was left behind. After so many years in captivity, he'd grown close to his Spanish captors, and Cheap accused him of having converted to Catholicism and shifted his allegiance from England to Spain. If true, members of the *Wager*'s company had now perpetrated virtually every grave sin under the Articles of War—including treason.

As Cheap, Byron, and Hamilton made their way back home, they sailed past Wager Island and round Cape Horn, as if they were journeying through their ravaged past. Yet in the everlasting mystery of the sea, this time the passage was relatively calm. When they reached Dover, Byron immediately set out for London on a loaned horse. Now twenty-two, he was dressed like a pauper, and with no spare change he sped past the tollgates. He later recalled that he had been "obliged to defraud, by riding as hard as I could through them all, not paying the least regard to the men, who called out to stop me." Clattering along the muddy cobblestone roads, he raced through fields and hamlets, through suburbs spreading outward from London, the largest city in Europe with a population approaching

700,000. The city—that "great and monstrous thing," Defoe called it—had grown even in the years since Byron had been gone, the old houses and churches and shops now crowded amid new brick buildings and tenements and stores; the streets were jammed with coaches and carriages, with noblemen and traders and shopkeepers. London was the pulsing heart of an island empire built on the toll of seamen and slavery and colonialism.

Byron reached Great Marlborough Street, in a fashionable area in central London. He went to an address where a few of his closest friends had lived. The place was boarded up. "Having been absent so many years, and in all that time never having heard a word from home, I knew not who was dead, or who was living, or where to go next," Byron wrote. He stopped at a dry-goods shop that his family used to frequent and inquired about his siblings. He was informed that his sister, Isabella, had gotten married to a lord and was living nearby in Soho Square, an aristocratic neighborhood with large stone houses built around a bucolic garden. Byron walked there as quickly as he could and knocked on the door of his sister's house, but the porter looked askance at the alien figure. Byron prevailed upon the man to let him inside, where Isabella was standing. A thin, elegant woman who later wrote a book on etiquette, she looked bewilderedly at her visitor, then realized it was none other than her dead brother. "With what surprise and joy my sister received me," he wrote. The sixteen-year-old boy she had last seen was now a hardened seaman.

David Cheap made his way to London as well. He was nearly fifty, and during his long time in captivity he had seemingly kept revisiting every disastrous incident, every cruel snub. Now he discovered that John Bulkeley had accused him—in a book, no less—of being an incompetent and murderous commander, a charge that could end not only his military career but his life. Cheap, in a letter to an Admiralty official, decried Bulkeley and his associates as liars: "For what can be expected of such poltroons... after most inhumanly abandoning us and destroying at their departure everything they thought could be of any use to us."

Cheap burned to tell his own version. But he wouldn't play Bulkeley's game and publish a book. Instead, he would save his testimony—and fury—for a forum more determinative: a court-martial composed of a panel of judges, all of them commanding officers like him. He prepared a sworn deposition detailing his allegations, and in a letter to the secretary of the Admiralty, he insisted that once a judicial hearing was complete, "I flatter myself... that my conduct will appear unblameable both before and after our shipwreck." In one of his few public comments, he remarked, "I have nothing to say for nor against the villains, until the day of trial"—when, he added, there would be nothing to stop these men from hanging.

The story—or stories—of the expedition continued to capture the public imagination. The press had grown exponentially, fueled by the loosening of government censorship and by wider literacy. And to satisfy the public's insatiable thirst for news, there had emerged a professional class of scribblers who earned a living from sales rather than from aristocratic patronage, and whom the old literary establishment derided as "Grub Street hacks." (Grub Street had been part of a poor area in London with doss-houses and brothels and fly-by-night publishing ventures.) And Grub Street, sniffing a good story, now seized on the so-called affair of the *Wager.*

The *Caledonian Mercury* reported that Bulkeley and the mutinous crew had physically attacked not only Cheap and Hamilton but also their entire faction—"bound them hand and foot," before leaving them to "the disposal of more merciful barbarians." Another story offered Hamilton's view that Cheap's behavior was "often mysterious and always arrogant and high"; looking back now, though, it was clear to Hamilton that the captain had "always acted under the guidance of a sagacious foresight."

Once the broadsheet newspapers and periodicals were filled with breathless reports, book publishers competed to release first-hand accounts from the former castaways. Shortly after Cheap returned to England, Campbell arrived in another vessel from Chile. He published his own narrative exceeding a hundred pages, called *The Sequel to Bulkeley and Cummins's Voyage to the South-Seas*, in which he defended himself from allegations of treason. But soon after, he fled the country and joined the Spanish military.

John Byron believed that Bulkeley had tried to justify what "could not be considered in any other light than that of direct mutiny." And though Byron might have released his own version, he seemed reluctant to speak poorly of his superior officers and indulge in what he called "egotism." Meanwhile, other accounts proliferated. One booklet by a Grub Street hack, *An Affecting Narrative of the Unfortunate Voyage and Catastrophe of His Majesty's Ship Wager*, noted that it had been "compiled from authentic journals, and transmitted, by letter, to a merchant in London, from a person who was an eye witness of all the affair." However, as the scholar Philip Edwards has pointed out, the account is a perverse rehashing—sometimes word for word—of Bulkeley's journal in which every detail is spun to support Cheap's perspective and uphold the longstanding systems of authority. In a war of words, the gunner's journal had been refashioned into a weapon against him.

Because of the sheer number of accounts—including those of dubious provenance—perceptions of the *Wager* affair varied from reader to reader. Bulkeley, whose journal kept being pilfered by hacks, was incensed when he realized that it was increasingly being regarded with suspicion, as if it, too, might be fake.

Within days of Cheap's return to England, the Admiralty issued a summons, publicized in newspapers, for all the *Wager*'s surviving officers, petty officers, and seamen to appear in Portsmouth for a court-martial. The trial, to commence in just a few weeks, would have to pierce through the fog of narratives—the contradictory, the shaded, even the fictitious—to discern what had really happened and thus mete out justice. As the writer Janet Malcolm once observed, "The law is the guardian of the ideal of unmediated truth, truth stripped bare of the ornament of narration.... The story that can best withstand the attrition of the rules of evidence is the story that wins." Yet, no matter which story prevailed, the trial would surely expose how the officers and seamen—part of that vanguard of the British Empire—had descended into anarchy and savagery. The sad spectacle might even supplant the glorious tale of Anson's capturing the galleon.

CHAPTER 24

The Docket

AFTER BULKELEY HAD READ in the newspaper about the court-martial summons, he was informed by an attorney that the Admiralty had issued a warrant for his detention. At the time, Bulkeley was in London, and he went to find the marshal who was looking for him. When he tracked him down, Bulkeley pretended to be a relative of one of the castaways who had made the journey in the longboat to Brazil. He inquired what should happen to these men now that Captain Cheap had returned.

"Hanged," the marshal replied.

"For God's sake, for what?" Bulkeley cried. "For not being drowned? And is a murderer at last come home to be their accuser?"

"Sir, they have been guilty of such things to Captain Cheap whilst a prisoner that I believe the gunner and carpenter will be hanged, if nobody else."

Bulkeley finally admitted that he was "the unfortunate gunner of the *Wager*."

The marshal, stunned, said that he had no choice but to take him into custody. Bulkeley was confined until several other officers from the *Wager* had been rounded up, among them Lieutenant Baynes; the carpenter, Cummins; and the boatswain, King. Then they were all transported to Portsmouth—the marshal warned to "take particular care that the gunner and carpenter did not make their escape." At the harbor, a transport boat rowed them out to HMS *Prince George,* a ninety-gun man-of-war anchored beyond the harbor. They were sequestered onboard, imprisoned once more by the sea. Bulkeley complained that he was not allowed to receive letters from family or friends.

Byron was also summoned, as were other members of the crew. Cheap boarded the ship on his own volition but likely had to surrender his sword. He had been suffering from gout and respiratory issues since the expedition, but he had regained some of his formidable presence, with his elegant officer's waistcoat and severe eyes and taut lips.

It was the first time that these men had been together since the island. Now each of them would have to, as Bulkeley had said, "give account of his actions," and let "justice take place." Eighteenth-century British naval law has a reputation for being draconian, but it was often more flexible and forgiving in reality. Under the Articles of War, many transgressions, including falling asleep on watch, were punishable by death, yet there was usually an important caveat: a court could hand down a lesser sentence if it saw fit. And although overthrowing a captain was a grave crime, "mutinous" behavior often applied to minor insubordinations not deemed worthy of severe punishment.

Nevertheless, the case against all of the men of the *Wager* seemed overwhelming. They were not accused of negligible misconduct but, rather, of a complete breakdown of naval order, from the highest levels of command to the rank and file. And though they had each tried to shape their stories in ways that justified their actions, the legal system was designed to strip these narratives down to the bare, hard, unemotive facts. In *Lord Jim*, Joseph Conrad writes of an official naval inquiry: "They wanted facts. Facts! They demanded facts." And all the former castaways' accounts contained, at their core, certain incontrovertible facts. Neither side disputed that Bulkeley, Baynes, and their party had tied up their captain and left him on the island, or that Cheap had shot an unarmed man without any legal proceedings or even any warning. These were the facts!

Bulkeley and his party appeared to have violated the most statutes of the Articles of War: Article 19, which barred "mutinous assemblies upon any pretence whatsoever, upon pain of death"; Article 20, which said that no one "shall conceal any traitorous or mutinous practices, designs, or words"; Article 21, which forbade quarreling or striking a superior officer; and Article 17, which decreed that any seaman who runs away "shall be punished with death." A stringent prosecutor could tack on more charges, including cowardice, for defying Cheap's orders to pursue their Spanish enemies and come to the aid of Anson; theft, for taking the transport boats and other supplies; and even "scandalous actions in derogation of God's honour, and corruption of good manners." Moreover, Cheap had accused Bulkeley and his party not just of a full-fledged mutiny but also of attempted murder, because they had abandoned him and his followers on the island.

Yet Cheap himself would surely face the most damning charge of all: homicide. It was one of the few statutes that offered no leniency for violators. Article 28 stated unequivocally, "All murders and willful killing of any person in the ship shall be punished with death."

Even Byron could not rest easy. He himself had briefly mutinied when he initially deserted Cheap on the island and went off with Bulkeley and his party. He had turned back, but was that enough?

Although many of the defendants had written accounts in attempts to clear their names, they were rife with glaring omissions. Cheap's report never explicitly acknowledged the shooting of Cozens—it merely noted that their altercation had led to "extremities." Bulkeley's journal described his abandonment of Cheap on the island as if he had been dutifully complying with his captain's wishes.

Even worse, many of the legalistic documents produced by the defendants during the expedition indicated a consciousness of guilt. These men knew the rules and regulations, knew exactly what they were doing, and after each violation had tried to create a paper trail to help them escape the consequences.

A naval court-martial was intended to do more than adjudicate the innocence or guilt of those on trial; it was meant to uphold and reinforce discipline throughout the service. As one expert put it, the system was "contrived to convey the majesty and strength of the state," and to ensure that the few who were guilty of serious crimes would serve as examples: "The underlying theory was that simple mariners, having witnessed these spectacles, would be left trembling at the prospect that such tremendous force—the power of life and death—might one day be used against them in the event that they violated the law."

After the famous mutiny on HMS *Bounty*, in 1789, the Admiralty dispatched a ship all the way to the Pacific to hunt down the suspects and bring them to justice in England. Following a court-martial, three were sentenced to die. On a ship moored in Portsmouth, they were led up to the forecastle, where three nooses dangled, neck high, from a yardarm. The crew of the ship stood on deck, looking on solemnly. A yellow flag was hoisted—the signal of death—and other vessels in the harbor assembled around the ship; their companies were obliged to watch, too. Crowds of spectators, including children, observed from the shore.

After the condemned men prayed, they were asked if they had any last words. One of them was reported by a witness to have said, "Brother seamen, you see before you three lusty young fellows about to suffer a shameful death for the dreadful crime of mutiny and desertion. Take warning by our example never to desert your officers, and should they behave ill to you, remember it is not their cause, it is the cause of your country you are bound to support."

Each mutineer had a bag placed over his head. A plaited noose was then looped around his neck. Shortly before noon, at the sound of a gun, several crewmen began to pull the ropes, lifting the mutineers high above the sea. The nooses tightened. The men strained for air and their legs and arms convulsed until they suffocated. Their bodies were left to swing for two hours.

One Sunday, while the men from the *Wager* were still waiting on the *Prince George* for the trial to commence, they attended a religious service on deck. The chaplain noted that a man who goes to sea often descends into the troubled depths where his "soul is melted." And he warned the rattled congregants that they should not hold on to "vain notions or expectations of a reprieve or pardon." The survivors of the *Wager* had every reason to expect to be hanged—or, as Bulkeley put it, to "fall by the violence of power."

CHAPTER 25

The Court-Martial

ON APRIL 15, 1746, a Union Jack flag was hoisted atop one of the *Prince George*'s masts and a cannon fired. The court-martial was beginning. The sea novelist Frederick Marryat, who entered the Royal Navy in 1806 at the age of fourteen and rose to captain, once wrote that the pomp of such proceedings was calculated to "strike the mind with awe—even of a captain himself." He added, "The ship is arranged with the greatest nicety; her decks are as white as snow—her hammocks are stowed with care—her ropes are taut—her yards square—her guns run out—and a guard of marines, under the orders of a lieutenant, prepared to receive every member of the court with the honour due to his rank.... The great cabin is prepared, with a long table covered with a green cloth. Pens, ink, paper, prayer-books, and the Articles of War are laid round to every member."

The thirteen judges assigned to the *Wager* trial appeared on deck in their formal dress. All were officers of high rank: captains and commodores, and the lead judge, the so-called president, was Sir James Steuart, a nearly seventy-year-old vice-admiral who was commander-in-chief of all His Majesty's Ships at Portsmouth. These men clearly seemed more like peers of Cheap than of Bulkeley and his followers, yet judges were known to punish a fellow officer. In 1757, Admiral John Byng would be executed after being found guilty of failing to "do his utmost" during battle, prompting Voltaire to remark in *Candide* that the English believed it proper to "kill an admiral from time to time in order to encourage the others."

Steuart sat at the head of the table, and the other judges placed themselves on either side of him, in a descending order of seniority. The judges swore to uphold their duty to administer justice without favor or affection. A prosecutor was present, and so was a judge advocate who helped to run the tribunal and provide its members with legal advice.

George Anson was not there, but a year earlier, during his steady ascent through the ranks, he had been appointed to the powerful Board of the Admiralty, which oversaw the general policy of naval discipline. And he undoubtedly had a deep interest in the proceedings involving his former men, especially his protégé Cheap. Over the years, Anson had proven an astute judge of character, and many of the men in the squadron whom he promoted would go on to become some of the most illustrious commanders of the Navy—among them, the *Centurion*'s lieutenant, Charles Saunders, the midshipman Augustus Keppel, and the *Severn*'s midshipman Richard Howe. But the man Anson had chosen to command the *Wager* was at risk of being convicted as a murderer.

Cheap had earlier sent Anson a letter, congratulating him on his victory over the *Covadonga* and the promotions "you so justly deserve in the opinion of all mankind." He wrote, "I take the liberty to assure you that no man on earth wishes your prosperity with a warmer heart than I do," and then added, "I must beg your favour and protection which I flatter myself I shall have whilst I behave myself as I ought, and when I behave otherwise I shall expect neither." Anson told a relative of Cheap that he remained supportive of his former lieutenant.

Cheap and the other defendants were brought in to face the court. As was then customary, they were not represented by attorneys: they had to defend themselves. But they could receive legal advice from the court or a colleague. Crucially, they could call and cross-examine witnesses.

Prior to the hearing, each defendant had been required to give a statement of facts, which was then presented into evidence. When

Bulkeley was called to record his, he protested that he still did not know exactly what charges were being filed against him. Ever conscious of his rights, he said, "I always thought, or at least the laws of my country tell me, that when a man is a prisoner, he must be accused." Bulkeley complained that he had no way to properly prepare a defense. He was told that at the moment, he simply needed to provide a deposition on the cause of the shipwreck. Whenever one of His Majesty's Ships was lost, an inquiry was held to determine if any of the officers or crew were responsible.

Now, as the trial began, Cheap was the first to answer questions. On the limited matter regarding the wrecking of the *Wager*, he leveled just one accusation: that Lieutenant Baynes had been derelict in his duties by, among other things, failing to inform him that the carpenter, Cummins, had reported seeing land the day before the ship struck the rocks.

A judge asked Cheap, "Do you charge any officer besides the lieutenant with being in any degree accessory to the loss of the *Wager*?"

"No, sir, I acquit them all of *that*," he replied.

He was not pressed on his other allegations. And before long it was Bulkeley's turn. He, too, was interrogated only about the loss of the *Wager*. A judge asked him why, before the ship ran aground, he had not tried with others to release its anchor.

"The cable was foul," Bulkeley replied.

"Have you anything to object to the conduct of the captain or officers, or to his proceedings in all respects for the good and preservation of the ship and crew?"

Bulkeley had already answered this question by publishing his journal—in those pages he had pointedly blamed Cheap for the wreck, alleging that the captain had refused to alter their course out of stubbornness and a blind obedience to orders. These temperamental shortcomings, Bulkeley believed, had only worsened during the tempestuous interlude on the island, fueling the mayhem and culminating with Cheap's committing murder and his ouster from power. Yet now, as Bulkeley spoke before the thirteen judges, he seemed to sense that something about the legal proceedings was fundamentally amiss. He had not been charged with mutiny—or, indeed, with anything at all. It was as if he were being offered an unspoken bargain. And so Bulkeley, though he had given an oath to tell the whole truth and was not one to hold his tongue, decided to leave some things unspoken as well. "I can lay nothing to the charge of any officer," he said.

Thus it went. The carpenter, Cummins, considered one of the ringleaders of the mutiny, was asked, "Have you anything to lay to the charge of the captain or any of the officers, for neglecting the preservation of the ship?"

"No," he replied, passing over the fact that he had once accused Cheap directly to his face of causing the wreck, not to mention having called him a murderer in print.

The boatswain, King, was summoned. He had been among the unruliest castaways—he had stolen liquor and officers' clothing, and during the rebellion he had physically assaulted Cheap. But King was not brought up on a single charge, and was simply asked, "Have you anything to say against your captain . . . for the loss of the ship?"

"No, the captain behaved very well. I have nothing to say against him or any other officer."

When it was John Byron's turn, he was not asked about any of the horrors he had witnessed: those dark acts that he had learned men—supposed gentlemen—were capable of. After a few technical questions about the ship's operations, he was dismissed.

Lieutenant Baynes was the only one facing any accusation whatsoever. He insisted that he had not reported the sighting of land to Cheap because he had thought it was no more than a speck of clouds on the horizon. "Otherwise, I would have certainly told the captain," he said.

After a brief adjournment, the court returned. It had reached a unanimous verdict. A paper was handed to the judge advocate, who read the decision aloud: "that Captain David Cheap had done his duty, and used all means in his power to have preserved His Majes-

Wager Island

(Above) In this 1805 engraving, the castaways are shown building their encampment on Wager Island. (Left) Mount Misery can be seen looming over the men in this eighteenth-century illustration.

The castaways found Wager Island's mountainous terrain (top) virtually barren of food. They were forced to consume bits of seaweed (right) and celery (below).

(Left) A Kawésqar man hunting sea lions, photographed by the anthropologist Martin Gusinde in the early twentieth century

(Below) The indigenous people in the region spent much of their time in canoes and survived almost exclusively off marine resources.

A coastal Kawésqar camp,
photographed by the anthropologist Gusinde

Murderous violence erupted among the *Wager*'s castaways,
as depicted in this 1745 engraving.

Magellan Straight
The North Sea

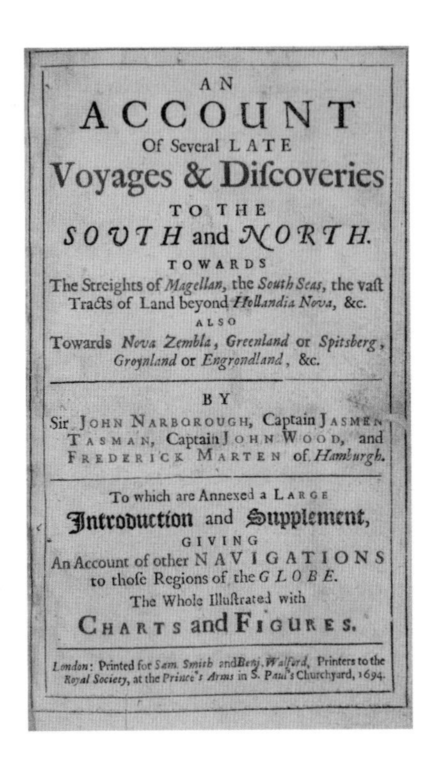

AN
ACCOUNT
Of Several LATE
Voyages & Diſcoveries
TO THE
SOUTH and NORTH.
TOWARDS
The Streights of *Magellan*, the *South Seas*, the vaſt Tracts of Land beyond *Hollandia Nova*, &c.
ALSO
Towards *Nova Zembla*, *Greenland* or *Spitsberg*, *Groynland* or *Engrondland*, &c.

BY
Sir JOHN NARBOROUGH, Captain JASMEN TASMAN, Captain JOHN WOOD, and FREDERICK MARTEN of *Hamburgh*.

To which are Annexed a LARGE
Introduction and **Supplement**,
GIVING
An Account of other NAVIGATIONS to thoſe Regions of the *GLOBE*.
The Whole Illuſtrated with
CHARTS and FIGURES.

London: Printed for *Sam. Smith* and *Benj. Walford*, Printers to the *Royal Society*, at the *Prince's Arms* in S. *Paul's* Churchyard, 1694.

OPPOSITE (Top) An eighteenth-century painting of the *Centurion* engaged in battle, its sails and British flag torn from cannon fire

OPPOSITE (Bottom) George Anson led the British squadron that included the *Wager*.

(Above) A remnant of the *Wager* wreck that was discovered in 2006

(Left and below) The castaways had a copy of John Narborough's account of his British expedition to Patagonia, and they carefully studied his map of the Strait of Magellan.

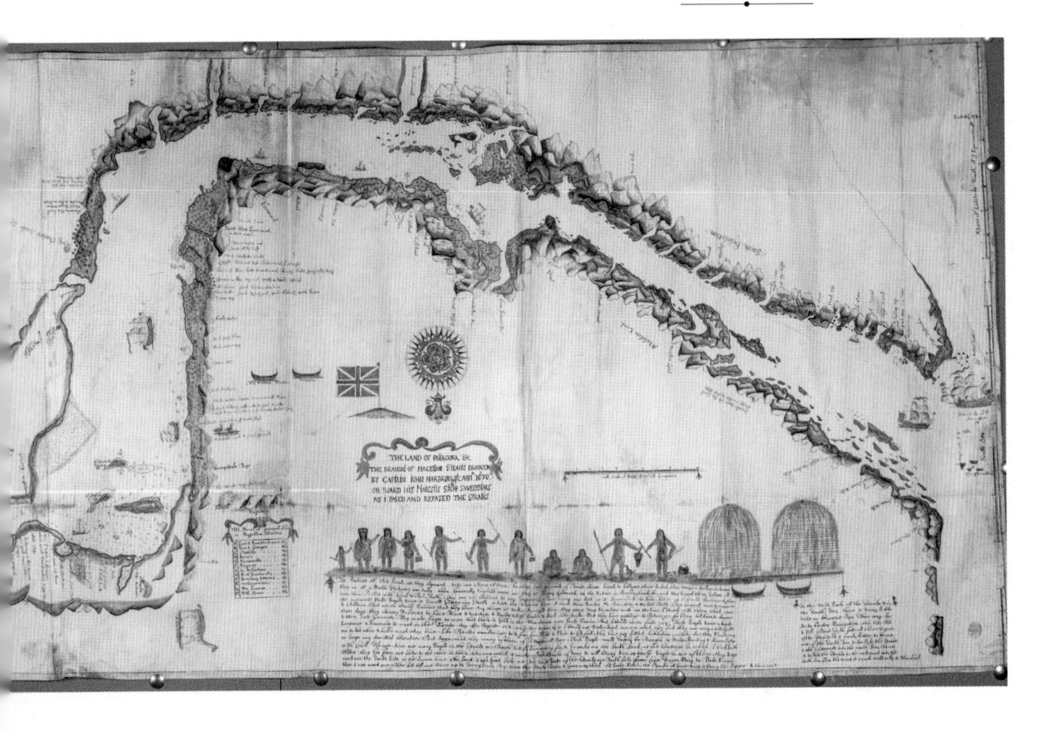

An eighteenth-century painting of men crowded in a small transport boat, similar to the one that the survivors on Wager Island used

To escape, the castaways from the *Wager* would have to navigate through the violent seas along the Chilean coast of Patagonia.

ty's Ship *Wager* under his command." All the other officers and crew were also absolved on this count—except for Baynes, who received a mere reprimand.

Bulkeley was overjoyed by the verdict. He boasted that he had been "honourably acquitted," and declared, "In this day's proceedings we beheld the great and glorious power of the Almighty, in pleading our cause, and defending us from falling by the violence of men." Cheap must have been alerted beforehand of the court's limited focus, for he never pressed his allegations against Bulkeley and his men. Though Cheap was denied his long-sought retribution, he, too, had been spared any punishment. He hadn't even been stripped of his cherished title of captain.

There were no further proceedings—no adjudication of whether Cheap had been guilty of murder or whether Bulkeley and his followers had mutinied and attempted to kill their commander. There was not even a hearing on whether any of the men had been guilty of desertion or quarreling with a superior officer. The British authorities, it seemed, didn't want *either* side's story to prevail. And to justify this outcome, they relied on a murky facet of the regulations: because naval rules stated that, after a shipwreck, the seamen onboard were no longer entitled to wages, the castaways might have assumed that they were not subject to naval law on the island. Yet this bureaucratic reasoning, which the historian Glyndwr Williams called an "escape clause," baldly ignored an addendum to the rule: if seamen were still able to procure supplies from a wreck, then they continued to be on the Navy's payroll. C. H. Layman, a British rear admiral and an authority on the *Wager* case, later concluded there was "an uncomfortable whiff of justification" in the Admiralty's decision not to prosecute a conspicuous mutiny.

It is impossible to know for sure what transpired behind the scenes, but there were certainly reasons for the Admiralty to want the case to disappear. Ferreting out and documenting all the incontrovertible facts of what had happened on the island—the marauding, the stealing, the whippings, the murders—would have undercut the central claim on which the British Empire tried to justify its rule of other peoples: namely, that its imperial forces, its civilization, were inherently superior. That its officers were gentlemen, not brutes.

Moreover, a proper trial would have offered an unwelcome reminder that the War of Jenkins' Ear had been a calamity—another ignoble chapter in the long, grim history of nations sending their troops off on ill-conceived, poorly funded, bungled military adventures. Five years before the court-martial, Admiral Vernon had led, as planned, Britain's massive assault with nearly two hundred ships on the South American city of Cartagena. But plagued by mismanagement, infighting between military leaders, and the constant menace of yellow fever, the siege had resulted in the loss of more than ten thousand men. After sixty-seven days of failing to capture the city, Vernon declared to his surviving crew that they were "surrounded with the toils of death." He then ordered a humiliating retreat.

Even Anson's expedition, with its vaunted haul of treasure, had largely been a catastrophe. Of the nearly two thousand men who had set sail, more than thirteen hundred had perished—a shocking death rate, even for such a long voyage. And though Anson had returned with some 400,000 pounds' worth of booty, the war had cost taxpayers 43 million pounds. One British newspaper had dissented from the celebrations of Anson's victory by publishing a poem:

Deluded Britons! Wherefore should you boast
Of treasure, purchased at a treble cost?
Will this, while centering in a private hand,
Restore to wealth, your much impoverished land?
To purchase this, think how much treasure's gone;
Think on the mighty mischiefs it hath done . . .
Of Albion's sons, unprofitably lost.
Then will your boastings into sorrow turn.

Not only had British men and boys been sent to their death, but the war itself had been rooted at least partly in a deception. The merchant captain Robert Jenkins had indeed been attacked by the Spanish, but this had occurred in 1731, eight years before the outbreak of the war. The incident had originally drawn little attention—and was forgotten until British politicians and business interests clamoring for war dredged it up. In 1738, when Jenkins was summoned to testify before the House of Commons, it was widely reported afterward that he had held up his ear in a jar of brine and delivered his rousing remarks about sacrificing himself for his country. But though he was certainly called to testify, no transcript exists of what occurred, and some historians have suggested that he was out of the country at the time.

British political and economic interests had their own ulterior motivations for war. Although English merchants had been widely prevented from trading in Spanish-controlled ports in Latin America, they had found a sinister way in. In 1713, the British South Sea Company had received from Spain what was known as an *asiento*—a license to sell nearly five thousand African people a year as slaves in Spain's Latin American colonies. Because of this abhorrent new agreement, English merchants were able to use their ships to smuggle such goods as sugar and wool. As the Spanish increasingly retaliated by seizing vessels that sold forbidden goods, British merchants and their political allies began searching for a pretext to rally the public for war to expand Britain's colonial holdings and monopolies on trade. And "the fable of Jenkins's ear," as Edmund Burke later dubbed it, provided a righteous sheen to their scheme. (The historian David Olusoga had noted that the unseemly aspects of the war's origin have largely been "expunged from the mainstream narrative of British history.")

By the time of the *Wager* court-martial, the stalemated War of Jenkins' Ear had already been subsumed into another, wider imperial struggle, known as the War of the Austrian Succession, in which all the European powers were jockeying for dominance. Over the next several decades, British naval victories would transform the small island nation into an empire with maritime supremacy—what the poet James Thomson called an "empire of the deep." By the early 1900s, Great Britain had become the largest empire in history, ruling over 400 million people and a quarter of the earth's landmass. But in 1746 the government was preoccupied with maintaining public support after so many dreadful losses.

A mutiny, especially in times of war, can be so threatening to the established order that it is not even officially recognized as one. During the First World War, French troops in various units on the western front refused to fight, in one of the largest mutinies in history. But the government's official account described the incident merely as "Disturbances and the Rectification of Morale." The military records were sealed for fifty years, and it wasn't until 1967 that an authoritative account was published in France.

The official inquiry into the *Wager* affair was permanently closed. Cheap's deposition detailing his allegations eventually disappeared from the court-martial files. And the upheaval on Wager Island became, in the words of Glyndwr Williams, "the mutiny that never was."

CHAPTER 26

The Version That Won

LOST AMID THE CONTROVERSY over the *Wager* affair was the story of another mutiny—one witnessed by the very last castaways to straggle home. Three months after the court-martial, three long-lost crew members from Bulkeley's party, including the midshipman Isaac Morris, astonishingly arrived on a ship in Portsmouth.

It had been more than four years since these men had swum ashore in Patagonia with a small party from the *Speedwell* to gather provisions—only to be left behind on the beach. Bulkeley and other survivors onboard the boat had told their version of what had happened: that stormy seas and a broken rudder had made it impossible for them to steer close enough to the coast to retrieve the men. After Bulkeley's crew had sent ashore a barrel filled with some munitions and an explanatory note, Morris and his companions, watching the *Speedwell* sail away, had sunk to their knees. Morris later called their desertion "the greatest act of cruelty." At the time, Morris's group had included seven other men. They'd already been castaways for eight months; now, as Morris wrote, they found themselves on "a wild desolate part of the world, fatigued, sickly, and destitute of provisions."

Four of them perished, but Morris and three others clung to life by hunting and foraging. They tried to reach Buenos Aires, several hundred miles to the north, but gave up in exhaustion. One day, after eight months of being lost in the wilderness, Morris spotted men on horses galloping toward him: "I imagined nothing but death approaching, and prepared to meet it with all the resolution I could muster up." Instead of an attack, he was greeted warmly by a party of native Patagonians. "They treated us with great humanity: killed a horse for us, kindled a fire, and roasted a part of it," Morris recalled. "They also gave each of us a piece of an old blanket to cover our nakedness."

The castaways were led from one village to another, often staying for months in one place. And in May 1744, two and a half years after the *Speedwell* left them behind, three of the men safely reached the capital—for the Spanish to take them as prisoners. They were confined for more than a year. Finally, the Spaniards gave them permission to return home, and they were transported to Spain as prisoners in a sixty-six-gun warship under the command of Don José Pizarro, the officer who had once pursued Anson's squadron. In addition to a crew of nearly five hundred, there were onboard eleven indigenous men, including a chief named Orellana, who had been forced into slavery and made to work on the ship.

Few records endure detailing the enslaved men's lives, and those that exist are filtered through the eyes of Europeans. According to the most in-depth report, which was based on the eyewitness testimony of Morris and his fellow castaways, they came from a tribe outside Buenos Aires that had long resisted colonization. About three months before Pizarro's return voyage, they had been captured by Spanish soldiers. On the ship, they were treated, as the report put it, with "great insolence and barbarity."

One day Orellana was ordered to climb the mast. When he refused, an officer beat him until he was dazed and bloodied. The report stated that officers had repeatedly lashed him and his men "most cruelly, on the slightest pretences, and oftentimes only to exert their superiority."

On the third night of the voyage, Morris was down below when he heard a commotion coming from on deck. One of his companions wondered if a mast had fallen, and rushed up a ladder to see what was happening. As he emerged, someone struck him on the back of the head and he fell, smacking the deck. Then a body dropped beside him—that of a dead Spanish soldier. Cries rang through the ship: "A mutiny! A mutiny!"

Morris also came on deck, and was amazed by what he saw: Orellana and his ten men were storming the quarterdeck. They were vastly outnumbered, and they had no muskets or pistols—only some knives that they had covertly gathered, and a few slingshots they had fashioned from wood and cords. Yet they fought one man after another until Pizarro and several of his officers barricaded themselves in a cabin, snuffing out the lanterns and hiding in the dark. Some of the Spaniards concealed themselves amid the cattle penned up onboard, while others scurried up the rigging and took refuge in the tops of the masts. "These eleven Indians, with a resolution perhaps without example, possessed themselves almost in an instant of the quarterdeck of a ship mounting sixty-six guns, with a crew of near five hundred men," the report noted.

It was one of hundreds of documented slave rebellions and indigenous insurrections that had taken place in the Americas—true mutinies. As the historian Jill Lepore has noted, occupied peoples had "revolted again and again and again," asking the "same question, unrelentingly: *By what right are we ruled?*"

On the Spanish ship, Orellana and his party continued to maintain control over the command center, blocking the gangplanks and resisting incursions. But they had no way to maneuver the ship and no place to go, and after more than an hour Pizarro and his forces began to regroup. In the cabin, some men found a bucket and tied it to a long rope, which they lowered through a porthole down to the powder room, where the gunner filled it with munitions. The officers quietly pulled it upward. Once fully armed, they cracked open the cabin door, glimpsing Orellana. He had removed the western clothing he had been forced to wear and was standing nearly naked with his men, breathing in the evening air. The officers poked out the barrels of their pistols and began to fire—sudden flashes in the darkness. A bullet hit Orellana. He staggered and fell, his blood running over the deck. "Thus was the insurrection quelled," the report stated, "and the possession of the quarterdeck regained, after it had been full two hours in the power of this great and daring chief, and his gallant and unhappy countrymen." Orellana had been killed. And his remaining men, rather than be enslaved again, climbed onto the railings of the ship, let out defiant cries, and leapt overboard to their deaths.

After Morris returned to England, he published a forty-eight-page narrative, adding to the ever-growing library of accounts about the *Wager* affair. The authors rarely depicted themselves or their companions as the agents of an imperialist system. They were consumed with their own daily struggles and ambitions—with working the ship, with gaining promotions and securing money for their families, and, ultimately, with survival. But it is precisely such unthinking complicity that allows empires to endure. Indeed, these imperial structures require it: thousands and thousands of ordinary people, innocent or not, serving—and even sacrificing themselves for—a system many of them rarely question.

Strikingly, there was one surviving castaway who never had a chance to record his testimony in any form. Not in a book or in a deposition. Not even in a letter. And that was John Duck, the free Black seaman who had gone ashore with Morris's abandoned party.

Duck had withstood the years of deprivation and starvation, and he had managed with Morris and two others to trek to the outskirts of Buenos Aires. But there his fortitude was of no avail, and he suffered what every free Black seaman dreaded: he was kidnapped and sold into slavery. Morris didn't know where his friend had been taken, whether to the mines or to the fields—Duck's fate was unknown, as is the case for so many people whose stories can never be told. "I believe he will end his days" in bondage, Morris wrote, "there being no prospect of his ever returning to England." Empires preserve their power with the stories that they tell, but just as critical are the stories they don't—the dark silences they impose, the pages they tear out.

Meanwhile, there was already a competition underway in England to publish the definitive narrative of Anson's globe-spanning expedition. Richard Walter, the *Centurion*'s chaplain, let it be known that he was writing such a chronicle, and the ship's schoolmaster, Pascoe Thomas, complained that Walter was attempting to dissuade others from printing their own versions, so that he could "make a monopoly of this voyage." In 1745, Thomas preempted Walter by releasing *A True and Impartial Journal of a Voyage to the South-Seas, and Round the Globe, in His Majesty's Ship the Centurion, Under the Command of Commodore George Anson.* Another chronicle, likely polished by a Grub Street hack, hailed Anson's voyage as "undoubtedly of the greatest worth and importance."

In 1748, two years after the court-martial, Reverend Walter finally published his account, *A Voyage Round the World in the Years 1740–1744 by George Anson.* At nearly four hundred pages, it was the longest and most detailed of the various narratives, and it was illustrated with beautiful sketches made during the expedition by a lieutenant on the *Centurion.* Like many travelogues of the time, the book suffers from stilted prose and the tedious minutiae of a logbook, but it successfully conveys the pulsing drama of Anson and his men confronting one disaster after another. In a brief discussion of the *Wager* affair, the account sympathizes with Cheap, arguing that he had "done his utmost" to save the crew and only shot Cozens because he was the "ringleader" of a band of violent agitators. Walter also lent credence to the reason that none of the castaways were ever prosecuted, claiming that the "men conceived, that by the loss of the ship, the authority of the officers was at an end." Ultimately, in Walter's hands, the sinking of the *Wager* becomes just one more impediment in the

Centurion's quest to capture the galleon. The book concludes with the stirring words: "Though prudence, intrepidity, and perseverance united are not exempted from the blows of adverse fortune," in the end they "rarely fail of proving successful."

But there is something odd about the book. For the work of a clergyman, it contains conspicuously little mention of God. And though the narrator writes in the first person while describing the *Centurion*'s engagement with the galleon, Walter was not present for this battle—he had departed from China for England shortly before the engagement. Later, sleuthing historians discovered that Walter was not the book's sole author; much of it had been ghostwritten by a pamphleteer and mathematician named Benjamin Robins.

In fact, there was yet another hidden force behind the book—none other than Admiral Anson himself. He had what he admitted was an "aversion to writing," and in his dispatch after capturing the galleon, he had offered little more than "I got sight of her and gave chase." Anson, however, had engineered Walter's book—providing the source materials, choosing the reverend to compile it, reportedly paying Robins a thousand pounds to breathe life into it, and making sure that it reflected his perspective on every page.

The expedition was touted as "an enterprise of so very singular a nature," and Anson himself was depicted throughout as a commander who "constantly exerted his utmost endeavours" and "always kept up his usual composure"—a man who was as "remarkable for his lenity and humanity" as for "his resolution and courage." Moreover, the book is one of the few accounts that seems deeply conscious of Britain's imperial interests, praising, on the first page, the country for once more demonstrating its "manifest superiority" over its enemies, "both in commerce and glory." The account was secretly Anson's version of the events, designed to burnish not only his reputation but also that of the British Empire. Even the book's illustration of the battle between the *Centurion* and the galleon, which became an iconic image, altered the dimensions of the vessels to make it look as if the galleon was the larger and more formidable of the two, rather than the other way around.

The book went through one printing after another and was translated around the world—a best-selling smash, in today's parlance. An official of the Admiralty noted, "Everybody has heard of, and multitudes have read, 'Anson's Voyage Round the World.'" The book influenced Rousseau, who, in one of his novels, described Anson as "un capitaine, un soldat, un pilote, un sage, un grand homme!" Montesquieu wrote a forty-plus-page annotated summary of the book. Captain James Cook, who described Reverend Walter as "the ingenious author of Lord Anson's voyage," carried a copy on the *Endeavour* during his first expedition around the world, and so did Darwin on his journey on the *Beagle.* The book was hailed by critics and historians as "a classic story of adventure," "one of the pleasantest little books in the world's library," and "the most popular travel book of its time."

Just as people tailor their stories to serve their interests—revising, erasing, embroidering—so do nations. After all the grim and troubling narratives about the *Wager* disaster, and after all the death and destruction, the empire had finally found its mythic tale of the sea.

Epilogue

IN ENGLAND, THE MEN from the *Wager* resumed their lives as if the sordid affair had never happened. With Admiral Anson's support, David Cheap was made captain of a forty-four-gun man-of-war. On Christmas Day in 1746, eight months after the court-martial, he was sailing off Madeira with another British ship when he spotted a thirty-two-gun Spanish vessel. Cheap and the other British ship gave chase, and for a moment he resembled the leader that he had always wanted to be: perched on the quarterdeck, guns ready, barking out orders to his men. He later informed the Admiralty that it was his "honour" to reveal that his party had overtaken the enemy in "about half-an-hour." Moreover, he reported that he had discovered onboard the vessel more than a hundred chests of silver. Cheap had finally captured what he called "so valuable a prize." After receiving a substantial share of the money, he retired from the Navy, bought a large estate in Scotland, and married. Yet even after his victory he could not entirely purge the stain of the *Wager*. When he died in 1752, at the age of fifty-nine, an obituary noted that after being shipwrecked he had shot one man "dead on the spot."

John Bulkeley escaped to a land where migrants could discard their burdensome pasts and reinvent themselves: America. He moved to the colony of Pennsylvania, that future hotbed of rebellion, and in 1757 he published an American edition of his book. He included an extract from an account that Isaac Morris had written, though he cut out the part in which Morris accused him of cruelly abandoning him and his party. After the American publication, Bulkeley vanished from history as abruptly as he had inserted himself. The last time his voice can be heard is in the new dedication to his book, in which he mentions that he hopes to find in America "the Garden of the Lord."

John Byron, who married and had six children, stayed in the Navy, serving for more than two decades and ascending the ranks all the way to vice-admiral. In 1764, he was asked to lead an expedition around the globe; one of his orders was to keep an eye out in the unlikely event that any *Wager* castaways had survived on the shores of Patagonia. He completed the voyage without losing a ship, but wherever he went at sea, he was hounded by dreadful storms. His nickname became Foul-Weather Jack. An eighteenth-century naval biographer wrote that Byron had "the universal and justly acquired reputation of a brave and excellent officer, but of a man extremely unfortunate." Nevertheless, in the cloistered wooden world he seemed to find what he had longed for—a sense of fellowship. And he was widely praised for what one officer called his tenderness and his care toward his men.

Bound by naval tradition, he kept quiet about the *Wager* affair, carrying with him his anguishing memories: how his friend Cozens had gripped his hand after being shot; how the dog that he found was slaughtered and eaten; and how some of his companions had turned, as a last resort, to cannibalism. In 1768, two decades after the court-martial—and long after Cheap had died—Byron finally published his own version of the events. It was called *The Narrative of the Honourable John Byron . . . Containing an Account of the Great Distresses Suffered by Himself and His Companions on the Coast of Patagonia, from the Year 1740, Till Their Arrival in England, 1746.* With Cheap no longer alive, he could be more candid about his former captain's dangerously "rash and hasty" conduct. Marine Lieutenant Hamilton, who continued to vehemently defend Cheap's conduct, accused Byron of doing a "great injustice" to the captain's memory.

The book was praised by critics. One called it "simple, interesting, affecting, and romantic." And though it never received a lasting readership, it cast a spell on Byron's grandson, whom he never met. In *Don Juan*, the poet wrote that the protagonist's "hardships were comparative / To those related in my grand-dad's 'Narrative.'" He also once wrote:

Reversed for me our grandsire's fate of yore,—
He had no rest at sea, nor I on shore.

Admiral George Anson went on to win more naval victories. During the War of the Austrian Succession, he captured an entire French fleet. But his greatest impact came not as a commander but as an administrator. While serving for two decades on the Board of the Admiralty, he helped to reform the Navy, addressing many of the problems that had caused so many calamities during the War of Jenkins' Ear. The changes included professionalizing the service and establishing a permanent marine corps under Admiralty control, which would avoid invalids being sent to sea and the kind of hazy command structure that had contributed to the disorder on Wager Island. Anson was hailed as the "Father of the British Navy." Streets and towns were named in his honor, including Ansonborough in South Carolina. John Byron named his second son George Anson Byron.

Yet within decades even the fame of Byron's old commodore began to wane, overshadowed by subsequent generations of commanders such as James Cook and Horatio Nelson, with their own mythic tales of the sea. After the *Centurion* was decommissioned and broken apart, in 1769, its sixteen-foot wooden lion's head was given to the Duke of Richmond, who had it placed on a pedestal at a local inn with a plaque that read:

Stay, traveller, awhile, and view
One who has travelled more than you:
Quite round the globe, through each degree,
Anson and I have ploughed the sea

Later, at the King's request, the lion's head was moved to Greenwich Hospital, in London, and placed in front of a ward for seamen, which was named for Anson. But over the next hundred years the artifact's significance faded, and it was eventually dumped in a shed, where it decayed into pieces.

Occasionally, a great teller of sea tales would be drawn to the saga of the *Wager*. In his 1850 novel *White-Jacket*, Herman Melville notes that the "remarkable and most interesting narratives" of the castaways' suffering make for fine reading on "a boisterous March night, with the casement rattling in your ear, and the chimney-stacks blowing down upon the pavement, bubbling with rain-drops." In 1959, Patrick O'Brian published *The Unknown Shore*, a novel inspired by the *Wager* disaster. Though a fledgling, less polished work, it provided O'Brian with a template for his subsequent masterful series set during the Napoleonic Wars.

Yet the *Wager* affair, despite these occasional reminders, has now been all but forgotten by the public. Maps of the Golfo de Penas contain references that are baffling to most contemporary seamen. Near the northernmost headlands, which Cheap and his group tried futilely to row past, four small islands are identified as Smith, Hertford, Crosslet, and Hobbs—the names of the four marines left behind when there wasn't room for them on the one remaining transport boat. They had cried out "God bless the King" before disappearing forever. There is Canal Cheap and Byron Island—the place where Byron had made his fateful choice to leave Bulkeley's party and return to his captain.

Gone from the coastal waters are the nomads of the sea. By the late nineteenth century, the Chono had been wiped out by contact with Europeans, and by the early twentieth century there were only a few dozen Kawésqar, who had settled at a hamlet about a hundred miles south of the Golfo de Penas.

Wager Island remains a place of wild desolation. Today, it looks no less forbidding, its shores still battered by unrelenting winds and waves. The trees are knotted and twisted and bent, and many have been blackened by lightning. The ground is sodden from rain and sleet. A near-permanent mist enshrouds the top of Mount Anson and the other peaks, and it sometimes creeps down the slopes to the rocks along the water's edge, as if the whole island were being consumed by smoke. Few creatures seem to move in the haze, except for a white-chinned petrel or other aquatic bird that flies over the surf.

Near Mount Misery, where the castaways built their outpost, a few stalks of celery still sprout, and you can forage for scattered limpets like those the men survived on. And a short way inland, partially buried in an icy stream, are several rotted wooden planks that, hundreds of years ago, washed up onto the island. About five yards long and hammered with treenails, these boards are from the skeletal frame of an eighteenth-century hull—His Majesty's Ship the *Wager*. Nothing else remains of the ferocious struggle that once took place there, or of the ravaging dreams of empires.

Acknowledgments

Writing a book can sometimes feel like navigating a ship on a long, stormy voyage. And I'm grateful to so many people who kept me afloat.

The distinguished British naval historian Brian Lavery patiently gave me tutorials on everything from eighteenth-century shipbuilding to seamanship, and he generously reviewed my manuscript before publication and offered his wise comments. Daniel A. Baugh, a leading naval historian, provided enormous insights and guidance during my research. And so many other historians and experts kindly answered my pestering calls, including Denver Brunsman and Douglas Peers. Rear Admiral C. H. Layman, who has done his own considerable research into the *Wager* affair, responded to my inquiries and allowed me to reprint several illustrations from his collection.

In 2006, Colonel John Blashford-Snell, who runs the Scientific Exploration Society, organized a joint British and Chilean expedition to uncover the wreck of the *Wager.* He shared with me critical information, and so did Chris Holt, one of the leaders of the party, who also allowed me to reprint several of his photographs.

Yolima Cipagauta Rodríguez, a whirlwind explorer who had helped to arrange the society's expedition, assisted me in organizing my own three-week journey to the island. We departed from Chiloé Island on a small boat, which was heated by a wood stove. The vessel was operated by a skilled and knowledgeable captain, Noel Vidal Landeros, and his two extremely capable crew members, Hernán Videla and Soledad Nahuel Arratia. Because of their remarkable abilities and the aid of Rodríguez, I was able to reach Wager Island, locating pieces of the wreck and better understanding what the castaways had experienced.

I am also indebted to the numerous archivists who made this book possible, including at the British Library, the British National Archives, the National Library of Scotland, the Oregon Historical Society, the University of St. Andrews Library's Special Collections, and the National Maritime Museum in Greenwich.

Several individuals were particularly invaluable to the project. Len Barnett tirelessly assisted in finding and copying naval records. Carol McKinven was a wunderkind with genealogical research. Cecilia Mackay tracked down numerous photos and illustrations. Aaron Tomlinson sharpened several of my photographs of Wager Island. Stella Herbert kindly shared with me information about her ancestor Robert Baynes. And Jacob Stern, Jerad W. Alexander, and Madeleine Baverstam—all gifted young reporters—helped locate numerous books and articles.

I can never thank David Kortava enough. An extraordinary journalist, he not only relentlessly fact-checked the book but was an endless source of insight and support. I asked, as always, too much of my friends and fellow writers Burkhard Bilger, Jonathan Cohn, Tad Friend, Elon Green, David Greenberg, Patrick Radden Keefe, Raffi Khatchadourian, Stephen Metcalf, and Nick Paumgarten.

Every page benefited from the wisdom of John Bennet, an editor and a friend, who tragically died, in 2022. I will never forget the lessons he imparted to me as a writer, and I hope this book will stand as a small part of his vast legacy.

Ever since I joined *The New Yorker,* in 2003, I've been blessed to work with Daniel Zalewski, an editor revered among writers. Without his advice and friendship, I would feel marooned, and he gave this book his magical touches, burnishing sentences, removing infelicities, and sharpening my thoughts.

In a sometimes-turbulent industry, I've been steadied by my agents, Kathy Robbins and David Halpern, at the Robbins Office, and Matthew Snyder, at CAA. They have been at my side for decades, guiding and supporting me. I'm also so lucky to have the backing of Nancy Aaronson and Nicole Klett-Angel at the Leigh Bureau.

There's been no greater leader to follow than Bill Thomas, my longtime publisher and editor at Doubleday. He made this book, and all my books, possible. Uncannily smart and unwavering in his backing, he has helped me not only to find the right stories but how to best tell them. He and Maya Mavjee, the president and publisher of the Knopf Doubleday Group, and Todd Doughty, my publicist extraordinaire, are a writer's gift, and so is the entire team at Doubleday. I especially want to thank John Fontana, who designed the book's cover; Maria Carella, who did the interior design; the copyeditor Patrick Dillon; the managing editors Vimi Santokhi and Kathy Hourigan; the production editor Kevin Bourke; the assistant editor Khari Dawkins; Jeffrey L. Ward, who made the maps; and the incredible marketing force of Kristin Fassler, Milena Brown, Anne Jaconette, and Judy Jacoby.

Nina and John Darnton remain the most loving in-laws. They read each rough chapter, showing me ways to improve it and giving me the encouragement to forge on. John's brother, Robert Darnton, who is among the greatest historians, took time to read the manuscript and make wonderful suggestions. My sister, Alison, and my brother, Edward, are my anchors, as is my mother, Phyllis, who, more than anyone, stirred my love of reading and writing. My father, Victor, is no longer alive, but this book was inspired by our many wondrous sailing adventures together. He was always a captain of grace and kindness.

Finally, there are the three people who are everything to me: Kyra, Zachary, and Ella. No words can express my gratitude to them, and for once, as a writer, I must end in awed silence.

Notes

A NOTE ON THE SOURCES

One day several years ago, I made a visit to the British National Archives, in Kew, where I put in a request. Hours later, I received a box; inside was a dusty, moldering manuscript. To avoid damaging it further, I gently pried open the cover with a paper marker. Each page was arranged in columns, with such headings as "month and year," ship's "course," and "Remarkable Observations and Incidents." The entries, composed with a quill and ink, were now smudged, and the writing was so small and squirrely that I strained to decipher it.

On April 6, 1741, with the ship trying to round Cape Horn, an officer wrote under observations, "All the sails and rigging was bad and men very sickly." Several days later, the officer noted, "Lost sight of the *Commodore* and all the squadron." With each passing day, the notes grew bleaker—the ship was breaking apart, the men were running out of drinking water. On April 21, the entry read: "Timothy Picaz, seaman, departed this life... Thomas Smith, invalid, departed this life... John Paterson, invalid, and John Fiddies, seaman, departed this life."

The book was just one of the many harrowing logs that had survived from the expedition led by George Anson. Even after more than two and a half centuries have passed, there is a surprising trove of firsthand documents, including those detailing the *Wager*'s calamitous wreck on a desolate island off the coast of Patagonia. These records include not only logbooks, but also correspondence, diaries, muster books, court-martial testimony, Admiralty reports, and other government records. Added to them are numerous contemporaneous newspaper accounts, sea ballads, and sketches made during the voyage. And, of course, there are the vivid sea narratives that many of the participants themselves published.

The book you are holding is drawn extensively from these rich materials. My descriptions of Wager Island and the surrounding seas were further enhanced by my own three-week journey there, which provided at least a glimpse of the wonder and terror that the castaways experienced.

To depict life inside the wooden world during the eighteenth century, I also relied on both published and unpublished journals of other mariners. And I benefited from the work of several superb historians. Glyn Williams's book *The Prize of All the Oceans* remains invaluable, as does his edited collection of primary records, *Documents Relating to Anson's Voyage Round the World.* Other essential sources included Daniel Baugh's groundbreaking *British Naval Administration in the Age of Walpole;* Denver Brunsman's illuminating history of impressment, *The Evil Necessity;* Brian Lavery's brilliant studies of shipbuilding and naval life, among them *The Arming and Fitting of English Ships of War, 1600–1815* and his edited collection of primary documents, *Shipboard Life and Organisation, 1731–1815;* and N. A. M. Rodger's monumental *The Wooden World.* Rear Admiral C. H. Layman has also reprinted several key records in his edited collection of primary documents, *The Wager Disaster.* In addition, I relied on many extensive interviews with these and other experts.

In the bibliography, I have delineated any important sources. If I was especially indebted to a book or article, I tried to cite it in the notes as well. Anything that appears in the text between quotation marks comes directly from a journal, log, diary, letter, or some other source. For clarity, I have modernized archaic spellings and punctuation, such as the random capitalization of words and the use of the *f*-like version of *s* that was common in the eighteenth century. Any quotations are cited in the notes.

ARCHIVAL AND UNPUBLISHED SOURCES

BL	British Library
ADD MSS	Additional Manuscripts
ERALS	East Riding Archives and Local Studies
HALS	Hertfordshire Archives and Local Studies, Hertfordshire
JS	Joseph Spence papers in the James Marshall and Marie-Louise Osborn Collection, Beinecke Rare Book and Manuscript Library, Yale University
LOC	Library of Congress, Washington, DC
NMM	National Maritime Museum, Greenwich, London
ADM B	Letters from the Navy Board to the Admiralty
ADM L	Admiralty: Lieutenants' Logs
HER	Heron-Allen Collection, containing letters and engraved portraits of naval officers
HSR	Manuscript documents
JOD	Journals and diaries

LBK	Letter books of naval officers
PAR/162/1	Personal collection of Sir William Parker, Admiral of the Fleet, 1781–1866
POR	Portsmouth Dockyard letters and reports
NLS	National Library of Scotland, Edinburgh
NRS	National Records of Scotland, Edinburgh
CC8	Wills and testaments
JC26/135	Court records
SIG1	Land records
OHS	Oregon Historical Society, Portland
TNA	The National Archives, Kew, Surrey
ADM 1	Admiralty official correspondence and papers
ADM 1/5288	Admiralty court-martial records
ADM 3	Admiralty board minutes
ADM 6	Admiralty service records, registers, returns, and certificates
ADM 8	Admiralty list books
ADM 30	Navy Board: Navy Pay Office
ADM 33	Navy Board pay books for ships
ADM 36	Admiralty muster books for ships
ADM 51	Admiralty captains' logs
ADM 52	Admiralty masters' logs
ADM 55	Admiralty supplementary logs and journals of ships on exploration
ADM 106	Navy Board: in letters
HCA	High Court of Admiralty records
PROB 11	Copies of wills from the Prerogative Court of Canterbury
SP	Records assembled by the State Paper Office, including papers of the Secretaries of State
RLSA	Rochdale Local Studies and Archive, Rochdale, England
SL	State Library of New South Wales, Australia
USASC	University of St. Andrews Special Collections, Scotland
WSRO	West Sussex Record Office, England

PROLOGUE

3 the strange object: My description of the arrival of the vessels is drawn largely from the survivors' journals, dispatches, published accounts, and private correspondence. For more information, see John Bulkeley and John Cummins's *A Voyage to the South Seas;* John Byron's *The Narrative of the Honourable John Byron*; Alexander Campbell's *The Sequel to Bulkeley and Cummins's "Voyage to the South Seas"*; C. H. Layman's *The Wager Disaster*; and records in TNA-ADM 1 and JS.

4 "human nature": Bulkeley and Cummins, *A Voyage to the South Seas*, xxxi.

John Cummins, the carpenter on the *Wager*, is listed as coauthor of the journal, but Bulkeley was the one who actually wrote it.

4 "quite lost himself": Byron, *The Narrative of the Honourable John Byron*, 170.

5 "dark and intricate": Bulkeley and Cummins, *A Voyage to the South Seas*, xxiv.

5 "faithful narrative": Campbell, *The Sequel to Bulkeley and Cummins's "Voyage to the South Seas,"* cover page.

5 "I have been": Ibid., vii–viii.

5 "imperfect narrative": Bulkeley and Cummins, *A Voyage to the South Seas*, 72.

5 "blackened us": Ibid.

5 "We stand": Ibid., xxiv.

CHAPTER 1

9 David Cheap: Little has previously been published about Cheap's background, and my portrait of him is drawn mostly from unpublished records. They include his family's papers, his private correspondence, and his logbooks and dispatches. I've also drawn from several of the journals and accounts composed by his friends and enemies. For more information, see records at JS, TNA, NMM, USASC, NLS, and NRS. Also see Bulkeley and Cummins's *A Voyage to the South Seas*; Byron's *The Narrative of the Honourable John Byron*; Campbell's *The Sequel to Bulkeley and Cummins's "Voyage to the South-Seas"*; and Alexander Carlyle's *Anecdotes and Characters of the Times.*

9 Cheap: The traditional spelling of his surname was Cheape. But in both contemporaneous and modern accounts of the voyage, it is generally spelled Cheap, and I've used that spelling throughout to avoid confusion.

10 George Anson: My portrait of Anson is drawn from the unpublished written records he has left behind, including his correspondence with the Admiralty and the logbooks from his voyages. I've also relied upon descriptions of him in letters, diaries, and other writings composed by his family members, fellow seamen, and contemporaries. Moreover, I benefited from several published accounts. These include Walter Vernon Anson's *The Life of Admiral Lord Anson: The Father of the British Nav, 1697–1762*; John Barrow's *The Life of Lord George Anson*; N. A. M. Rodger's entry about Anson in the *Oxford Dictionary of National Biography* as well as in *Precursors of Nelson,* edited by Peter Le Fevre and Richard Harding; Andrew D. Lambert's *Admirals: The Naval Commanders Who Made Britain Great*; Brian Lavery, *Anson's Navy: Building a Fleet for Empire 1744 –1763*; Richard Walter's *A Voyage Round the World*; S. W. C. Pack's *Admiral Lord Anson: The Story of Anson's Voyage and Naval Events of His Day*; and Glyn Williams's *The Prize of All the Oceans.* Finally, I'm grateful to the historian Lavery, who shared with me an unpublished essay he had written about Anson.

10 did not wield: Although Anson didn't carry the sort of family connections that greased the rise of many officers, he was not totally devoid of them. His aunt was married to the Earl of Macclesfield. Later, through his meritori-

ous naval service, he also developed several influential backers, including Philip Yorke, the first Earl of Hardwicke.

10 propelled many officers: A letter one captain sent to a colleague perfectly captures how this patronage, or "interest," worked in the Navy. "I must beg you will now use all your interest with your great and noble friends that I may at this time be promoted to a Flag Officer," the captain wrote.

10 "Anson, as usual": Quoted in Barrow, *The Life of Lord George Anson*, 241.

10 "He loved reading": Quoted in Rodger, "George, Lord Anson," in *Precursors of Nelson*, ed. Le Fevre and Harding, 198.

10 "round it": Ibid., 181.

11 "He had high": Ibid., 198.

11 "act up to": Thomas Keppel, *The Life of Augustus, Viscount Keppel, Admiral of the White, and First Lord of the Admiralty in 1782–3*, vol. 1, 172.

11 "No man will": Quoted in James Boswell, *The Life of Samuel Johnson*, 338.

12 "The sooner he": Unpublished autobiography of Andrew Massie, which I had translated from Latin into English, NLS.

12 "unhappy fate": Report from Cheap to Richard Lindsey, Feb. 26, 1744, JS.

12 few pirates: One captain under whom Cheap served had written an account describing how a band of pirates had stormed his ship in the Caribbean. "The enemy came in furiously with their lances and cutlasses and fell cutting me and my people in a most barbarous manner," the captain reported, adding, "Besides two musket balls which I received in the middle of the action through my right thigh, I was cut in three places of my head."

12 "vaporing manner": Carlyle, *Anecdotes and Characters of the Times*, 100.

12 "a man of": Ibid., 99.

12 The conflict: For more information on the war, see Craig S. Chapman, *Disaster on the Spanish Main*, and Robert Gaudi, *The War of Jenkins' Ear: The Forgotten War for North and South America.*

13 pickled in a jar: The poet Alexander Pope further enshrined the story, writing that "the Spaniards did a waggish thing" when they "cropt our ears, and sent them to the King."

13 "my cause": Quoted in Philip Stanhope Mahon, *History of England: From the Peace of Utrecht to the Peace of Versailles*, vol. 2, 268.

13 round Cape Horn: The instructions also mentioned alternatively going through the Strait of Magellan, a treacherous passageway between the end of the South American mainland and Tierra del Fuego. But Commodore Anson planned to round Cape Horn.

13 "taking, sinking, burning": Instructions to Commodore Anson, 1740, printed in Glyndwr Williams, ed., *Documents Relating to Anson's Voyage Round the World*, 35.

14 who later compiled: For simplicity's sake, I subsequently refer to this narrative as Reverend Walter's account.

14 "the most desirable": Walter, *A Voyage Round the World*, 246. This quote is ren-

dered slightly different in one edition, and I've quoted it how it standardly appears.

14 "if it shall": Ibid., 37.

14 "most secret": Extract from "A Journal of My Proceedings," by Sir John Norris, 1739–40, printed in Williams, ed., *Documents Relating to Anson's Voyage Round the World*, 12.

14 "essential maxim": Walter, *A Voyage Round the World*, 95–96.

15 "Whosoever commands": Quoted in Luc Cuyvers, *Sea Power*, xiv.

16 "no chance": Keppel, *The Life of Augustus, Viscount Keppel, Admiral of the White, and First Lord of the Admiralty in 1782–3*, vol. 1, 155.

16 The royal dockyards: There is no more important study of the Navy's administration during this period than Daniel Baugh's book *British Naval Administration in the Age of Walpole*. I drew on this account as well as his edited collection of primary-source documents, *Naval Administration, 1715–1750*. I also drew on extensive interviews with Baugh.

16 they were largely made: For more information on how men-of-war were built and fitted out, see the invaluable works by Brian Lavery, especially *Building the Wooden Walls: The Design and Construction of the 74-Gun Ship Valiant*, and *The Arming and Fitting of English Ships of War, 1600–1815*. Lavery also generously helped me with countless interviews and fact-checking these sections of the book.

16 might be felled: The kind of thick oaks necessary for the hull—including the coveted compass oak, which had the natural curves for the frame—took about a hundred years to reach maturity. Shipwrights scoured the earth for timber. Many of the masts—the "great sticks," which were cut from more flexible woods, such as pine—were imported from the American colonies. In 1727, the Navy's contractor in New England reported that in one winter alone, "not less than thirty thousand pine trees were cut down," and that in seven years, if the rate continued, "there will not be a thousand mast trees standing in all those provinces." It is an early glimpse of deforestation.

16 ate through hulls: It would be several decades before the Navy began to regularly sheathe the bottom of its vessels in copper rather than wood.

16 "in danger": Samuel Pepys, *Pepys' Memoires of the Royal Navy, 1679–1688*, ed. J. R. Tanner, 11.

16 "general state": Julian Slight, *A Narrative of the Loss of the Royal George at Spithead*, 79.

16 "so much worm-eaten": Letter from Jacob Acworth to Secretary of the Admiralty Josiah Burchett, August 15, 1739, NMM-ADM B.

17 "much rat eaten": Anson's logbook on the *Centurion*, NMM-ADM L.

17 "do not like": Anselm John Griffiths, *Observations on Some Points of Seamanship*, 158.

17 "very strange": Letter from Cheap to the Admiralty, June 17, 1740, TNA-ADM 1/1439.

18 "both action": Extract from "A Journal of My Proceedings," by John Norris,

1739–40, printed in Williams, ed., *Documents Relating to Anson's Voyage Round the World*, 12.

18 "I lay three": Quoted in Sarah Kinkel, *Disciplining the Empire: Politics, Governance, and the Rise of the British Navy*, 98–99.

18 "tumbled over": Captain Dandy Kidd's logbook on the *Wager,* TNA-ADM 51/1082.

19 down the Thames: For more information on what it was like to pilot down the Thames, see G. J. Marcus's excellent book *Heart of Oak.*

19 merciless oglers: The *Centurion* midshipman Augustus Keppel, who would later rise to admiral, remarked of a passing ship, "She still retains a fat buttock."

19 exhausted its supply: For more information on the extraordinary manning crisis and the naval administration at this time, see Baugh's *British Naval Administration in the Age of Walpole* and his edited collection of documents, *Naval Administration, 1715–1750.*

20 first prime minister: Though the term prime minister was not then in use, he is today generally regarded by historians as the country's first prime minister.

20 "Oh! seamen": Quoted in Baugh, *British Naval Administration in the Age of Walpole*, 186.

20 "catching at": Thomas Gibbons Hutchings, *The Medical Pilot, or, New System*, 73.

20 "very indifferent": Report from Cheap to Lindsey, Feb. 26, 1744, JS.

20 a devastating epidemic: For more information on the impact of the typhus epidemic on the Royal Navy, see Baugh's *British Naval Administration in the Age of Walpole.* Also see James Lind's *An Essay on the Most Effectual Means of Preserving the Health of Seamen in the Royal Navy.*

20 transported unwashed recruits: James Lind, the naval surgeon who revolutionized methods of hygiene in the service, wrote that one sick recruit would infect a ship, which became a "seminary of contagion to the whole fleet."

20 "In this miserable": Quoted in Baugh, *British Naval Administration in the Age of Walpole,* 181.

21 "more violent": Ibid., 148.

21 "seize all straggling": Admiralty Memorial to the King in Council, January 23, 1740, printed in Baugh, ed., *Naval Administration, 1715–1750*, 118.

21 "What ship": Robert Hay, *Landsman Hay: The Memoirs of Robert Hay*, ed. Vincent McInerney, 195.

21 Press gangs headed out: An officer on the *Centurion* wrote in his log, "The second Lieutenant and 27 men sailed hence to impress seamen."

21 "I would rather": Quoted in Marcus, *Heart of Oak*, 80.

21 extraordinary lengths: Sometimes bloodshed ensued during pressing. One captain reported resisters firing upon his press gang when they tried to board their ship. "I then ordered my men to enter with cutlasses," he wrote. Five of them were killed.

22 "an old gentlewoman's": Quoted in Denver Brunsman, *The Evil Necessity: British Naval Impressment in the Eighteenth-Century Atlantic World,* 184.

22 "In this place": William Robinson, *Jack Nastyface: Memoirs of an English Seaman*, 25–26.

22 "In my life": Pepys, *Everybody's Pepys: The Diary of Samuel Pepys*, ed. O. F. Morshead, 345.

22 deserted at: If deserters were caught, they faced the prospect of being hanged—or, as a captain had once petitioned the Admiralty, "some punishment more terrible than death." Yet rarely were deserters executed. The Navy couldn't afford to kill so many seamen when it desperately needed them. And the few apprehended were usually returned to their ships. But in one instance on Anson's squadron, an officer reported, a deserter had "seduced several of our people to run away & did his utmost to prevent others returning," and after being caught for this and other offenses had to be chained to one of the ringbolts—"a great punishment to him."

23 "go off as": Quoted in Baugh, *British Naval Administration in the Age of Walpole*, 184.

23 Altogether, more than: This figure is based on my analysis of the muster books from the squadron's five men-of-war and the *Trial* scouting sloop.

23 "I would give": Quoted in Peter Kemp, *The British Sailor: A Social History of the Lower Deck*, 186.

23 "honour, courage": Report from Cheap to Lindsey, Feb. 26, 1744, JS.

23 "full of the": Quoted in Baugh, *British Naval Administration in the Age of Walpole*, 165.

23 the government sent: For my description of the marines and invalids, I've drawn on the firsthand accounts of members of the expedition. I also benefited from Glyn Williams's superb historical work *The Prize of All the Oceans.* According to hospital records he uncovered, one of the invalids had previously been "wounded in the Right Thigh," and his left leg and stomach "hurt by a bombshell." Another was listed as a "paraletic & very infirm."

23 they were "useless": Quoted in Williams, *The Prize of All the Oceans,* 22.

24 "old, lame": Michael Roper, *The Records of the War Office and Related Departments*, 71.

24 "most decrepit": Walter, *A Voyage Round the World*, 7–8.

24 "All those": Ibid.

24 "They would": Ibid.

24 "everything being": Anon., *A Voyage to the South-Seas, and to Many Other Parts of the World, Performed from the Month of September in the Year 1740, to June 1744, by Commodore Anson*, 12.

24 the *Trial*: The archaic spelling of the ship's name was often Tryal or Tryall, but I've used the modern spelling, which is *Trial.*

25 "waiting for": London *Daily Post*, September 5, 1740.

25 "The men were": Bulkeley and Cummins, *A Voyage to the South Seas*, 1.

CHAPTER 2

27 John Byron was: My study of Byron is drawn primarily from his journals; his correspondence with family and friends; his reports to the Admiralty over the years; the logbooks kept on the various ships in which he sailed; the firsthand accounts published by his fellow officers and seamen; and contemporaneous newspaper accounts. In addition, I drew on several books about Byron and his family's history, including Emily Brand's *The Fall of the House of Byron: Scandal and Seduction in Georgian England;* Fiona MacCarthy's *Byron: Life and Legend*; and A. L. Rowse's *The Byrons and Trevanions.*

28 "plates, glasses": Doris Leslie, *Royal William: The Story of a Democrat*, 10.

28 "so perverse": Bulkeley and Cummins, *A Voyage to the South Seas*, 135.

29 Newstead Abbey: Washington Irving described the Byron family estate as "one of the finest specimens in existence of those quaint and romantic piles, half castle, half convent, which remain as monuments of the olden times of England."

29 "The mansion's self": George Gordon Byron, *The Poetical Works of Lord Byron*, 732.

29 "The hall": Ibid., 378.

29 "honourable service": Pepys, *The Diary of Samuel Pepys*, ed. Robert Latham and William Matthews, vol. 2, 114.

30 a "perversion": Quoted in N. A. M. Rodger, *The Wooden World: An Anatomy of the Georgian Navy*, 115.

30 "Ye gods": Frederick Chamier, *The Life of a Sailor*, 10.

30 "unwholesome ill smells": Quoted in N. A. M. Rodger, *The Safeguard of the Sea*, 408.

31 "the champion of": John Bulloch, *Scottish Notes and Queries*, 29.

31 There were men: Women were prohibited from serving in the Navy, though some tried to disguise themselves; and occasionally officers brought their wives along.

31 enlisted free Black men: For more information on Black seamen during this period, see W. Jeffrey Bolster's *Black Jacks: African American Seamen in the Age of Sail* and the edited collection of Olaudah Equiano's work, *The Interesting Narrative and Other Writings.*

32 "A man-of-war may": Quoted in Henry Baynham, *From the Lower Deck*, 116.

33 "The captain had": Dudley Pope, *Life in Nelson's Navy*, 62.

33 Robert Baynes: The *Wager*'s lieutenant, Baynes, left behind limited correspondence and testimony, and so much of what is known about his conduct comes from the accounts of others on the ship. A good deal of information exists about his family. Among other sources, see Derek Hirst's "The Fracturing of the Cromwellian Alliance: Leeds and Adam Baynes"; John Yonge Akerman's *Letters from Roundhead Officers Written from Scotland and Chiefly Addressed to Captain Adam Baynes, July MDCL–June MDCLX;* and Henry Reece's *The Army in Cromwellian England, 1649–1660.* I also interviewed Derek

Hirst about the Baynes family and spoke to a descendant of Baynes, Stella Herbert, who kindly shared with me information that she had gathered about Robert Baynes.

33 On the bottom: There was also a third group of seamen that consisted of the afterguard men. Though positioned on the quarterdeck, they were order takers, not givers. They performed such rudimentary tasks as bracing the mizzenmast sails or scrubbing the deck with holystones—bricklike rocks the men kneeled over as if in prayer.

34 "set of *human*": Samuel Leech, *Thirty Years from Home, or, A Voice from the Main Deck*, 40.

34 a mysterious civilization: My portrait of shipboard life is drawn from numerous published and unpublished sources. I'm particularly indebted to Rodger's groundbreaking work of history, *The Wooden World*; Adkins and Adkins's *Jack Tar*; Lavery's *Shipboard Life and Organisation, 1731–1815*, a terrific collection of primary documents; and the firsthand accounts and journals and logs of seamen—among them those who went on Anson's voyage. I also benefited from interviews with experts in the field, among them Lavery, Rodger, Baugh, and Brunsman.

34 "always asleep": Quoted in Rodger, *The Wooden World*, 37.

34 "It is a mistaken": Edward Thompson, *Sailor's Letters*, vol. 1, 155–56.

35 curse like one: In an essay published in 1702, an author complained that officers cursed their men as "sons of eternal whores" and "bloods of eternal bitches," adding that they also "swear by the Lord Jesus Christ... with many other impious expressions not fit to be mentioned."

36 the food: Without refrigeration, that miraculous invention of the nineteenth century, the only way to preserve food was to dry it, salt it, or pickle it.

36 "I never knew": Byron, *The Narrative of the Honourable John Byron*, 39.

36 a fiddler: Byron recalled how on one voyage an officer "played on the fiddle & some of our people danced."

36 *They cut off:* Charles Harding Firth, *Naval Songs and Ballads*, 172.

37 "the most surprising": Robert E. Gallagher, ed., *Byron's Journal of His Circumnavigation, 1764–1766*, 35.

37 "They struck": Thompson, *Sailor's Letters*, vol. 2, 166.

37 "I can bear": Bulkeley and Cummins, *A Voyage to the South Seas*, 77.

39 "The first time": Herman Melville, *Redburn: His First Voyage: Being the Sailor-Boy Confession and Reminiscences of the Son-of-a-Gentleman, in the Merchant Service*, 132–33.

39 As Byron now: After many repetitions climbing the mainmast, Byron would write with cool nonchalance how he "went up immediately."

40 "designed by Providence": Walter, *A Voyage Round the World*, 17.

40 "The difficulties": Ibid., 11.

40 "Having been": Letter from Captain Norris to Anson, Nov. 2, 1740, TNA-ADM 1/1439.

40 "Cowardice, Negligence": N. A. M. Rodger, *Articles of War: The Statutes Which Governed Our Fighting Navies, 1661, 1749, and 1886*, 24.

40 "rather a puny": John Nichols, *Literary Anecdotes of the Eighteenth Century*, 782.

40 "Fye upon it": Berkenhout, "A Volume of Letters from Dr. Berkenhout to His Son, at the University of Cambridge," 116.

40 "quit" his: Walter, *A Voyage Round the World*, 18.

40 "greatest signs": "An Appendix to the Minutes Taken at a Court-Martial, Appointed to Enquire into the Conduct of Captain Richard Norris," 24.

40 "remove that infamy": Letter from Captain Norris to the Admiralty, Sept. 18, 1744, TNA-ADM 1/2217.

41 "worthy and humane": Anon., *A Voyage to the South-Seas, and to Many Other Parts of the World, Performed from the Month of September in the Year 1740, to June 1744, by Commodore Anson . . . by an Officer of the Squadron*, 18.

41 "courting the favour": W. H. Long, ed., *Naval Yarns of Sea Fights and Wrecks, Pirates and Privateers from 1616–1831 as Told by Men of Wars' Men*, 86.

42 all the "intelligence": Andrew Stone to Anson, Aug. 7, 1740, printed in Williams, ed., *Documents Relating to Anson's Voyage Round the World*, 53.

42 "intended to put": Walter, *A Voyage Round the World*, 19.

42 "In strength": Ibid., 20.

CHAPTER 3

43 "never seen": Quoted in Adkins and Adkins, *Jack Tar*, 270.

43 the ship's great guns: For more information on how the men on British naval warships prepared for battle, see Adkins and Adkins's *Jack Tar*; Patrick O'Brian's *Men-of-War: Life in Nelson's Navy*; Tim Clayton's *Tars: The Men Who Made Britain Rule the Waves*; G. J. Marcus's *Heart of Oak*; Lavery's *Shipboard Life and Organisation*; and Rodger's *The Wooden World*. Also see the many firsthand accounts by seamen, including those by William Dillon and Samuel Leech.

44 guns were blazing: During practice, many guns fired blanks to conserve ammunition.

45 "laugh at vindictive": Chamier, *The Life of a Sailor*, 93.

45 "A gunner at": William Monson, *Sir William Monson's Naval Tracts: In Six Books*, 342.

45 "Garden of the": Bulkeley and Cummins, *A Voyage to the South Seas*, xxi.

45 "prayer had been": Ibid., 45.

46 "make a man": Thomas à Kempis, *The Christian's Pattern, or, A Treatise of the Imitation of Jesus Christ*, 19.

46 "the life": Ibid., 20.

46 "the terror of": Bulkeley and Cummins, *A Voyage to the South Seas*, xxi.

46 "sober, careful": William Mountaine, *The Practical Sea-Gunner's Companion, or, An Introduction to the Art of Gunnery*, ii.

46 "lowest station": Ibid.

46 "Tho' I was": Bulkeley and Cummins, *A Voyage to the South Seas*, 5.

46 "degenerate" practice: Ibid., xxiii.

46 "In the time-honoured": Rodger, *The Wooden World*, 20.

47 "He compelled": Bulkeley and Cummins, *A Voyage to the South Seas*, 136.

47 "These volumes": For my understanding of logbooks and sea narratives, I'm especially indebted to two excellent sources. They are Philip Edwards's *The Story of the Voyage: Sea-Narratives in Eighteenth-Century England* and Paul A. Gilje's *To Swear Like a Sailor: Maritime Culture in America, 1750–1850.*

47 "tedious accounts": Daniel Defoe, *The Novels and Miscellaneous Works of Daniel Defoe*, 194.

48 *Bold were:* Bulkeley and Cummins, *A Voyage to the South Seas*, front page.

48 "logbooks of memory": Gilje, *To Swear Like a Sailor*, 66.

48 "carefully kept": R. H. Dana, *The Seaman's Friend: A Treatise on Practical Seamanship*, 200.

48 These logbooks: For more information on the growing interest in sea narratives during this era, see Edwards's *The Story of the Voyage.*

48 "in our present": Quoted in Edwards, *The Story of the Voyage*, 3.

49 "unequal" he: Lawrence Millechamp, *A Narrative of Commodore Anson's Voyage into the Great South Sea and Round the World,* NMM-JOD/36.

49 line of battle: For more information on naval battle tactics, see Sam Willis's insightful book *Fighting at Sea in the Eighteenth Century: The Art of Sailing Warfare.*

49 This formation: The naval historian Sam Willis writes that this line of battle formation was considered "the holy grail of fleet performance."

49 "surprise and confound": Quoted in Willis, *Fighting at Sea in the Eighteenth Century*, 137.

49 "Masthead there": Leech, *Thirty Years from Home*, 83.

50 invisible siege: For more information on the typhus epidemic that bedeviled the expedition, see, among other sources, Heaps's *Log of the Centurion*; Keppel's *The Life of Augustus, Viscount Keppel, Admiral of the White, and First Lord of the Admiralty in 1782–3*, vol. 1; Pascoe Thomas's *A True and Impartial Journal of a Voyage to the South-Seas*; Boyle Somerville's *Commodore Anson's Voyage into the South Seas and Around the World*; Walter's *A Voyage Round the World*; and Williams's *The Prize of All the Oceans.* Also see the various logbooks and muster books kept on each ship in Anson's squadron, which provide a vivid and unnerving record of the enormous toll.

50 "Our men grew": Keppel, *The Life of Augustus, Viscount Keppel, Admiral of the White, and First Lord of the Admiralty in 1782–3*, vol. 1, 24.

51 "machine for reducing": Henry Ettrick, "The Description and Draught of a Machine for Reducing Fractures of the Thigh," *Philosophical Transactions* 459, XLI (1741), 562.

51 "flow of words": Pascoe Thomas, *A True and Impartial Journal of a Voyage to the South-Seas*, 142.

52 "for a man": Millechamp, *A Narrative of Commodore Anson's Voyage into the Great South Sea and Round the World,* NMM-JOD/36.

52 "These a certain": *The Spectator*, August 25 and September 1, 1744.

52 "I was much": Tobias Smollett, *The Works of Tobias Smollett: The Adventures of Roderick Random*, vol. 2, 54.

52 "dropping silent tears": Quoted in H. G. Thursfield, ed., *Five Naval Journals, 1789–1817*, 35.

52 According to tradition: For further information on the rituals for burial at sea, see, among other sources, Adkins and Adkins's *Jack Tar*; Baynham's *From the Lower Deck*; Joan Druett's *Rough Medicine: Surgeons at Sea in the Age of Sail*; Pope's *Life in Nelson's Navy*; Rex Hickox's *18th Century Royal Navy*; and Thursfield's *Five Naval Journals, 1789–1817*.

53 "Death is at": Dana, *Two Years Before the Mast, and Twenty-Four Years After*, 37.

54 "sinners from": John Woodall's *De Peste, or the Plague*, preface.

54 "The *Industry* store-ship": Bulkeley and Cummins, *A Voyage to the South Seas*, 2.

55 more than sixty-five: The tally of the deaths is based on my examination of the muster books of the *Pearl*, the *Centurion*, the *Severn*, and the *Gloucester*. Because many of the *Wager*'s records were lost during the wreck, it is not possible to give a precise number of the deaths its company suffered from typhus, though they were considerable. I also do not include any deaths suffered on the *Trial* sloop and the two cargo ships, the *Industry* and the *Anna*. As a result, the figure I cite is conservative, and even so it shows that the toll was much greater than has generally been reported.

55 "not only terrible": Walter, *A Voyage Round the World*, 42.

55 "looked like blood": Bulkeley and Cummins. *A Voyage to the South Seas*, 4.

55 "We saw the": Ibid., 3.

56 "fled hither": Thomas, *A True and Impartial Journal of a Voyage to the South-Seas*, 12.

56 "very singular bird": Quoted in Keppel, *The Life of Augustus, Viscount Keppel, Admiral of the White, and First Lord of the Admiralty in 1782–3*, vol. 1, 26.

56 "One might imagine": Ibid.

56 the sickness: Typhus was no longer the sole cause of their suffering. Some of them had likely contracted yellow fever and malaria. Though the men complained of venomous mosquitoes, they did not realize these insects transmitted such potentially fatal illnesses. Instead, many officers attributed the fevers to the atmospheric conditions—what the schoolmaster, Thomas, called the "violent heat of the climate, and the bad air." The very name malaria reflects this misconception: it derives from the Italian words *mala* and *aria*, meaning bad air.

56 "absolutely necessary": Thomas, *A True and Impartial Journal of a Voyage to the South-Seas*, 10.

57 "cut and bruised": Millechamp, *A Narrative of Commodore Anson's Voyage into the Great South Sea and Round the World*, NMM-JOD/36.

57 "We lost sight": Bulkeley and Cummins, *A Voyage to the South Seas*, 3.

57 "They came within": Lieutenant Salt's report to the Admiralty, July 8, 1741, TNA-ADM 1/2099.

58 "I regret to": Somerville, *Commodore Anson's Voyage into the South Seas and Around the World*, 28.

58 "brave fellows": Anon., *A Voyage to the South-Seas, and to Many Other Parts of*

the World, Performed from the Month of September in the Year 1740, to June 1744, by Commodore Anson . . . by an Officer of the Squadron, 19.

58 "advancement in": Will and testament of Dandy Kidd, TNA-PROB 11.

58 those despots: Tyrannical captains were much less common than widely portrayed over the years. When a captain earned a reputation for excessive cruelty, he quickly found few would go to sea with him. The Admiralty also tried to root out these figures, if not for humane reasons, then for practical ones: an unhappy ship was an ineffectual one. One forecastle man observed that well-treated crews always outperformed those who felt "so degraded at being wantonly and unmanly beaten about, that their spirits were partly broken."

58 "How shall thy": Kempis, *The Christian's Pattern*, 41.

58 "It would end": Bulkeley and Cummins, *A Voyage to the South Seas*, 4.

CHAPTER 4

61 "command of temper": Scott, *Recollections of a Naval Life*, 41.

61 "faithful to that": Joseph Conrad, *Complete Short Stories*, 688.

62 Articles of War: For more information on these rules and regulations, see Rodger's *Articles of War: The Statutes Which Governed Our Fighting Navies, 1661, 1749, and 1886.*

62 round Cape Horn: In describing the conditions around Cape Horn, I relied on the firsthand journals and logbooks of seamen, especially those on Anson's voyage. I also benefited from various published accounts, including Adrian Flanagan's *The Cape Horners' Club: Tales of Triumph and Disaster at the World's Most Feared Cape*; Richard Hough's *The Blind Horn's Hate*; Robin Knox-Johnston's *Cape Horn: A Maritime History*; Dallas Murphy's *Rounding the Horn: Being a Story of Williwaws and Windjammers, Drake, Darwin, Murdered Missionaries and Naked Natives—a Deck's Eye View of Cape Horn;* and William F. Stark and Peter Stark's *The Last Time Around Cape Horn: The Historic 1949 Voyage of the Windjammer Pamir.*

63 a British expedition: Francis Drake on his expedition passed through the Strait of Magellan, but on the western coast of Patagonia his ship got caught in a storm and was blown near Cape Horn. Though he didn't round the Horn, he found the route, which was later named the Drake Passage.

63 "the most mad": Quoted in David Laing Purves, *The English Circumnavigators: The Most Remarkable Voyages Round the World*, 59.

63 "At those ends": Melville, *White-Jacket*, 151–53.

63 "blind Horn's hate": Rudyard Kipling, *The Writings in Prose and Verse of Rudyard Kipling*, 168.

63 To determine his: For more information on navigating and longitude, see Dava Sobel's comprehensive account, *Longitude: The True Story of a Lone Genius Who Solved the Greatest Scientific Problem of His Time.* Also see two other excellent sources: Lloyd A. Brown's *The Story of Maps*, and William J. H. Andrewes's *The Quest for Longitude.*

64 first to circumnavigate: Magellan himself did not complete the voyage around the world. In 1521, he was killed during a fight with inhabitants of what is today the Philippines, who had resisted his attempts to convert them to Christianity.

64 "will not speak": Quoted in Sobel, *Longitude*, foreword, xiii.

64 "By reason of": Ibid., 52.

65 "yelps of": Ibid., 7.

65 "very ingenious": Quoted in Lloyd A. Brown, *The Story of Maps*, 232.

65 "the technique of": Sobel, *Longitude*, 14.

66 "We had here": Thomas, *A True and Impartial Journal of a Voyage to the South-Seas*, 18.

66 "The only things": Millechamp, *A Narrative of Commodore Anson's Voyage into the Great South Sea and Round the World,* NMM-JOD/36.

67 "crafty lawyers": Quoted in Samuel Bawlf, *The Secret Voyage of Sir Francis Drake, 1577–1580*, 104.

67 "Lo! This": Ibid., 106.

67 "seat of infernal": Journal of Saumarez, printed in Williams, ed., *Documents Relating to Anson's Voyage Round the World*, 165.

67 "half fish": Millechamp, *A Narrative of Commodore Anson's Voyage into the Great South Sea and Round the World,* NMM-JOD/36.

67 "It is incredible": Gallagher, ed., *Byron's Journal of His Circumnavigation, 1764–1766*, 62.

67 "rather a dangerous": Ibid., 59.

68 "a pleasing dreadful": Millechamp, *A Narrative of Commodore Anson's Voyage into the Great South Sea and Round the World,* NMM-JOD/36.

68 "The land sometimes": Ibid.

68 "one cheerful": Thomas, *A True and Impartial Journal of a Voyage to the South-Seas*, 19.

68 "so tall that": Antonio Pigafetta and R. A. Skelton, *Magellan's Voyage: A Narrative of the First Circumnavigation*, 46.

69 "you will answer": Orders from Anson to Captain Edward Legge on Jan. 18, 1741, TNA-ADM 1/2040.

69 "for islands of": Journal of Saumarez, printed in Williams, ed., *Documents Relating to Anson's Voyage Round the World*, 165.

70 "Though Tierra": Walter, *A Voyage Round the World*, 79.

70 "loomed up": Melville, *White-Jacket*, 183.

70 "a proper nursery": Millechamp, *A Narrative of Commodore Anson's Voyage into the Great South Sea and Round the World,* NMM-JOD/36.

70 *Instead of the:* Samuel Taylor Coleridge, *The Rime of the Ancient Mariner*, 18.

70 "I remember one": Millechamp, *A Narrative of Commodore Anson's Voyage into the Great South Sea and Round the World,* NMM-JOD/36.

71 "The morning of": Walter, *A Voyage Round the World*, 80–81.

71 "a prodigious fine": Logbook of Captain Matthew Mitchell of the *Gloucester*, March 8, 1741, TNA-ADM 51/402.

71 "We could not": Walter, *A Voyage Round the World*, 80.

71 "The force of": William F. Stark and Peter Stark, *The Last Time Around Cape Horn: The Historic 1949 Voyage of the Windjammer Pamir*, 176–77.

72 "crushing the lives": John Kenlon, *Fourteen Years a Sailor*, 216.

72 "very near being": Byron, *The Narrative of the Honourable John Byron*, 4.

72 "excellent seaman": Bulkeley and Cummins, *A Voyage to the South Seas*, 73.

CHAPTER 5

73 "Below forty degrees": *Los Angeles Times*, Jan. 5, 2007.

74 "such violence": Gallagher, ed., *Byron's Journal of His Circumnavigation, 1764–1766*, 32.

74 "a luxuriance": Walter, *A Voyage Round the World*, 109.

74 "with such excessive": Thomas, *A True and Impartial Journal of a Voyage to the South-Seas*, 142.

74 "the most violent": Gallagher, ed., *Byron's Journal of His Circumnavigation, 1764–1766*, 116.

74 "Still more astonishing": Walter, *A Voyage Round the World*, 109.

75 "strange dejection": Ibid., 108.

75 "the falling down": Quoted in Lamb, *Scurvy*, 56.

75 descend into lunacy: During the outbreak, Lieutenant Saumarez observed that some of the ailing men displayed "idiotism, lunacy, convulsions."

75 "got into their": Anon., *A Voyage to the South-Seas, and to Many Other Parts of the World, Performed from the Month of September in the Year 1740, to June 1744, by Commodore Anson . . . by an Officer of the Squadron*, 233.

75 They were suffering: For more information on scurvy, see several excellent sources. They include Kenneth J. Carpenter's *The History of Scurvy and Vitamin C*; David Harvie's *Limeys: The Conquest of Scurvy*; Stephen R. Bown's *Scurvy: How a Surgeon, a Mariner, and a Gentleman Solved the Greatest Medical Mystery of the Age of Sail*; Jonathan Lamb's *Scurvy: The Disease of Discovery*, which is especially insightful on the psychic effects of the disorder on seamen; James Watt's "The Medical Bequest of Disaster at Sea: Commodore Anson's Circumnavigation, 1740–44"; and Eleanora C. Gordon's "Scurvy and Anson's Voyage Round the World, 1740–1744: An Analysis of the Royal Navy's Worst Outbreak." To understand how the disease was perceived and misperceived during the Age of Sail, I also drew on medical texts from that period, such as James Lind's *An Essay on the Most Effectual Means of Preserving the Health of Seamen in the Royal Navy*; Richard Mead's *The Medical Works of Richard Mead*; and Thomas Trotter's *Medical and Chemical Essays*. For how the disease specifically ravaged Anson's squadron, see the crew members' diaries, correspondence, and logbooks.

75 "the plague": Quoted in Kenneth J. Carpenter, *The History of Scurvy and Vitamin C*, 17.

75 "I cannot": Letter from Anson to James Naish, December, 1742, printed in Williams, ed., *Documents Relating to Anson's Voyage Round the World*, 152.

75 "The greatest part": Byron, *The Narrative of the Honourable John Byron*, 8–9.

76 "bones, after the": Anon., *A Voyage to the South-Seas, and to Many Other Parts of the World, Performed from the Month of September in the Year 1740, to June 1744, by Commodore Anson . . . by an Officer of the Squadron*, 233.

76 "black and yellow": Richard Mead, *The Medical Works of Richard Mead*, 441.

76 the cause: Others speculated that scurvy was the result of food supplies that had begun to spoil. Another, crueler theory held by some officers was that the sick seamen themselves were to blame—that their lethargy, rather than being a symptom of the disease, had caused it. On the verge of death, these poor men were kicked and beaten while being cussed as idle, lazy, skulking dogs.

76 "entire secret": Thomas, *A True and Impartial Journal of a Voyage to the South-Seas*, 143.

76 "It was a": Bulkeley and Cummins, *A Voyage to the South Seas*, 6.

76 the bizarre sight: Another unfounded cure for scurvy was perhaps even more disconcerting to behold. Patients were submerged, as a text for sea surgeons recommended, "in a good bath of the blood of beasts, either cows, horse, asses, goats or sheeps."

76 "twenty men's heads": A. Beckford Bevan and H. B. Wolryche-Whitmore, eds., *The Journals of Captain Frederick Hoffman, R.N., 1793–1814*, 80.

76 "many marvelous": Marjorie H. Nicolson, "Ward's 'Pill and Drop' and Men of Letters," *Journal of the History of Ideas* 29, no. 2 (1968), 178.

76 "very violently": Thomas, *A True and Impartial Journal of a Voyage to the South-Seas*, 143.

77 "I could plainly": Journal of Saumarez, printed in Williams, ed., *Documents Relating to Anson's Voyage Round the World*, 166.

77 "died before they": Walter, *A Voyage Round the World*, 110.

78 "Nothing was": Millechamp, *A Narrative of Commodore Anson's Voyage into the Great South Sea and Round the World*, NMM-JOD/36.

78 "So miserable": Logbook of Captain Matthew Mitchell of the *Gloucester*, TNA-ADM 51/402.

78 "so weak": Captain Edward Legge to Secretary of the Admiralty, July 4, 1741, TNA-ADM 1/2040.

78 "So great": John Philips, *An Authentic Journal of the Late Expedition Under the Command of Commodore Anson*, 46.

78 "great diligence": Captain Legge to Secretary of the Admiralty, July 4, 1741, TNA-ADM 1/2040.

79 "I have omitted": Keppel, *The Life of Augustus, Viscount Keppel, Admiral of the White, and First Lord of the Admiralty in 1782–3*, vol. 1, 31.

79 "Henry Cheap": *Centurion*'s muster book, TNA-ADM 36/0556.

79 "my grand-dad's": George Gordon Byron, *The Complete Works of Lord Byron*, 720.

79 "Without a grave": Ibid., 162.

79 "total destruction": Walter, *A Voyage Round the World*, 107.

79 "Getting thither": Ibid., 113.

80 "When his clothes": Woodes Rogers, *A Cruising Voyage Round the World*, 128.

80 "so that he": Ibid., 126.

80 "the absolute monarch": Ibid., 131.

80 As a tale: The reverberations of the stories of Selkirk and Crusoe continue into the modern age. See, for instance, the 2015 survival film *The Martian.*

80 "long wished": Millechamp, *A Narrative of Commodore Anson's Voyage into the Great South Sea and Round the World,* NMM-JOD/36.

80 "like two black": Logbook of Captain Mitchell of the *Gloucester,* TNA-ADM 51/402.

80 "Our seamen": Millechamp, *A Narrative of Commodore Anson's Voyage into the Great South Sea and Round the World,* NMM-JOD/36.

CHAPTER 6

82 "perfect hurricane": Byron, *The Narrative of the Honourable John Byron,* 9. The Reverend Walter account also refers to the storms as the "perfect hurricane."

82 "We had": Bulkeley and Cummins, *A Voyage to the South Seas,* 5.

82 "greater sea": Captain Legge to secretary of the Admiralty, July 4, 1741, TNA-ADM 1/2040.

82 to describe it: One officer in the squadron said simply of the conditions, "A more violent storm never blew from the heavens."

82 "A raging sea": Thomas, *A True and Impartial Journal of a Voyage to the South-Seas,* 24.

83 "Down I came": Ibid., 25.

83 where he lay: Even after Schoolmaster Thomas recovered from the fall, he continued to suffer. "I have ever since had a violent pain in that shoulder, very often accompanied with an inability to pull on my own garments, to turn my hand behind my back, or even to lift a pound of weight with it," he wrote in his journal.

83 "carried me": Bulkeley and Cummins, *A Voyage to the South Seas,* 6.

83 "Do nothing": Ibid.

84 lost his grip: He was not the only member of the expedition to fall overboard and drown. Many others did as well. In one instance, the *Centurion*'s midshipman Keppel wrote in his logbook, "Martin Enough, a brisk seaman, in going up the main-shrouds, fell overboard, and was lost—much wanted, and regretted."

84 "He might continue": Walter, *A Voyage Round the World,* 85.

84 *Wash'd headlong:* Eva Hope, ed., *The Poetical Works of William Cowper,* 254.

85 "so much worm-eaten": Thomas, *A True and Impartial Journal of a Voyage to the South-Seas,* 145.

85 "if it had": Captain Murray's report to Admiralty, July 10, 1741, TNA-ADM 1/2099.

85 "A quick, subtle": Keppel, *The Life of Augustus, Viscount Keppel, Admiral of the White, and First Lord of the Admiralty in 1782–3,* vol. 1, 32.

85 "crazy ship": Walter, *A Voyage Round the World,* 114.

86 "My rigging": Bulkeley and Cummins, *A Voyage to the South Seas*, 6.
87 "My ship's company": Report from Cheap to Richard Lindsey, Feb. 26, 1744, JS.
87 "resolution not": Captain Murray's report to Admiralty, July 10, 1741, TNA-ADM 1/2099.
87 "Lost sight": Bulkeley and Cummins, *A Voyage to the South Seas*, 5.
88 "lag designedly": Thomas, *A True and Impartial Journal of a Voyage to the South-Seas*, 24.
88 "on some desolate": Walter, *A Voyage Round the World*, 106.
88 "This was the": Bulkeley and Cummins, *A Voyage to the South Seas*, 7.

CHAPTER 7

89 "rheumatism" and "asthma": Report from Cheap to Lindsey, Feb. 26, 1744, JS.
90 "cut and run": This is another nautical term, which derived from when a captain, to hastily escape an enemy, would order his men to "cut" the anchor cable and "run" speedily downwind.
90 "My attachment to": Campbell, *The Sequel to Bulkeley and Cummins's "Voyage to the South Seas,"* 20.
90 "Let the fate": Report from Cheap to Lindsey, Feb. 26, 1744, JS.
90 "stubborn defiance": Byron, *The Narrative of the Honourable John Byron*, 7.
90 "We can't be": Bulkeley and Cummins, *A Voyage to the South Seas*, 9.
91 "condition the ship": Ibid., 39.
91 "I would have": This and subsequent quotes in scene, ibid., 9–10.
91 "a very great": Ibid., 8.
92 it was "impossible": Ibid., 10.
92 "I saw the": Ibid., 11.
92 "Sway the foreyard": Ibid.
93 execute a jibe: seamen then used the term to "wear" when referring to jibing.
93 "I was taken": Report from Cheap to Lindsey, Feb. 26, 1744, JS.
94 "dreadful beyond": Byron, *The Narrative of the Honourable John Byron,* 18.
94 "In this dreadful": Ibid., 10.
94 "Six foot of": John Cummins's court-martial testimony, April 15, 1746, TNA-ADM 1/5288.
94 "full of water": Report from Cheap to Lindsey, Feb. 26, 1744, JS.
95 "bereaved of all": Byron, *The Narrative of the Honourable John Byron*, 12.
95 "My friends": Ibid., 13.
96 "made a scene": George Gordon Byron, *The Complete Works of Lord Byron*, 695.
96 "Providentially we": Byron, *The Narrative of the Honourable John Byron*, 14.

CHAPTER 8

99 "willfulness, negligence": Rodger, *Articles of War*, 17.
99 "contrary to my": Report from Cheap to Lindsey, Feb. 26, 1744, JS.

99 "We expected": Bulkeley and Cummins, *A Voyage to the South Seas*, 13.
100 "sign of culture": Byron, *The Narrative of the Honourable John Byron*, 17.
100 "We now thought": Ibid., 14.
100 four such vessels: For the estimated size of these transport boats, see Layman, *The Wager Disaster.* For more detailed descriptions of the making and design of these boats, see Lavery, *The Arming and Fitting of English Ships of War, 1600–1815.*
100 "Go and save": Campbell, *The Sequel to Bulkeley and Cummins's "Voyage to the South Seas,"* 13.
100 "Don't mind": Ibid.
100 "if the people's": John Jones's court-martial testimony, April 15, 1746, TNA-ADM 1/5288.
100 "He gave his": Byron, *The Narrative of the Honourable John Byron*, 15.
101 lifted the barge: Bulkeley wrote that the barge was freed first, but other accounts indicate that it was the yawl.
101 "We had several": Bulkeley and Cummins, *A Voyage to the South Seas*, 13.
102 "We have good": Ibid., 14.
102 "I was forced": Byron, *The Narrative of the Honourable John Byron*, 16.
102 "We helped him": Campbell, *The Sequel to Bulkeley and Cummins's "Voyage to the South Seas,"* 14.
103 The castaways huddled: Bulkeley and the carpenter, Cummins, joined the group a bit later, because they had been on the ship gathering supplies.
103 "It is natural": Byron, *The Narrative of the Honourable John Byron*, 17–18.
104 "faint, benumbed": Ibid, 18.
104 tangled, marshy grass: My descriptions of the island are based not only on the accounts of the castaways but also on my own voyage to the island and extensive exploration of it.
104 "Our uncertainty": Byron, *The Narrative of the Honourable John Byron*, 18.
104 "certainly lost": Campbell, *The Sequel to Bulkeley and Cummins's "Voyage to the South Seas,"* 14.
105 "Some were singing": Ibid.
105 "Damn ye!": Ibid., 15.
106 "like a parcel": Bulkeley and Cummins, *A Voyage to the South Seas*, 14.

CHAPTER 9

107 "We had most": Byron, *The Narrative of the Honourable John Byron*, 19.
107 "The very sea": Ibid., vi–vii.
107 "seized with the": Ibid., 20.
108 "the soul": P. Parker King, *Narrative of the Surveying Voyages of His Majesty's Ships Adventure and Beagle*, vol. 1, 179. In his quote, King is borrowing a line from the poet James Thomson.
108 "Being strongly": Byron, *The Narrative of the Honourable John Byron*, 21.
108 "hideous spectacles": Ibid., 26.
108 "It rained so": Bulkeley and Cummins, *A Voyage to the South Seas*, 14.

108 "impossible for us": Byron, *The Narrative of the Honourable John Byron*, 25.
109 "to contrive something": Bulkeley and Cummins, *A Voyage to the South Seas*, 15.
109 "murmurings and discontent": Ibid., 18.
109 "things began": Ibid., xxviii.
109 "their own masters": Ibid.
109 "we might probably": Ibid., 21.
109 "always acted": Ibid., xxiv.
110 *Presence of mind:* Ibid., 212.
110 "The wood here": Byron, *The Narrative of the Honourable John Byron*, 53.
111 "large kind of": Ibid., 51.
111 "the only feathered": Ibid.
111 "As if to": Anne Chapman, *European Encounters with the Yamana People of Cape Horn, Before and After Darwin*, 104–5.
111 "The woods were": Byron, *The Narrative of the Honourable John Byron*, 52.
111 "very large": Ibid., 53.
111 "As for food": Bulkeley and Cummins, *A Voyage to the South Seas*, 15.
111 "scarce to be": Byron, *The Narrative of the Honourable John Byron*, vi.
112 "a scene": Ibid., 32.

CHAPTER 10

113 Minnesota Starvation Experiment: For more information on the experiment, see Ancel Keys, Josef Brozek, Austin Henschel, and Henry Longstreet Taylor's study, *The Biology of Human Starvation;* David Baker and Natacha Keramidas's "The Psychology of Hunger," *American Psychological Association* 44, no. 9 (October 2013), 66; Nathaniel Philbrick's *In the Heart of the Sea: The Tragedy of the Whaleship Essex*; and Todd Tucker's *The Great Starvation Experiment: Ancel Keys and the Men Who Starved for Science.*
113 "How many people": Quoted in Todd Tucker, *The Great Starvation Experiment: Ancel Keys and the Men Who Starved for Science*, 139.
114 "I'm going": Ibid., 102.
114 "how thin": Quoted in Philbrick, *In the Heart of the Sea*, 171.
114 their environment: When Charles Darwin later visited Patagonia, he marveled at how the "inanimate works of nature—rock, ice, snow, wind, and water—all warring with each other, yet combined against man—here reigned in absolute sovereignty."
114 "every man": Thomas Hobbes, *Leviathan, or, The Matter, Forme, & Power of a Common-wealth Ecclesiasticall and Civil*, 91.
114 "mutinous assemblies": Rodger, *Articles of War*, 16–17.
114 "My first care": Report from Cheap to Lindsey, Feb. 26, 1744, JS.
115 "The difficulties": Byron, *The Narrative of the Honourable John Byron*, 27.
115 "Found several": Bulkeley and Cummins, *A Voyage to the South Seas*, 19.
115 "Got out several": Ibid., 17.
115 "By the Captain's": Campbell, *The Sequel to Bulkeley and Cummins's "Voyage to the South Seas,"* 21.

116 "in our situation": Ibid., 29.
116 "blown up": Bulkeley and Cummins, *A Voyage to the South Seas*, 18.
116 "They were so": Ibid., 16.
117 "the most frugal": Byron, *The Narrative of the Honourable John Byron*, 27.
117 "Our stomachs": Bulkeley and Cummins, *A Voyage to the South Seas*, 58.
117 "expressed the greatest": Campbell, *The Sequel to Bulkeley and Cummins's "Voyage to the South Seas,"* 19.
117 "If it had": Ibid., 21.
117 "a good and": Bulkeley and Cummins, *A Voyage to the South Seas*, 55.
117 "I had the": Campbell, *The Sequel to Bulkeley and Cummins's "Voyage to the South Seas,"* 31.
117 "This poor stuff": Ibid.
118 "punts, cask-boats": Bulkeley and Cummins, *A Voyage to the South Seas*, 47.
118 "in quest of": Byron, *The Narrative of the Honourable John Byron*, 48.
119 steamer duck: Charles Darwin compared the way this type of bird scurries across the sea to how "the common house-duck escapes when pursued by a dog."
119 "the velocity": Byron, *The Narrative of the Honourable John Byron*, 51.
119 "This is a rich": Bulkeley and Cummins, *A Voyage to the South Seas*, 30.
120 "Providence made": Ibid., 174.
120 "careful in writing": Ibid., 14.
120 "irregular habitations": Byron, *The Narrative of the Honourable John Byron*, 99.
120 "a kind of village": Ibid.
121 "Hunting all": Quote extracts come from the journals of Byron and Bulkeley.
122 "Ill humour and": Byron, *The Narrative of the Honourable John Byron*, 35.
122 "The store tent": Bulkeley and Cummins, *A Voyage to the South Seas*, 27.
122 "most heinous crime": Byron, *The Narrative of the Honourable John Byron*, 67.

CHAPTER 11

123 "It freezes": Bulkeley and Cummins, *A Voyage to the South Seas*, 17.
123 "Their clothing": Byron, *The Narrative of the Honourable John Byron*, 33–34.
123 "cur-like looking": Ibid., 137.
123 "It was evident": Ibid., 33.
124 They were a: For information concerning the Kawésqar and other inhabitants of the region, I drew on several sources. They included Junius B. Bird's *Travels and Archaeology in South Chile*; Lucas E Bridges's *Uttermost Part of the Earth: Indians of Tierra del Fuego*; Arnoldo Canclini's *The Fuegian Indians: Their Life, Habits, and History*; Chapman's *European Encounters with the Yamana People of Cape Horn, Before and After Darwin*; John M. Cooper's *Analytical and Critical Bibliography of the Tribes of Tierra del Fuego and Adjacent Territory*; Joseph Emperaire's *Los Nomades del Mar*; Martin Gusinde's *The Lost Tribes of Tierra del Fuego: Selk'nam, Yamana, Kawésqar*; Diego Carabias Amor's essay "The Spanish Attempt Salvage," published in Layman's *The Wager Disaster*; Samuel Kirkland Lothrop's *The Indians of Tierra del Fuego*; Colin McEwan,

Luis Alberto Borrero, and Alfredo Prieto's edited *Patagonia: Natural History, Prehistory, and Ethnography at the Uttermost End of the Earth*; Omar Reyes's *The Settlement of the Chonos Archipelago, Western Patagonia, Chile*; and Julian H. Steward's *Handbook of South American Indians*. In addition, I benefited from the detailed information and exhibits about the Kawésqar and Yaghan at the Martin Gusinde Anthropological Museum and the Chilean Museum of Pre-Columbian Art.

124 party of Kawésqar: Over the years foreigners often referred to these people by other names as well, including Alacaluf. The descendants, however, consider Kawésqar their authentic name.

125 no credible evidence: The Yaghan didn't even consume vultures, because they might have pecked on human carcasses.

126 "Home could": Chapman, *European Encounters with the Yamana People of Cape Horn, Before and After Darwin*, 186.

126 "happy people": Instructions to Commodore Anson, 1740, printed in Williams, ed., *Documents Relating to Anson's Voyage Round the World*, 41.

127 "When they": Pigafetta and Skelton, *Magellan's Voyage*, 48.

127 several Kawésqar were abducted: In 2008, the remains of five of these kidnap victims were discovered in a collection at the Anthropological Institute and Museum at the University of Zurich. They were eventually returned to Chile and given a proper Kawésqar burial—the bones anointed with oil, placed in protective sea-lion skins and reed baskets, and deposited in a cave. For more information, see "Remains of Indigenous Abductees Back Home After 130 Years," *Spiegel*, Jan. 13, 2010.

127 "signs of friendship": Byron, *The Narrative of the Honourable John Byron*, 33.

127 tried to communicate: For more information on the Kawésqar's distinctive language, see Jack Hitt's piece "Say No More," published in *The New York Times Magazine*, February 29, 2004. He notes how the Kawésqar had numerous subtle distinctions for denoting the past: "You can say, 'A bird flew by.' And by the use of different tenses, you can mean a few seconds ago, a few days ago, a time so long ago that you were not the original observer of the bird (but you know the observer yourself) and, finally, a mythological past, a tense the Kawésqar use to suggest that the story is so old that it no longer possesses fresh descriptive truth but rather that other truth which emerges from stories that retain their narrative power despite constant repetition."

127 "They uttered no": Byron, *The Narrative of the Honourable John Byron*, 34.

128 "They were strangely": Ibid., 33.

128 "extremely courteous": Campbell, *The Sequel to Bulkeley and Cummins's "Voyage to the South Seas,"* 20.

128 "treated them": Ibid., 19.

128 "the largest and": Bulkeley and Cummins, *A Voyage to the South Seas*, 16.

128 "good example": Campbell, *The Sequel to Bulkeley and Cummins's "Voyage to the South Seas,"* 20.

128 "much reconciled": Byron, *The Narrative of the Honourable John Byron*, 45.

128 "They bend": Ibid., 125–26.

128 brought this bark: The Kawésqar also often used pelts from seals to cover the roofs and walls of their dwellings.
129 "The Indians are": Bulkeley and Cummins, *A Voyage to the South Seas*, 27.
129 "Diving to the": Byron, *The Narrative of the Honourable John Byron*, 133.
129 "from which several": Ibid., 134.
129 "Their agility": Bulkeley and Cummins, *A Voyage to the South Seas*, 28.
129 "it seems as": Byron, *The Narrative of the Honourable John Byron*, 133.
130 "very sagacious": Ibid., 100.
130 "This method": Bulkeley and Cummins, *A Voyage to the South Seas*, 58.
130 "now subject": Byron, *The Narrative of the Honourable John Byron*, 45.
130 "Could we have": Ibid.

CHAPTER 12

131 "This creature grew": Byron, *The Narrative of the Honourable John Byron*, 36.
131 "shorter allowance": Bulkeley and Cummins, *A Voyage to the South Seas*, 29.
131 "Our living": Ibid., 54.
131 "beat with such": Ibid., 56.
132 "ever met": Ibid, 30.
132 "are so extremely": Ibid., 46.
132 "we thought no": Ibid., 55.
132 "The pressing calls": Byron, *The Narrative of the Honourable John Byron*, 47.
132 *What could they*: George Gordon, Lord Byron, *The Complete Works of Lord Byron*, 715.
133 "rambled wither": Campbell, *The Sequel to Bulkeley and Cummins's "Voyage to the South Seas,"* 20.
133 "stabbed in": Byron, *The Narrative of the Honourable John Byron*, 40.
133 "no less than": Ibid., 38.
133 "the spirits": Ibid, 102–3.
133 "continually exclaiming": Campbell, *The Sequel to Bulkeley and Cummins's "Voyage to the South Seas,"* 20.
134 "state of anarchy": Ibid., 17.
134 "absolutely uncertain": Ibid., 20.
134 "Liking none": Byron, *The Narrative of the Honourable John Byron*, 36.
134 "really make": Bulkeley and Cummins, *A Voyage to the South Seas*, 57.
134 "lest he": Thomas à Kempis, *The Christian's Pattern, or, A Treatise of the Imitation of Jesus Christ*, 20.
135 "in the same": Bulkeley and Cummins, *A Voyage to the South Seas*, 44.
135 "villainous practices": Ibid., 47.
135 to "consult": Ibid.
136 "Strict orders": Ibid., 20.
136 "fatigued with": Byron, *The Narrative of the Honourable John Byron*, 28.
136 "disturbed by": Ibid., 53.
136 "deep and plain": Ibid., 56.

136 "upwards of": Bulkeley and Cummins, *A Voyage to the South Seas*, 44.
137 "I really think": Ibid.
137 "This was not": Ibid.
137 "governed by": Ibid., 60.
137 public trial: For more information on how courts-martial were run, see John D. Byrn, *Crime and Punishment in the Royal Navy*; Markus Eder, *Crime and Punishment in the Royal Navy of the Seven Years' War, 1755–1763*; David Hannay, *Naval Courts Martial*; John M'Arthur, *Principles and Practice of Naval and Military Courts Martial*; Rodger, *Articles of War*; and Rodger, *The Wooden World*.
137 several officers: Cheap and other naval officers oversaw the courts-martial of seamen, while Pemberton and his officers presided over any trials of marines.
137 "crime did not": Bulkeley and Cummins, *A Voyage to the South Seas*, 44.
137 "I am sure": Quoted in Henry Baynham, *From the Lower Deck*, 63.
138 "a way next": Bulkeley and Cummins, *A Voyage to the South Seas*, 44.
138 "lacerated back": Leech, *Thirty Years from Home*, 116.
138 "When a poor": Quoted in H. G. Thursfield, ed., *Five Naval Journals, 1789–1817*, 256.
139 "I endeavoured": Report from Cheap to Lindsey, Feb. 26, 1744, JS.
139 "We, in compassion": Byron, *The Narrative of the Honourable John Byron*, 67.
139 "dead and stiff": Ibid., 68.

CHAPTER 13

140 "perpetuate their": Byron, *The Narrative of the Honourable John Byron*, 36–37.
140 "all sense": Report from Cheap to Lindsey, Feb. 26, 1744, JS.
140 "the people": Bulkeley and Cummins, *A Voyage to the South Seas*, 20.
141 "the repeated troubles": Report from Cheap to Lindsey, Feb. 26, 1744, JS.
141 "jealous to the": Byron, *The Narrative of the Honourable John Byron*, 41.
141 "With what": Bulkeley and Cummins, *A Voyage to the South Seas*, 19.
141 "This day": Ibid., 18.
142 "Though Shelvocke": Ibid., 19.
142 "proceeded to extremities": Report from Cheap to Lindsey, Feb. 26, 1744, JS.

CHAPTER 14

143 "weltering in": Byron, *The Narrative of the Honourable John Byron*, 40.
143 "took me": Ibid.
143 "notorious disrespectful": Bulkeley and Cummins, *A Voyage to the South Seas*, 22.
143 "The unhappy victim": Byron, *The Narrative of the Honourable John Byron*, 42.
143 "But, on consideration": Bulkeley and Cummins, *A Voyage to the South Seas*, 21.
144 "I see you": Ibid., 22.
144 "open sedition": Byron, *The Narrative of the Honourable John Byron*, 41.

144 "smothered for": Ibid., 42.
144 "are always compound": John Woodall, *The Surgions Mate*, 140.
145 "This was looked": Bulkeley and Cummins, *A Voyage to the South Seas*, 23.
145 "who seeth": Woodall, *The Surgions Mate*, 2.
145 "If he lives": Bulkeley and Cummins, *A Voyage to the South Seas*, 24.
145 "for God is": Woodall, *The Surgions Mate*, 139.
146 "Departed this": Bulkeley and Cummins, *A Voyage to the South Seas*, 25.
146 "greatly beloved": Byron, *The Narrative of the Honourable John Byron*, 42.
146 "extremely affected": Ibid., 41.
146 "sundry ways": Bulkeley and Cummins, *A Voyage to the South Seas*, 25.
146 "We buried": Ibid.

CHAPTER 15

147 "the love of": Bulkeley and Cummins, *A Voyage to the South Seas*, xxviii.
147 "any composure": Ibid., 52.
148 "In this affair": Ibid., 20.
148 "so necessary": Byron, *The Narrative of the Honourable John Byron*, 43–44.
149 honed the design: For how the vessel was constructed, I benefited from the deep expertise of Brian Lavery, a leading naval historian and authority on shipbuilding, who patiently guided me through the process.
149 "They are in": Bulkeley and Cummins, *A Voyage to the South Seas*, 46.
150 "We need not": Ibid., 66.
150 "At any time": Narborough, Tasman, Wood, and Martens, *An Account of Several Late Voyages and Discoveries to the South and North*, 116.
151 "mad undertaking": Bulkeley and Cummins, *A Voyage to the South Seas*, xxviii.
151 "A man may": Narborough, Tasman, Wood, and Martens, *An Account of Several Late Voyages and Discoveries to the South and North*, 118.
151 "desperate diseases": Bulkeley and Cummins, *A Voyage to the South Seas*, xxviii.
151 "here are ducks": Narborough, Tasman, Wood, and Martens, *An Account of Several Late Voyages and Discoveries to the South and North*, 119.
151 "Our going": Bulkeley and Cumamins, *A Voyage to the South Seas*, 31.
153 "The loss": Ibid., 73.
153 WE, whose: Ibid., 33.
154 "This paper": For this and subsequent quotes in scene, ibid., 36–40.
156 as "bribery": Ibid., 48.
156 "all in a": Campbell, *The Sequel to Bulkeley and Cummins's "Voyage to the South Seas,"* 17.
157 "We believe": Bulkeley and Cummins, *A Voyage to the South Seas*, 45.

CHAPTER 16

158 "violent shocks": Bulkeley and Cummins, *A Voyage to the South Seas*, 48.
158 "the rules": Ibid., 60.

159 "A mutiny is": Quoted in Elihu Rose, "The Anatomy of Mutiny," *Armed Forces & Society*, 561.

159 "treasonable practices": David Farr, *Major-General Thomas Harrison: Millenarianism, Fifth Monarchism and the English Revolution, 1616–1660*, 258.

160 "We imagined": Bulkeley and Cummins, *A Voyage to the South Seas*, 61.

160 "justify himself": Ibid., 49.

160 "which must": Ibid.

161 "in the most": Ibid., 67.

161 "For England": For this and subsequent quotes in scene, ibid., 51–52.

161 "Yes, sir": Ibid., 56.

161 "my mutineers": Report from Cheap to Lindsey, Feb. 26, 1744,

162 "compelled for": Bulkeley and Cummins, *A Voyage to the South Seas*, 52.

162 "Here the Captain": Ibid.

162 "I sat": Byron, *The Narrative of the Honourable John Byron*, 111.

163 "last extremity": Ibid., 30.

163 a solution: According to Brian Lavery, the authority on shipbuilding, this was the method they had to employ.

164 "somewhat rudely": Campbell, *The Sequel to Bulkeley and Cummins's "Voyage to the South Seas,"* 23.

164 "dangerous to suffer": Bulkeley and Cummins, *A Voyage to the South Seas*, 62.

164 "Gentlemen, do": For this and subsequent quotes in scene, ibid., 63–64.

165 "We now looked": Campbell, *The Sequel to Bulkeley and Cummins's "Voyage to the South Seas,"* 26.

166 "Our flour": Byron, *The Narrative of the Honourable John Byron*, 60–61.

166 "the good of": Bulkeley and Cummins, *A Voyage to the South Seas*, 67.

167 "rather be shot": Ibid., 66.

167 "Let him stay": Ibid., 67.

167 "in so small": Ibid., 74.

167 "all in pieces": Report from Cheap to Lindsey, Feb. 26, 1744, JS.

167 "a very small": Ibid.

168 Just seven seceders: Bulkeley notes that there were eight seceders, but all other accounts, including those by Cheap, Byron, and Campbell, indicate there were seven of them.

168 "We are so": Bulkeley and Cummins, *A Voyage to the South Seas*, 76–77.

168 "utmost insolence": Report from Cheap to Lindsey, Feb. 26, 1744, JS.

168 "This was the": Bulkeley and Cummins, *A Voyage to the South Seas*, 72.

CHAPTER 17

173 "I had all": Byron, *The Narrative of the Honourable John Byron*, 59.

176 "the Honourable": Bulkeley and Cummins, *A Voyage to the South Seas*, 76.

176 "Damn you!": Campbell, *The Sequel to Bulkeley and Cummins's "Voyage to the South Seas,"* 28.

176 "John!": Bulkeley and Cummins, *A Voyage to the South Seas*, 77.

CHAPTER 18

178 "makes the air": Bulkeley and Cummins, *A Voyage to the South Seas*, 81.
178 "the greatest": Ibid., 84.
179 "Nothing but": Ibid.
179 "what Providence": Ibid., 107.
180 "We are now": Ibid., 84.
180 "new life": Ibid., 85.
181 "Great uneasiness": Ibid., 97.
181 "all persons": Ibid., 88.
181 "the preservation": Ibid., 87.
182 "so desolate": Narborough, Tasman, Wood, and Martens, *An Account of Several Late Voyages and Discoveries to the South and North*, 78.
182 "I never": Bulkeley and Cummins, *A Voyage to the South Seas*, 89.
182 "intolerable tempest": Francis Drake and Francis Fletcher, *The World Encompassed by Sir Francis Drake, Being His Next Voyage to That to Nombre de Dois*, 82.
182 "We prayed": Bulkeley and Cummins, *A Voyage to the South Seas*, 90.
183 "We call": Ibid.
183 "If we are": Ibid., 87.
183 "ripe for": Ibid., 86.
183 "The people": Ibid.
183 "raw as soon": Ibid., 95.
183 "This poor creature": Ibid., 93.
184 "Persons who": Ibid., 94–95.
184 "if ever there": Ibid., 96.

CHAPTER 19

185 "riotous applications": Byron, *The Narrative of the Honourable John Byron*, 65.
185 "He now became": Campbell, *The Sequel to Bulkeley and Cummins's "Voyage to the South Seas,"* 31.
185 "I then began": Report from Cheap to Lindsey, Feb. 26, 1744, JS.
186 "One night": Byron, *The Narrative of the Honourable John Byron*, 102–3.
186 "all my heart": Campbell, *The Sequel to Bulkeley and Cummins's "Voyage to the South Seas,"* 35.
187 "Here we have": Ibid., 37.
189 "I was": Byron, *The Narrative of the Honourable John Byron*, 82.
189 "Here we lay": Ibid., 83.
189 "The marines": Campbell, *The Sequel to Bulkeley and Cummins's "Voyage to the South Seas,"* 46.
189 "This was": Ibid., 45–46.
190 "Perceiving now": Byron, *The Narrative of the Honourable John Byron*, 88.
190 "We were now": Ibid., 90.
190 "all thoughts": Ibid., 89.

190 "We considered": Campbell, *The Sequel to Bulkeley and Cummins's "Voyage to the South Seas,"* 48.
190 "This bay": Byron, *The Narrative of the Honourable John Byron,* 89.
190 "We had now": Campbell, *The Sequel to Bulkeley and Cummins's "Voyage to the South Seas,"* 47.
191 "consigning one": Byron, *The Narrative of the Honourable John Byron,* 103.
191 *The lots were:* George Gordon Byron, *The Complete Works of Lord Byron,* 623.

CHAPTER 20

192 "It is enough": Bulkeley and Cummins, *A Voyage to the South Seas,* 98.
192 "At eight saw": Ibid., 105.
192 "landsman dream": Darwin and Amigoni, *The Voyage of the Beagle,* 230.
193 "died like": Quoted in Richard Hough, *The Blind Horn's Hate,* 149.
193 "as large as": Bulkeley and Cummins, *A Voyage to the South Seas,* 101.
194 "peaked-up rock": Ibid., 106.
195 "The people eating": Ibid.
195 "To go from": Ibid., 109.
196 "We still": Ibid.
196 "on the coast": Ibid., 112–13.
196 "Hadst thou": Thomas à Kempis, *The Christian's Pattern, or, A Treatise of the Imitation of Jesus Christ,* 33.
196 "There are": Bulkeley and Cummins, *A Voyage to the South Seas,* 108.
196 "Our poor fellows": Letter from Lieutenant Baynes to his brother, October 6, 1742, ERALS-DDGR/39/52.
197 "I believe": Bulkeley and Cummins, *A Voyage to the South Seas,* 120.
197 "They were surprised": Ibid.
198 "justly deserves": Ibid., 103.
198 "the day of": Ibid., 120.
198 "We think": Ibid., 121.
198 "This wonder": Ibid., 120.
198 "at his own": Ibid., 124.

CHAPTER 21

201 "Here we": Bulkeley and Cummins, *A Voyage to the South Seas,* 137.
201 "an improper season": Ibid., 137–38.
202 "either to": Ibid., 138.
202 "people who had": Ibid., 136.
202 "give account": Ibid., 127.
202 "We were even": Ibid., xxix.
203 "they found": Ibid.
203 "We were confident": Ibid., xxix.

203 "We thought": Ibid., 151.
203 "imperfect narrative": Ibid., 72.
204 "If things": Ibid., 152.
204 "to make": Ibid., 153.
204 "We have strictly": Ibid., 158.
204 "Our families": Ibid., 151–52.
204 "After surviving": Ibid., xxiii–xxiv.
205 "lest your Lordships": Ibid., 161.
205 "We don't set": Ibid., xxix.
205 "It has been hinted": Ibid., xxx.
206 "too busy": Ibid., xxix.
206 "Our confining": Ibid., xxviii.
206 "taken care": Ibid., xxxi.
206 "a plain maritime": Ibid., xxiii.
207 "Money is": Ibid., 159.
207 "How dare": Ibid., 172.
207 "We are ready": *The Universal Spectator,* August 25 and Sept. 1, 1744.
208 "a true ring": Arthur D. Howden Smith's introduction to Bulkeley and Cummins, *A Voyage to the South Seas,* vi.

CHAPTER 22

209 "no other light": Captain Murray's report to Admiralty, July 10, 1741, TNA-ADM 1/2099.
209 never condemned them: A brother of the *Severn*'s captain was grateful that Anson had stood by his relative and protected him from "the cavils of those children of ease who sit at home and, without risking themselves, blame every man's conduct they do not and cannot understand."
210 "as melancholy": Leo Heaps, *Log of the Centurion: Based on the Original Papers of Captain Philip Saumarez on Board HMS Centurion, Lord Anson's Flagship During His Circumnavigation, 1740–44,* 175.
210 "She burnt": Millechamp, *A Narrative of Commodore Anson's Voyage into the Great South Sea and Round the World,* NMM-JOD/36.
210 "like rotten sheep": *The Gentleman's Magazine,* June 1743.
210 "I should": Letter from Anson to Lord Hardwicke, June 14, 1744, BL-ADD MSS.
211 "We had the": *The Universal Spectator,* Aug. 25 and Sept. 1, 1744.
211 "It is almost": Millechamp, *A Narrative of Commodore Anson's Voyage into the Great South Sea and Round the World,* NMM-JOD/36.
211 "Unless we wish": Somerville, *Commodore Anson's Voyage into the South Seas and Around the World,* 183–84.
211 "the meanest sailor": *The Universal Spectator,* Aug. 25 and Sept. 1, 1744.
211 "endeavour to": Millechamp, *A Narrative of Commodore Anson's Voyage into the Great South Sea and Round the World,* NMM-JOD/36.
211 Now, while sailing: My description of the chase of the galleon and the sub-

sequent battle scene is drawn largely from the numerous firsthand accounts and reports of those who were present. For more information, see Anson's letters and dispatches; Heaps's *Log of the Centurion*; Keppel's *The Life of Augustus, Viscount Keppel, Admiral of the White, and First Lord of the Admiralty in 1782–3*, vol. 1; Millechamp's *A Narrative of Commodore Anson's Voyage into the Great South Sea and Round the World*; Thomas's *A True and Impartial Journal of a Voyage to the South-Seas;* Walter's *A Voyage Round the World*; and Williams's *Documents Relating to Anson's Voyage Round the World.* My research also benefited from several excellent works of history, including Somerville's *Commodore Anson's Voyage into the South Seas and Around the World* and Williams's *The Prize of All the Oceans.*

212 "the English": Intelligence report sent to the governor of Manila, printed in Williams, ed., *Documents Relating to Anson's Voyage Round the World*, 207.

212 "Gentlemen, and": Somerville, *Commodore Anson's Voyage into the South Seas and Around the World*, 217.

212 "spirit in": Ibid.

212 "an act of": Williams, *The Prize of All the Oceans*, 161.

213 "Exercising our": Walter, *A Voyage Round the World*, 400.

213 "Keeping in": Ibid., 401.

213 "All hands": Journal of Saumarez, printed in Williams, ed., *Documents Relating to Anson's Voyage Round the World*, 197.

213 "Our ship": Millechamp, *A Narrative of Commodore Anson's Voyage into the Great South Sea and Round the World,* NMM-JOD/36.

216 "face death": Keppel, *The Life of Augustus, Viscount Keppel, Admiral of the White, and First Lord of the Admiralty in 1782–3*, vol. 1, 115.

217 "Nothing was": Millechamp, *A Narrative of Commodore Anson's Voyage into the Great South Sea and Round the World,* NMM-JOD/36.

217 "very well contrived": Thomas, *A True and Impartial Journal of a Voyage to the South-Seas,* 289.

218 "At the very": Quoted in Brian Lavery, *Anson's Navy: Building a Fleet for Empire, 1744–1763*, 102

219 "being frightened": Thomas, *A True and Impartial Journal of a Voyage to the South-Seas*, 282–83.

219 "It is too": Juan de la Concepción, *Historia General de Philipinas*, excerpted in Williams, ed., *Documents Relating to Anson's Voyage Round the World*, 218.

219 "promiscuously covered": Heaps, *Log of the Centurion*, 224.

219 "humane disposition": *The Universal Spectator,* Aug. 25 and Sept. 1, 1744.

220 grisly failures: In November 1739, at the very outset of the war, Admiral Edward Vernon and his forces captured the Spanish settlement of Portobelo, in what is now Panama, but this victory was soon followed by a string of calamitous defeats.

220 "GREAT BRITAIN'S": *Daily Advertiser,* July 5, 1744.

220 A share of: For information on estimates of the shares of prize money awarded to the seamen and officers, including Anson, see Williams, *The Prize of All the Oceans.*

221 "It was the": Rodger, *The Command of the Ocean: A Naval History of Britain, 1649–1815*, 239.

221 sea ballad: This song about Anson celebrates not just his taking of the galleon but also his capture of another wealthy prize four years later.

221 "The wagon": Firth, *Naval Songs and Ballads*, 196.

CHAPTER 23

222 "What could": Report from Cheap to Lindsey, Feb. 26, 1744, JS.

223 "five poor": Campbell, *The Sequel to Bulkeley and Cummins's "Voyage to the South Seas,"* 55.

223 "departed this": Ibid., 63.

223 "scraped a hole": Byron, *The Narrative of the Honourable John Byron*, 150–51.

223 "We durst": Campbell, *The Sequel to Bulkeley and Cummins's "Voyage to the South Seas,"* 58.

223 "Thus, in": Byron, *The Narrative of the Honourable John Byron*, 167.

224 "gave way": Ibid., 158.

224 "There ran": Ibid., 172.

225 "hardly appeared": Ibid., 169.

225 "I could compare": Ibid., 169–70.

225 "They made a": Ibid., 176.

225 "considerable service": Campbell, *The Sequel to Bulkeley and Cummins's "Voyage to the South Seas,"* 77.

225 "We all": Ibid., 70.

225 "We thought": Ibid., 78.

226 "I was now": Report from Cheap to Richard Lindsey, Feb. 26, 1744, JS.

226 "The officers of": Carlyle, *Anecdotes and Characters of the Times*, 100.

226 "condemned hole": Byron, *The Narrative of the Honourable John Byron*, 214.

226 "There was": Ibid.

226 "The soldiers": Ibid.

227 "Every day": Report from Cheap to Lindsey, Feb. 26, 1744, JS.

227 "my two faithful": Quoted in Layman, *The Wager Disaster*, 218.

227 "obliged to defraud": Byron, *The Narrative of the Honourable John Byron*, 262.

228 "great and monstrous": Defoe, *A Tour Through the Whole Island of Great Britain*, 135.

228 "Having been": Byron, *The Narrative of the Honourable John Byron*, 263.

228 "With what surprise": Ibid., 264.

229 "For what": Quoted in Layman, *The Wager Disaster*, 217.

229 "I flatter": Ibid., 216.

229 "I have nothing": Bulkeley and Cummins, *A Voyage to the South Seas*, 170.

229 the press: For more information on the publishing trade during this era, see Bob Clarke, *From Grub Street to Fleet Street: An Illustrated History of English Newspapers to 1899*; Robert Darnton, *The Literary Underground of the Old Regime*; Pat Rogers, *The Poet and the Publisher: The Case of Alexander Pope, Esq., of Twickenham versus Edmund Curll, Bookseller in Grub Street*; and Howard William

Troyer, *Ned Ward of Grub Street: A Study of Sub-Literary London in the Eighteenth Century.*

229 "bound them": *Caledonian Mercury*, February 6, 1744.

230 "often mysterious": Carlyle, *Anecdotes and Characters of the Times*, 100.

230 "could not be": Byron, *The Narrative of the Honourable John Byron*, x.

230 called "egotism": Ibid., ix.

231 "The law is": Janet Malcolm, *The Crime of Sheila McGough*, 3.

CHAPTER 24

232 "Hanged": This and other quotes in the scene come from Bulkeley and Cummins, *A Voyage to the South Seas*, 169–70.

233 British naval law: For more information on naval law and courts-martial, see Byrn, *Crime and Punishment in the Royal Navy*; Markus Eder, *Crime and Punishment in the Royal Navy of the Seven Years' War, 1755–1763*; David Hannay, *Naval Courts Martial*; John M'Arthur, *Principles and Practice of Naval and Military Courts Martial*; Rodger, *Articles of War*; and Rodger, *The Wooden World.*

233 "They wanted": Joseph Conrad, *Lord Jim*, 18.

234 "mutinous assemblies": For this and other quotes of regulations, see Rodger, *Articles of War*, 13–19.

235 "contrived to convey": Byrn, *Crime and Punishment in the Royal Navy*, 55.

235 mutiny on HMS *Bounty:* There are enough books on this mutiny to fill a vast library. I relied especially on Caroline Alexander's excellent account, *The Bounty: The True Story of the Mutiny on the Bounty.* For more information, also see Edward Christian and William Bligh, *The Bounty Mutiny.*

235 One of them: There are diverging accounts of what the condemned men said before the execution.

235 "Brother seamen": Quoted in Christian and Bligh, *The Bounty Mutiny*, 128.

236 "vain notions": Bulkeley and Cummins, *A Voyage to the South Seas*, 170.

236 to be hanged: A captain or other commissioned officer sentenced to death typically had the choice of whether to be hanged or shot.

236 "fall by the": Bulkeley and Cummins, *A Voyage to the South Seas*, 171.

CHAPTER 25

237 "strike the mind": Frederick Marryat, *Frank Mildmay, or, The Naval Officer*, 93.

237 "do his utmost": *The Trial of the Honourable Admiral John Byng, at a Court Martial, As Taken by Mr. Charles Fearne, Judge-Advocate of His Majesty's Fleet*, 298.

237 "kill an admiral": Voltaire, and David Wootton, *Candide and Related Texts*, 59.

238 "you so justly": Cheap to Anson, Dec. 12, 1745, printed in Layman, *The Wager Disaster*, 217-18.

239 "I always": Bulkeley and Cummins, *A Voyage to the South Seas*, 171.

239 "Do you charge": This and other quoted court-martial testimony come from TNA-ADM 1/5288.

239 "all of *that*": Italics added for emphasis.

241 "honourably acquitted": Bulkeley and Cummins, *A Voyage to the South Seas*, 172–73.

241 "escape clause": Williams, *The Prize of All the Oceans*, 101.

241 "an uncomfortable whiff": From my interview with Rear Admiral Layman.

242 "surrounded with": Quoted in Gaudi, *The War of Jenkins' Ear*, 277.

242 *Deluded Britons!*: London *Daily Post*, July 6, 1744.

242 the war itself: For more background on the origins of the war, see Chapman, *Disaster on the Spanish Main*; Gaudi, *The War of Jenkins' Ear*; and David Olusoga, *Black and British: A Forgotten History*.

243 "the fable of": Quoted in Justin McCarthy, *A History of the Four Georges and of William IV*, 185.

243 "expunged from": Olusoga, *Black and British*, 25.

244 "empire of the": Quoted in P. J. Marshall, *The Oxford History of the British Empire: The Eighteenth Century*, 5.

244 "Disturbances and": Quoted in Rose, "The Anatomy of Mutiny," *Armed Forces & Society*, 565.

244 "the mutiny that": Williams, *The Prize of All the Oceans*, 101.

CHAPTER 26

245 the very last castaways: In a surprising twist, Morris and the two other castaways discovered an unexpected person onboard the ship with them: Midshipman Alexander Campbell, who was returning to England after being left behind by Cheap.

245 "the greatest act": Morris, *A Narrative of the Dangers and Distresses Which Befel Isaac Morris, and Seven More of the Crew, Belonging to the Wager Store-Ship, Which Attended Commodore Anson, in His Voyage to the South Sea*, 10.

245 "a wild desolate": Ibid.

245 "I imagined": Ibid., 27–28.

246 "great insolence": Ibid., 42.

246 "most cruelly": Ibid.

247 "A mutiny!": Campbell, *The Sequel to Bulkeley and Cummins's "Voyage to the South Seas,"* 103.

247 "These eleven Indians": Morris, *A Narrative of the Dangers and Distresses Which Befel Isaac Morris*, 45.

247 "revolted again": Jill Lepore, *These Truths: A History of the United States*, 55.

248 "Thus was the": Morris, *A Narrative of the Dangers and Distresses Which Befel Isaac Morris*, 47.

248 "I believe": Ibid., 37.

249 "make a monopoly": Thomas, *A True and Impartial Journal of a Voyage to the South-Seas, and Round the Globe, in His Majesty's Ship the Centurion, Under the Command of Commodore George Anson*, 10.

249 "undoubtedly of the": Philips, *An Authentic Journal of the Late Expedition Under the Command of Commodore Anson*, ii. There was no one named John Philips

onboard the *Centurion,* but the account appears to have been based on an actual officer's logbook.

249 "done his utmost": Walter, *A Voyage Round the World,* 155.

249 the "ringleader": Ibid., 158.

249 "men conceived": Ibid., 156.

250 "Though prudence": Ibid., 444.

250 something odd: For more information on the mystery of who wrote *A Voyage Round the World*, see Barrow's *The Life of Lord George Anson* and Williams's *The Prize of All the Oceans.*

250 had been ghostwritten: Anson's biographer Barrow concluded that Walter "drew the cold and naked skeleton," while Robins "clothed it with flesh and muscles, and, by the warmth of his imagination . . . caused the blood to circulate through the veins."

250 "aversion to writing": Quoted in Lavery, *Anson's Navy,* 14.

250 "I got sight": Letter from Anson to Duke of Newcastle, June 14, 1744, TNA-SP 42/88.

250 "an enterprise": Walter, *A Voyage Round the World,* 2.

250 "constantly exerted": Ibid., 218.

250 "always kept up": Ibid., 342.

250 "remarkable for": Ibid., 174.

251 "Everybody has": Barrow, *The Life of Lord George Anson,* iii.

251 "un capitaine": Quoted in Mahon, *History of England,* vol. 3, 33.

251 "the ingenious author": James Cook, *Captain Cook's Journal During His First Voyage Round the World Made in H.M. Bark Endeavour, 1768–1771,* 48.

251 "a classic story": Glyndwr Williams's introduction to his edited version of *A Voyage Round the World,* ix.

251 "one of the": Thomas Carlyle, *Complete Works of Thomas Carlyle,* vol. 3, 491.

251 "the most popular": Bernard Smith, *Imagining the Pacific: In the Wake of the Cook Voyages,* 52.

EPILOGUE

253 "honour" to reveal: Letter from Cheap to Admiralty, January 13, 1747, printed in Layman, *The Wager Disaster,* 253–55.

253 "dead on the": *Derby Mercury,* July 24, 1752.

254 Foul-Weather Jack: A ballad about John Byron went:

Brave he may be, deny it who can,
Yet Admiral John is a luckless man;
And the midshipmen's mothers cry, "Out, alack!
My lad has sailed with Foulweather Jack!"

254 "the universal": John Charnock, *Biographia Navalis, or, Impartial Memoirs of the Lives and Characters of Officers of the Navy of Great Britain, from the Year 1660 to the Present Time,* 439.

254 "rash and hasty": Byron, *The Complete Works of Lord Byron,* 41.

254 "great injustice": Carlyle, *Anecdotes and Characters of the Times*, 100.

254 "simple, interesting": Quoted in Emily Brand, *The Fall of the House of Byron*, 112.

255 "hardships were": Byron, *The Complete Works of Lord Byron*, 720.

255 *Reversed for:* Byron, *The Collected Poems of Lord Byron*, 89.

255 *Stay, traveller:* Barrow, *The Life of Lord George Anson*, 419.

256 decayed into pieces: Nothing survived of the lion's head but a portion of the carved leg, which was salvaged by a descendant of Anson's.

256 "remarkable and most": Melville, *White-Jacket, or, The World in a Man-of-War*, 155–56.

256 Wager Island remains: The description of the island is based on my visit there.

257 rotted wooden planks: These remnants of the hull, some of which I observed during my own visit to the island, were first discovered in 2006 by an expedition organized by the Scientific Exploration Society with support of the Chilean Navy. For more information on its findings, see both "The Quest for HMS *Wager* Chile Expedition 2006," which was published by the Scientific Exploration Society, and "The Findings of the *Wager*, 2006," by Major Chris Holt, a member of the expedition, which is printed in Layman's *The Wager Disaster*.

Selected Bibliography

Adkins, Roy, and Lesley Adkins. *Jack Tar: Life in Nelson's Navy*. London: Abacus, 2009.

Akerman, John Yonge, ed. *Letters from Roundhead Officers Written from Scotland and Chiefly Addressed to Captain Adam Baynes, July MDCL–June MDCLX*. Edinburgh: W. H. Lizars, 1856.

Alexander, Caroline. *The Bounty: The True Story of the Mutiny on the Bounty*. New York: Penguin Books, 2004.

Andrewes, William J. H., ed. *The Quest for Longitude*. Cambridge, MA: Collection of Historical Scientific Instruments, Harvard University, 1996.

Anon. *An Affecting Narrative of the Unfortunate Voyage and Catastrophe of His Majesty's Ship Wager, One of Commodore Anson's Squadron in the South Sea Expedition ... The Whole Compiled from Authentic Journals*. London: John Norwood, 1751.

Anon. *An Authentic Account of Commodore Anson's Expedition: Containing All That Was Remarkable, Curious and Entertaining, During That Long and Dangerous Voyage ... Taken from a Private Journal*. London: M. Cooper, 1744.

Anon. *The History of Commodore Anson's Voyage Round the World ... by a Midshipman on Board the Centurion*. London: M. Cooper, 1767.

Anon. *A Journal of a Voyage Round the World, in His Majesty's Ship the Dolphin, Commanded by the Honourable Commodore Byron ... by a Midshipman on Board the Said Ship*. London: M. Cooper, 1767.

Anon. *Loss of the Wager Man of War, One of Commodore Anson's Squadron*. London: Thomas Tegg, 1809.

Anon. *A Voyage Round the World, in His Majesty's Ship the Dolphin, Commanded by the Honourable Commodore Byron ... by an Officer on Board the Said Ship*. London: Newbery and Carnan, 1768.

Anon. *A Voyage to the South-Seas, and to Many Other Parts of the World, Performed from the Month of September in the Year 1740, to June 1744, by Commodore Anson ... by an Officer of the Squadron*. London: Yeovil Mercury, 1744.

Anson, Walter Vernon. *The Life of Admiral Lord Anson: The Father of the British Navy, 1697–1762*. London: John Murray, 1912.

An Appendix to the Minutes Taken at a Court-Martial, Appointed to Enquire into the Conduct of Captain Richard Norris. London: Printed for W. Webb, 1745.

Atkins, John. *The Navy-Surgeon, or, A Practical System of Surgery.* London: Printed for Caesar Ward and Richard Chandler, 1734.

Barrow, John. *The Life of Lord George Anson.* London: John Murray, 1839.

Baugh, Daniel A. *British Naval Administration in the Age of Walpole.* Princeton: Princeton University Press, 1965.

———, ed. *Naval Administration, 1715–1750.* Great Britain: Navy Records Society, 1977.

Bawlf, Samuel. *The Secret Voyage of Sir Francis Drake, 1577–1580.* New York: Walker, 2003.

Baynham, Henry. *From the Lower Deck: The Royal Navy, 1780–1840.* Barre, MA: Barre Publishers, 1970.

Berkenhout, John. "A Volume of Letters from Dr. Berkenhout to His Son, at the University of Cambridge." *The European Magazine and London Review* 19 (February 1791).

Bevan, A. Beckford, and H. B. Wolryche-Whitmore, eds. *The Journals of Captain Frederick Hoffman, R.N., 1793–1814.* London: John Murray, 1901.

Bird, Junius B. *Travels and Archaeology in South Chile.* Iowa City: University of Iowa Press, 1988.

Blackmore, Richard. *A Treatise of Consumptions and Other Distempers Belonging to the Breast and Lungs.* London: Printed for John Pemberton, 1724.

Bolster, W. Jeffrey. *Black Jacks: African American Seamen in the Age of Sail.* Cambridge, MA: Harvard University Press, 1997.

Boswell, James. *The Life of Samuel Johnson.* Vol. 1. London: John Murray, 1831.

Bown, Stephen R. *Scurvy: How a Surgeon, a Mariner, and a Gentleman Solved the Greatest Medical Mystery of the Age of Sail.* New York: Thomas Dunne Books, 2004.

Brand, Emily. *The Fall of the House of Byron: Scandal and Seduction in Georgian England.* London: John Murray, 2020.

Bridges, E. Lucas. *Uttermost Part of the Earth: Indians of Tierra del Fuego.* New York: Dover Publications, 1988.

Brockliss, Laurence, John Cardwell, and Michael Moss. *Nelson's Surgeon: William Beatty, Naval Medicine, and the Battle of Trafalgar.* Oxford and New York: Oxford University Press, 2005.

Broussain, Juan Pedro, ed. *Cuatro relatos para un naufragio: La fragata Wager en el golfo de Penas en 1741.* Santiago, Chile: Septiembre Ediciones, 2012.

Brown, Kevin. *Poxed and Scurvied: The Story of Sickness and Health at Sea.* Barnsley: Seaforth, 2011.

Brown, Lloyd A. *The Story of Maps.* New York: Dover Publications, 1979.

Brunsman, Denver. *The Evil Necessity: British Naval Impressment in the Eighteenth-Century Atlantic World.* Charlottesville: University of Virginia Press, 2013.

Bulkeley, John, and John Cummins. *A Voyage to the South Seas.* 3rd ed. With introduction by Arthur D. Howden Smith. New York: Robert M. McBride & Company, 1927.

Bulloch, John. *Scottish Notes and Queries.* Vol. 1. 3 vols. Aberdeen: A. Brown & Co., 1900.

Burney, Fanny. *The Early Journals and Letters of Fanny Burney.* Edited by Betty Rizzo. Vol. 4. Oxford: Clarendon Press, 2003.

Byrn, John D. *Crime and Punishment in the Royal Navy: Discipline on the Leeward Islands Station, 1784–1812.* Aldershot: Scolar Press, 1989.

Byron, John. *The Narrative of the Honourable John Byron: Containing an Account of the Great Distresses Suffered by Himself and His Companions on the Coast of Patagonia, from the Year 1740, Till Their Arrival in England, 1746.* London: S. Baker and G. Leigh, 1769.

———. *Byron's Narrative of the Loss of the Wager: Containing an Account of the Great Distresses Suffered by Himself and His Companions on the Coast of Patagonia, from the Year 1740, Till Their Arrival in England, 1746.* London: Henry Leggatt & Co., 1832.

Byron, George Gordon. *The Collected Poems of Lord Byron.* Hertfordshire: Wordsworth, 1995.

———.*The Complete Works of Lord Byron.* Paris: Baudry's European Library, 1837.

———. *The Poetical Works of Lord Byron.* London: John Murray, 1846.

Camões, Luís Vaz de, and Landeg White. *The Lusíads.* Oxford World's Classics. Oxford and New York: Oxford University Press, 2008.

Campbell, Alexander. *The Sequel to Bulkeley and Cummins's "Voyage to the South-Seas."* London: W. Owen, 1747.

Campbell, John. *Lives of the British Admirals: Containing an Accurate Naval History from the Earliest Periods.* Vol. 4. London: C. J. Barrington, Strand, and J. Harris, 1817.

Canclini, Arnoldo. *The Fuegian Indians: Their Life, Habits, and History.* Buenos Aires: Editorial Dunken, 2007.

Canny, Nicholas P., ed. *The Oxford History of the British Empire: The Origins of Empire: British Overseas Enterprise to the Close of the Seventeenth Century.* Vol. 1. Oxford: Oxford University Press, 2001.

Carlyle, Alexander. *Anecdotes and Characters of the Times.* London: Oxford University Press, 1973.

Carlyle, Thomas. *Complete Works of Thomas Carlyle.* Vol. 3. New York: P. F. Collier & Son, 1901.

Carpenter, Kenneth J. *The History of Scurvy and Vitamin C.* Cambridge and New York: Cambridge University Press, 1986.

Chamier, Frederick. *The Life of a Sailor.* Edited by Vincent McInerney. London: Richard Bentley, 1850.

Chapman, Anne. *European Encounters with the Yamana People of Cape Horn, Before and After Darwin.* Cambridge: Cambridge University Press, 2013.

Chapman, Craig S. *Disaster on the Spanish Main: The Tragic British-American Expedition to the West Indies During the War of Jenkins' Ear.* Lincoln: Potomac Books, University of Nebraska Press, 2021.

Charnock, John. *Biographia Navalis, or, Impartial Memoirs of the Lives and Characters of Officers of the Navy of Great Britain, from the Year 1660 to the Present Time.* Vol. 5. Cambridge: Cambridge University Press, 2011.

Chiles, Webb. *Storm Passage: Alone Around Cape Horn.* New York: Times Books, 1977.

Christian, Edward, and William Bligh. *The Bounty Mutiny*. New York: Penguin Books, 2001.

Clark, William Mark. *Clark's Battles of England and Tales of the Wars*. Vol. 2. London: William Mark Clark, 1847.

Clarke, Bob. *From Grub Street to Fleet Street: An Illustrated History of English Newspapers to 1899*. Brighton: Revel Barker, 2010.

Clayton, Tim. *Tars: The Men Who Made Britain Rule the Waves*. London: Hodder Paperbacks, 2008.

Clinton, George. *Memoirs of the Life and Writings of Lord Byron*. London: James Robins and Co., 1828.

Cockburn, John. *The Unfortunate Englishmen*. Dundee: Chalmers, Ray, & Co., 1804.

Cockburn, William. *Sea Diseases, or, A Treatise of Their Nature, Causes, and Cure*. 3rd ed. London: Printed for G. Strahan, 1736.

Codrington, Edward. *Memoir of the Life of Admiral Sir Edward Codrington*. London: Longmans, Green, and Co., 1875.

Cole, Gareth. "Royal Navy Gunners in the French Revolutionary and Napoleonic Wars." *The Mariner's Mirror* 95, no. 3 (August 2009).

Coleridge, Samuel Taylor. *The Rime of the Ancient Mariner*. New York: D. Appleton & Co., 1857.

Conboy, Martin, and John Steel, eds. *The Routledge Companion to British Media History*. London and New York: Routledge, 2015.

Conrad, Joseph. *Lord Jim*. Ware, Hertfordshire: Wordsworth Editions, 1993.

———. *Complete Short Stories*. New York: Barnes & Noble, 2007.

Cook, James. *Captain Cook's Journal During His First Voyage Round the World Made in H.M. Bark Endeavour, 1768–1771*. London: Elliot Stock, 1893.

Cooper, John M. *Analytical and Critical Bibliography of the Tribes of Tierra del Fuego and Adjacent Territory*. Washington, DC: Government Printing Office, 1917.

Cuyvers, Luc. *Sea Power: A Global Journey*. Annopolis: Naval Institute Press, 1993.

Dana, R. H. *The Seaman's Friend: A Treatise on Practical Seamanship*. Boston: Thomas Groom & Co., 1879.

———. *Two Years Before the Mast, and Twenty-Four Years After*. London: Sampson Low, Son, & Marston, 1869.

Darnton, Robert. *The Literary Underground of the Old Regime*. Cambridge, MA, and London: Harvard University Press, 1982.

Darwin, Charles. *A Naturalist's Voyage*. London: John Murray, 1889.

———. *The Descent of Man*. Vol. 1. New York: D. Appleton and Company, 1871.

———, and David Amigoni. *The Voyage of the Beagle: Journal of Researches into the Natural History and Geology of the Countries Visited during the Voyage of HMS Beagle Round the World, Under the Command of Captain Fitz Roy, RN*. Wordsworth Classics of World Literature. Ware: Wordsworth Editions, 1997.

Davies, Surekha. *Renaissance Ethnography and the Invention of the Human: New Worlds, Maps and Monsters*. Cambridge: Cambridge University Press, 2016.

Defoe, Daniel. *The Earlier Life and Works of Daniel Defoe*. Edited by Henry Morley. Edinburgh and London: Ballantine Press, 1889.

———. *The Novels and Miscellaneous Works of Daniel Defoe*. London: George Bell & Sons, 1890.

———. *Robinson Crusoe*. Penguin Classics. London: Penguin, 2001.

———. *A Tour Through the Whole Island of Great Britain*. New Haven: Yale University Press, 1991.

Dennis, John. *An Essay on the Navy, or, England's Advantage and Safety, Prov'd Dependant on a Formidable and Well-Disciplined Navy, and the Encrease and Encouragement of Seamen*. London: Printed for the author, 1702.

Dickinson, H. W. *Educating the Royal Navy: Eighteenth- and Nineteenth-Century Education for Officers*. Naval Policy and History. London and New York: Routledge, 2007.

Dobson, Mary J. *Contours of Death and Disease in Early Modern England*. Cambridge: Cambridge University Press, 2002.

———. *The Story of Medicine: From Bloodletting to Biotechnology*. New York: Quercus, 2013.

Drake, Francis, and Francis Fletcher. *The World Encompassed by Sir Francis Drake, Being His Next Voyage to That to Nombre de Dois. Collated with an Unpublished Manuscript of Francis Fletcher, Chaplain to the Expedition*. London: The Hakluyt Society, 1854.

Druett, Joan. *Rough Medicine: Surgeons at Sea in the Age of Sail*. New York: Routledge, 2000.

Eder, Markus. *Crime and Punishment in the Royal Navy of the Seven Years' War, 1755–1763*. Hampshire, England, and Burlington, VT: Ashgate, 2004.

Edwards, Philip. *The Story of the Voyage: Sea-Narratives in Eighteenth-Century England*. Cambridge: Cambridge University Press, 1994.

Emperaire, Joseph, and Luis Oyarzún. *Los nomades del mar*. Biblioteca del bicentenario 17. Santiago de Chile: LOM Ediciones, 2002.

Ennis, Daniel James. *Enter the Press-Gang: Naval Impressment in Eighteenth-Century British Literature*. Newark: University of Delaware Press, 2002.

Equiano, Olaudah, and Vincent Carretta. *The Interesting Narrative and Other Writings*. New York: Penguin Books, 2003.

Ettrick, Henry. "The Description and Draught of a Machine for Reducing Fractures of the Thigh." *Philosophical Transactions* 459, XLI (1741).

Farr, David. *Major-General Thomas Harrison: Millenarianism, Fifth Monarchism and the English Revolution, 1616–1660*. London and New York: Routledge, 2016.

Firth, Charles Harding, ed. *Naval Songs and Ballads*. London: Printed for Navy Records Society, 1908.

Fish, Shirley. *HMS Centurion, 1733–1769: An Historic Biographical-Travelogue of One of Britain's Most Famous Warships and the Capture of the Nuestra Señora de Covadonga Treasure Galleon*. UK: AuthorHouse, 2015.

———. *The Manila-Acapulco Galleons: The Treasure Ships of the Pacific: With an Annotated List of the Transpacific Galleons, 1565–1815*. UK: AuthorHouse, 2011.

Flanagan, Adrian. *The Cape Horners' Club: Tales of Triumph and Disaster at the World's Most Feared Cape*. London: Bloomsbury Publishing, 2017.

Frézier, Amédée François. *A Voyage to the South-Sea and Along the Coasts of Chile and Peru, in the Years 1712, 1713, and 1714*. Cambridge: Cambridge University Press, 2014.

Friedenberg, Zachary. *Medicine Under Sail*. Annapolis: Naval Institute Press, 2002.

Frykman, Niklas Erik. "The Wooden World Turned Upside Down: Naval Mutinies in the Age of Atlantic Revolution." PhD diss., University of Pittsburgh, 2010.

Gallagher, Robert E., ed. *Byron's Journal of His Circumnavigation, 1764–1766*. London: Hakluyt Society, 1964.

Garbett, H. *Naval Gunnery: A Description and History of the Fighting Equipment of a Man-of-War*. London: George Bell and Sons, 1897.

Gardner, James Anthony. *Above and Under Hatches: The Recollections of James Anthony Gardner*. Edited by R. Vesey Hamilton and John Knox Laughton. London: Chatham, 2000.

Gaudi, Robert. *The War of Jenkins' Ear: The Forgotten War for North and South America*. New York: Pegasus Books, 2021.

Gilje, Paul A. *To Swear Like a Sailor: Maritime Culture in America, 1750–1850*. New York: Cambridge University Press, 2016.

Goodall, Daniel. *Salt Water Sketches; Being Incidents in the Life of Daniel Goodall, Seaman and Marine*. Inverness: Advertiser Office, 1860.

Gordon, Eleanora C. "Scurvy and Anson's Voyage Round the World, 1740–1744: An Analysis of the Royal Navy's Worst Outbreak." *The American Neptune* XLIV, no. 3 (Summer 1984).

Green, Mary Anne Everett, ed. *Calendar of State Papers, Domestic Series, 1655–6*. London: Longmans & Co, 1882.

Griffiths, Anselm John. *Observations on Some Points of Seamanship*. Cheltenham: J. J. Hadley, 1824.

Gusinde, Martin. *The Lost Tribes of Tierra del Fuego: Selk'nam, Yamana, Kawésqar*. New York: Thames & Hudson, 2015.

Hall, Basil. *The Midshipman*. London: Bell and Daldy, 1862.

Hannay, David. *Naval Courts Martial*. Cambridge: Cambridge University Press, 1914.

Harvie, David. *Limeys: The Conquest of Scurvy*. Stroud: Sutton, 2005.

Hay, Robert. *Landsman Hay: The Memoirs of Robert Hay*. Edited by Vincent McInerney. Barnsley, UK: Seaforth, 2010.

———. *Landsman Hay: The Memoirs of Robert Hay, 1789–1847*. Edited by M. D. Hay. London: Rupert Hart-Davis, 1953.

Haycock, David Boyd, and Sally Archer, eds. *Health and Medicine at Sea, 1700–1900*. Woodbridge, UK, and Rochester, NY: Boydell Press, 2009.

Hazlewood, Nick. *Savage: The Life and Times of Jemmy Button*. New York: St. Martin's Press, 2001.

Heaps, Leo. *Log of the Centurion: Based on the Original Papers of Captain Philip Saumarez on Board HMS Centurion, Lord Anson's Flagship During His Circumnavigation, 1740-44*. New York: Macmillan Publishing Co., 1971.

Hickox, Rex. *18th Century Royal Navy: Medical Terms, Expressions, and Trivia.* Bentonville, AR: Rex Publishing, 2005.

Hill, J. R., and Bryan Ranft, eds. *The Oxford Illustrated History of the Royal Navy.* Oxford: Oxford University Press, 1995.

Hirst, Derek. "The Fracturing of the Cromwellian Alliance: Leeds and Adam Baynes." *The English Historical Review,* 108 (1993).

Hoad, Margaret J. "Portsmouth—As Others Have Seen It." *The Portsmouth Papers,* no. 15 (March 1972).

Hobbes, Thomas. *Leviathan, or, The Matter, Forme, & Power of a Common-wealth Ecclesiasticall and Civil.* New York: Barnes & Noble Books, 2004.

Hope, Eva, ed. *The Poetical Works of William Cowper.* London: Walter Scott, 1885.

Hough, Richard. *The Blind Horn's Hate.* New York: W. W. Norton & Company, 1971.

Houston, R. A. "New Light on Anson's Voyage, 1740–4: A Mad Sailor on Land and Sea." *The Mariner's Mirror* 88, no. 3 (August 2002).

Hudson, Geoffrey L., ed. *British Military and Naval Medicine, 1600–1830.* Amsterdam: Rodopi, 2007.

Hutchings, Thomas Gibbons. *The Medical Pilot, or, New System.* New York: Smithson's Steam Printing Officers, 1855.

Hutchinson, J. *The Private Character of Admiral Anson, by a Lady.* London: Printed for J. Oldcastle, 1746.

Irving, Washington. *Tales of a Traveller.* New York: John B. Alden, 1886.

Jarrett, Dudley. *British Naval Dress.* London: J. M. Dent & Sons, 1960.

Jones, George. "Sketches of Naval Life." *The American Quarterly Review,* Vol. VI (December 1829).

Journal of the House of Lords. Vol. 27 (June 1746). London: His Majesty's Stationery Office.

Keevil, J. J. *Medicine and the Navy, 1200–1900.* Vol. 2. Edinburgh and London: E. & S. Livingstone, Ltd., 1958.

Kemp, Peter. *The British Sailor: A Social History of the Lower Deck.* London: Dent, 1970.

Kempis, Thomas à. *The Christian's Pattern, or, A Treatise of the Imitation of Jesus Christ.* Halifax: William Milner, 1844.

Kenlon, John. *Fourteen Years a Sailor.* New York: George H. Doran Company, 1923.

Kent, Rockwell. *Voyaging Southward from the Strait of Magellan.* New York: Halcyon House, 1924.

Keppel, Thomas. *The Life of Augustus, Viscount Keppel, Admiral of the White, and First Lord of the Admiralty in 1782–3.* 2 vols. London: Henry Colburn, 1842.

Keys, Ancel, Josef Brozek, Austin Henschel, and Henry Longstreet Taylor. *The Biology of Human Starvation.* Vol. 1. Minneapolis: University of Minnesota Press, 1950.

King, Dean. *Every Man Will Do His Duty: An Anthology of Firsthand Accounts from the Age of Nelson, 1793–1815.* New York: Open Road Media, 2012.

King, P. Parker. *Narrative of the Surveying Voyages of His Majesty's Ships Adventure and Beagle.* Vol. 1. London: Henry Colburn, 1839.

Kinkel, Sarah. *Disciplining the Empire: Politics, Governance, and the Rise of the British*

Navy. Harvard Historical Studies, vol. 189. Cambridge, MA, and London: Harvard University Press, 2018.

Kipling, Rudyard. *The Writings in Prose and Verse of Rudyard Kipling*. New York: Charles Scribner's Sons, 1899.

Knox-Johnston, Robin. *Cape Horn: A Maritime History*. London: Hodder & Stoughton, 1995.

Lambert, Andrew D. *Admirals: The Naval Commanders Who Made Britain Great*. London: Faber and Faber, 2009.

Lanman, Jonathan T. *Glimpses of History from Old Maps: A Collector's View*. Tring, England: Map Collector Publications, 1989.

Lavery, Brian. *Anson's Navy: Building a Fleet for Empire, 1744–1763*. Barnsley: Seaforth Publishing, 2021.

———. *The Arming and Fitting of English Ships of War, 1600–1815*. Annapolis: Naval Institute Press, 1987.

———. *Building the Wooden Walls: The Design and Construction of the 74-Gun Ship Valiant*. London: Conway, 1991.

———. *Royal Tars: The Lower Deck of the Royal Navy, 857–1850*. Annapolis: Naval Institute Press, 2011.

———, ed. *Shipboard Life and Organisation, 1731–1815*. Publications of the Navy Records Society, vol. 138. Aldershot, England: 1998.

———. *Wooden Warship Construction: A History in Ship Models*. Barnsley: Seaforth Publishing, 2017.

Layman, C. H. *The Wager Disaster: Mayhem, Mutiny and Murder in the South Seas*. London: Uniform Press, 2015.

Leech, Samuel. *Thirty Years from Home, or, A Voice from the Main Deck*. Boston: Tappan, Whittemore & Mason, 1843.

Lepore, Jill. *These Truths: A History of the United States*. New York and London: W. W. Norton & Company, 2018.

Leslie, Doris. *Royal William: The Story of a Democrat*. London: Hutchinson & Co., 1940.

Lind, James. *An Essay on the Most Effectual Means of Preserving the Health of Seamen in the Royal Navy*. London: D. Wilson, 1762.

———. *A Treatise on the Scurvy*. London: Printed for S. Crowder, 1772.

Linebaugh, Peter, and Marcus Rediker. *The Many-Headed Hydra: Sailors, Slaves, Commoners, and the Hidden History of the Revolutionary Atlantic*. Boston: Beacon Press, 2013.

Lipking, Lawrence. *Samuel Johnson: The Life of an Author*. Cambridge, MA: Harvard University Press, 1998.

Lloyd, Christopher, and Jack L. S. Coulter. *Medicine and the Navy, 1200–1900*. Vol. 4. Edinburgh and London: E. & S. Livingstone, 1961.

Long, W. H., ed. *Naval Yarns of Sea Fights and Wrecks, Pirates and Privateers from 1616–1831 as Told by Men of Wars' Men*. New York: Francis P. Harper, 1899.

Lothrop, Samuel Kirkland. *The Indians of Tierra del Fuego*. New York: Museum of the American Indian Heye Foundation, 1928.

MacCarthy, Fiona. *Byron: Life and Legend*. New York: Farrar, Straus and Giroux, 2002.

M'Arthur, John. *Principles and Practice of Naval and Military Courts Martial.* 2 vols. London: A. Strahan, 1813.

McCarthy, Justin. *A History of the Four Georges and of William IV.* Vol. 2. Leipzig: Bernhard Tauchnitz, 1890.

Magill, Frank N., ed. *Dictionary of World Biography.* Vol 4. Pasadena: Salem Press, 1998.

Mahon, Philip Stanhope. *History of England: From the Peace of Utrecht to the Peace of Versailles.* Vols. 2 and 3. London: John Murray, 1853.

Malcolm, Janet. *The Crime of Sheila McGough.* New York: Alfred A. Knopf, 1999.

Marcus, G. J. *Heart of Oak.* London: Oxford University Press, 1975.

Marryat, Frederick. *Frank Mildmay, or, The Naval Officer.* Classics of Nautical Fiction Series. Ithaca, NY: McBooks Press, 1998.

Marshall, P. J., ed. *The Oxford History of the British Empire: The Eighteenth Century.* Vol. 2. Oxford and New York: Oxford University Press, 1998.

Matcham, Mary Eyre, ed. *A Forgotten John Russell: Being Letters to a Man of Business, 1724–1751.* London: Edward Arnold, 1905.

McEwan, Colin, Luis Alberto Borrero, and Alfredo Prieto, eds. *Patagonia: Natural History, Prehistory, and Ethnography at the Uttermost End of the Earth.* Princeton Paperbacks. Princeton: Princeton University Press, 1997.

Mead, Richard. *The Medical Works of Richard Mead.* Dublin: Printed for Thomas Ewing, 1767.

Melby, Patrick. "Insatiable Shipyards: The Impact of the Royal Navy on the World's Forests, 1200–1850." Monmouth: Western Oregon University, 2012.

Melville, Herman. *Redburn: His First Voyage: Being the Sailor-Boy Confession and Reminiscences of the Son-of-a-Gentleman, in the Merchant Service.* New York: Modern Library, 2002.

———. *White-Jacket: or, The World in a Man-of-War.* London: Richard Bentley, 1850.

Miller, Amy. *Dressed to Kill: British Naval Uniform, Masculinity and Contemporary Fashions, 1748–1857.* London: National Maritime Museum, 2007.

Miyaoka, Osahito, Osamu Sakiyama, and Michael E. Krauss, eds. *The Vanishing Languages of the Pacific Rim.* Oxford Linguistics. Oxford and New York: Oxford University Press, 2007.

Monson, William. *Sir William Monson's Naval Tracts: In Six Books.* London: Printed for A. and J. Churchill, 1703.

Morris, Isaac. *A Narrative of the Dangers and Distresses Which Befel Isaac Morris, and Seven More of the Crew, Belonging to the Wager Store-Ship, Which Attended Commodore Anson, in His Voyage to the South Sea.* Dublin: G. and A. Ewing, 1752.

Mountaine, William. *The Practical Sea-Gunner's Companion, or, An Introduction to the Art of Gunnery.* London: Printed for W. and J. Mount, 1747.

Moyle, John. *Chirurgus Marinus, or, The Sea-Chirurgion.* London: Printed for E. Tracy and S. Burrowes, 1702.

———. *Chyrurgic Memoirs: Being an Account of Many Extraordinary Cures.* London: Printed for D. Browne, 1708.

Murphy, Dallas. *Rounding the Horn: Being a Story of Williwaws and Windjammers,*

Drake, Darwin, Murdered Missionaries and Naked Natives—a Deck's Eye View of Cape Horn. New York: Basic Books, 2005.

Narborough, John, Abel Tasman, John Wood, and Friedrich Martens. *An Account of Several Late Voyages and Discoveries to the South and North.* Cambridge: Cambridge University Press, 2014.

Nelson, Horatio. *The Dispatches and Letters of Vice Admiral Lord Viscount Nelson.* Edited by Nicholas Harris Nicolas. Vol. 3. London: Henry Colburn, 1845.

Newby, Eric. *The Last Grain Race.* London: William Collins, 2014.

Nichols, John. *Literary Anecdotes of the Eighteenth Century.* Vol. 9. London: Nichols, Son, and Bentley, 1815.

Nicol, John. *The Life and Adventures of John Nicol, Mariner.* Edited by Tim F. Flannery. New York: Grove Press, 2000.

Nicolson, Marjorie H. "Ward's 'Pill and Drop' and Men of Letters." *Journal of the History of Ideas* 29, no. 2 (1968).

O'Brian, Patrick. *The Golden Ocean.* New York: W. W. Norton & Company, 1996.

———. *Men-of-War: Life in Nelson's Navy.* New York: W. W. Norton & Company, 1995.

———. *The Unknown Shore.* New York: W. W. Norton & Company, 1996.

Oliphant, Margaret. "Historical Sketches of the Reign of George II." *Blackwood's Edinburgh Magazine* 104, no. 8 (December 1868).

Olusoga, David. *Black and British: A Forgotten History.* London: Macmillan, 2017.

Osler, William, ed. *Modern Medicine: Its Theory and Practice.* Vol. 2. Philadelphia and New York: Lea Brothers & Co., 1907.

Pack, S. W. C. *Admiral Lord Anson: The Story of Anson's Voyage and Naval Events of His Day.* London: Cassell & Company, 1960.

———. *The Wager Mutiny.* London: Alvin Redman, 1964.

Padfield, Peter. *Guns at Sea.* New York: St. Martin's Press, 1974.

The Parliamentary History of England from the Earliest Period to the Year 1803. Vol. 10. London: T. C. Hansard, 1812.

Peach, Howard. *Curious Tales of Old East Yorkshire.* Wilmslow, England: Sigma Leisure, 2001.

Peñaloza, Fernanda, Claudio Canaparo, and Jason Wilson, eds. *Patagonia: Myths and Realities.* Oxford and New York: Peter Lang, 2010.

Penn, Geoffrey. *Snotty: The Story of the Midshipman.* London: Hollis & Carter, 1957.

Pepys, Samuel. *The Diary of Samuel Pepys: A New and Complete Transcription. Vol. 2: 1661.* Edited by Robert Latham and William Matthews. London: HarperCollins, 2000.

———. *The Diary of Samuel Pepys: A New and Complete Transcription. Vol. 10: Companion.* Edited by Robert Latham and William Matthews. Berkeley and Los Angeles: University of California Press, 1983.

———. *Everybody's Pepys: The Diary of Samuel Pepys.* Edited by O. F. Morshead. New York: Harcourt, Brace & Company, 1926.

———. *Pepys' Memoires of the Royal Navy, 1679–1688.* Edited by J. R. Tanner. Oxford: Clarendon Press, 1906.

Philbrick, Nathaniel. *In the Heart of the Sea: The Tragedy of the Whaleship Essex*. New York: Penguin, 2001.

Philips, John. *An Authentic Journal of the Late Expedition Under the Command of Commodore Anson*. London: J. Robinson, 1744.

Pigafetta, Antonio, and R. A. Skelton. *Magellan's Voyage: A Narrative of the First Circumnavigation*. New York: Dover Publications, 1994.

Pope, Alexander. *The Works of Alexander Pope*. Vol. 4. London: Printed for J. Johnson, J. Nichols and Son, and others, 1806.

Pope, Dudley. *Life in Nelson's Navy*. London: Unwin Hyman, 1987.

Porter, Roy. *Disease, Medicine, and Society in England, 1550–1860*. Cambridge: Cambridge University Press, 1995.

Purves, David Laing. *The English Circumnavigators: The Most Remarkable Voyages Round the World*. London: William P. Nimmo, 1874.

Rediker, Marcus. *Between the Devil and the Deep Blue Sea: Merchant Seamen, Pirates and the Anglo-American Maritime World, 1700–1750*. Cambridge: Cambridge University Press, 2010.

Reece, Henry. *The Army in Cromwellian England, 1649–1660*. London: Oxford University Press, 2013.

Regulations and Instructions Relating to His Majesty's Service at Sea. 2nd ed. London, 1734.

Reséndez, Andrés. *The Other Slavery: The Uncovered Story of Indian Enslavement in America*. Boston and New York: Mariner Books, Houghton Mifflin Harcourt, 2017.

Reyes, Omar. *The Settlement of the Chonos Archipelago, Western Patagonia, Chile*. Cham, Switzerland: Springer Nature Switzerland AG, 2020.

Richmond, H. W. *The Navy in the War of 1739–48*. 3 vols. Cambridge: Cambridge University Press, 1920

Robinson, William. *Jack Nastyface: Memoirs of an English Seaman*. Annapolis: Naval Institute Press, 2002.

Rodger, N. A. M. *Articles of War: The Statutes Which Governed Our Fighting Navies, 1661, 1749, and 1886*. Homewell, Havant, Hampshire: Kenneth Mason, 1982.

———. *The Command of the Ocean: A Naval History of Britain, 1649–1815*. New York: W. W. Norton, 2005.

———. "George, Lord Anson." In *Precursors of Nelson: British Admirals of the Eighteenth Century*, edited by Peter Le Fevre and Richard Harding. Mechanicsburg, PA: Stackpole Books, 2000.

———. *The Safeguard of the Sea: 660-1649*. New York: W. W. Norton, 1999.

———. *The Wooden World: An Anatomy of the Georgian Navy*. New York: W. W. Norton, 1996.

Rogers, Nicholas. *The Press Gang: Naval Impressment and Its Opponents in Georgian Britain*. London: Continuum, 2007.

Rogers, Pat. *The Poet and the Publisher: The Case of Alexander Pope, Esq., of Twickenham versus Edmund Curll, Bookseller in Grub Street*. London: Reaktion Books, 2021.

Rogers, Woodes. *A Cruising Voyage Round the World*. London: Printed for A. Bell, 1712.

Roper, Michael. *The Records of the War Office and Related Departments, 1660–1964.* Public Record Office Handbooks, no. 29. Kew, UK: Public Record Office, 1998.

Rose, Elihu. "The Anatomy of Mutiny," *Armed Forces & Society* 8 (1982).

Roth, Hal. *Two Against Cape Horn.* New York: Norton, 1978.

Rowse, A. L. *The Byrons and Trevanions.* Exeter: A. Wheaton & Co., 1979.

Scott, James. *Recollections of a Naval Life.* Vol. 1. London: Richard Bentley, 1834.

Shankland, Peter. *Byron of the Wager.* New York: Coward, McCann & Geoghegan, 1975.

Slight, Julian. *A Narrative of the Loss of the Royal George at Spithead, August, 1782.* Portsea: S. Horsey, 1843.

Smith, Bernard. *Imagining the Pacific: In the Wake of the Cook Voyages.* New Haven: Yale University Press, 1992.

Smollett, Tobias. *The History of England, from the Revolution to the Death of George the Second.* Vol. 2. London: W. Clowes and Sons, 1864.

———. *The Miscellaneous Works of Tobias Smollett.* Vol. 4. Edinburgh: Mundell, Doig, & Stevenson, 1806.

———. *The Works of Tobias Smollett: The Adventures of Roderick Random.* Vol. 2. New York: George D. Sproul, 1902.

Sobel, Dava. *Longitude the Story of a Lone Genius Who Solved the Greatest Scientific Problem of His Time.* New York: Walker, 2007.

Somerville, Boyle. *Commodore Anson's Voyage into the South Seas and Around the World.* London and Toronto: William Heinemann, 1934.

Stark, William F., and Peter Stark. *The Last Time Around Cape Horn: The Historic 1949 Voyage of the Windjammer Pamir.* New York: Carroll & Graf, 2003.

Steward, Julian H., ed. *Handbook of South American Indians.* Vol. 1. Washington, DC: U.S. Government Printing Office, 1946.

Stitt, F. B. "Admiral Anson at the Admiralty, 1744–62." *Staffordshire Studies,* no. 4 (February 1991).

Styles, John. *The Dress of the People: Everyday Fashion in Eighteenth-Century England.* New Haven: Yale University Press, 2007.

Sullivan, F. B. "The Naval Schoolmaster During the Eighteenth Century and the Early Nineteenth Century." *The Mariner's Mirror* 62, no. 3 (August 1976).

Thomas, Pascoe. *A True and Impartial Journal of a Voyage to the South-Seas, and Round the Globe, in His Majesty's Ship the Centurion, Under the Command of Commodore George Anson.* London: S. Birt, 1745.

Thompson, Edgar K. "George Anson in the Province of South Carolina." *The Mariner's Mirror,* no. 53 (August 1967).

Thompson, Edward. *Sailor's Letters: Written to His Select Friends in England, During His Voyages and Travels in Europe, Asia, Africa, and America.* Dublin: J. Potts, 1767.

Thursfield, H. G., ed. *Five Naval Journals, 1789–1817.* Vol. 91. London: Publications of Navy Records Society, 1951.

The Trial of the Honourable Admiral John Byng, at a Court Martial, as Taken by Mr. Charles Fearne, Judge-Advocate of His Majesty's Fleet. Dublin: Printed for J. Hoey, P. Wilson, et al., 1757.

Trotter, Thomas. *Medical and Chemical Essays.* London: Printed for J. S. Jordan, 1795.

Troyer, Howard William. *Ned Ward of Grub Street: A Study of Sub-Literary London in the Eighteenth Century*. New York: Barnes & Noble, 1967.

Tucker, Todd. *The Great Starvation Experiment: Ancel Keys and the Men Who Starved for Science*. Minneapolis: University of Minnesota Press, 2007.

Velho, Alvaro, and E. G. Ravenstein. *A Journal of the First Voyage of Vasco Da Gama, 1497–1499*. Cambridge: Cambridge University Press, 2010.

Vieira, Bianca Carvalho, André Augusto Rodrigues Salgado, and Leonardo José Cordeiro Santos, eds. *Landscapes and Landforms of Brazil*. New York, Berlin and Heidelberg: Springer, 2015.

Voltaire, and David Wootton. *Candide and Related Texts*. Indianapolis: Hackett, 2000.

Walker, N. W. Gregory. *With Commodore Anson*. London: A. & C. Black, 1934.

Walker, Violet W., and Margaret J. Howell. *The House of Byron: A History of the Family from the Norman Conquest, 1066–1988*. London: Quiller Press, 1988.

Walpole, Horace. *The Letters of Horace Walpole*. Vol. 3. Philadelphia: Lea and Blanchard, 1842.

Walter, Richard. *A Voyage Round the World*. London: F. C. & J. Rivington, 1821.

———, George Anson, and Benjamin Robins. *A Voyage Round the World, in the Years MDCCXL, I, II, III, IV*. Edited by Glyndwr Williams. London and New York: Oxford University Press, 1974.

Ward, Ned. *The Wooden World*. 5th ed. Edinburgh: James Reid Bookseller, 1751.

Watt, James. "The Medical Bequest of Disaster at Sea: Commodore Anson's Circumnavigation, 1740–44." *Journal of the Royal College of Physicians of London* 32, no. 6 (December 1998).

Williams, Glyndwr, ed. *Documents Relating to Anson's Voyage Round the World*. London: Navy Records Society, 1967.

———. *The Prize of All the Oceans: Commodore Anson's Daring Voyage and Triumphant Capture of the Spanish Treasure Galleon*. New York: Penguin Books, 2001.

Willis, Sam. *Fighting at Sea in the Eighteenth Century: The Art of Sailing Warfare*. Woodbridge, Suffolk, UK: Boydell Press, 2008.

Wines, E. C. *Two Years and a Half in the American Navy: Comprising a Journal of a Cruise to England, in the Mediterranean, and in the Levant, on Board of the U.S. Frigate Constellation, in the Years 1829, 1830, and 1831*. Vol. 2. London: Richard Bentley, 1833.

Woodall, John. *De Peste, or the Plague*. London: Printed by J.L. for Nicholas Bourn, 1653.

———. *The Surgions Mate*. London: Kingsmead Press, 1978.

Yorke, Philip C. *The Life and Correspondence of Philip Yorke, Earl of Hardwicke, Lord High Chancellor of Great Britain*. Vol. 3. Cambridge: Cambridge University Press, 1913.

Zerbe, Britt. *The Birth of the Royal Marines, 1664–1802*. Woodbridge, Suffolk, and Rochester, NY: Boydell Press, 2013.

Index

ILLUSTRATION CREDITS

FIRST INSERT

PAGE 1

Portrait of John Byron by Joshua Reynolds, 1748. Newstead Abbey, Nottinghamshire.
Photo: Nottingham City Museums & Galleries / Bridgeman Images

PAGE 2

(top) *The Press Gang.* Painting by George Morland, 1790. Royal Holloway, University of London.
Photo: Bridgeman Images

(bottom) Portrait of David Cheap by Allan Ramsay, *c.* 1748. Reproduced with kind permission of the Strathyrum Trust.
Photo: C. H. Layman

PAGE 3

Painting of Deptford dockyard by John Cleveley, 1757. National Maritime Museum, Greenwich.
Photo: © National Maritime Museum, Greenwich, London

PAGE 4

(top) Gun deck.
Photo: © Nick Depree

(bottom) Copperplate engraving from Dr. Robert James, *A Medicinal Dictionary*, pub. T. Osborne, London, 1743.
Photo: Wellcome Collection, London

PAGE 5

The Burial at Sea of a Marine Officer. Painting by Eugène Isabey, 1836. The Montreal Museum of Fine Arts, purchase, Adrienne D'Amours Pineau and René Pineau Memorial Fund, the Museum Campaign 1988–1993 Fund, the Montreal Museum of Fine Arts' Volunteer Association Fund, and the Leacross Foundation Fund.
Photo: MMFA / Christine Guest

PAGE 6

(top) Logbook from the *Centurion.*
Photo: © National Maritime Museum, Greenwich, London

PAGES 6–7
(bottom, spread) Colored engraving by Piercy Brett, December 1740. Collection of Colin Paul.
Photo: © Michael Blyth

PAGE 7
(top) An albatross off Cape Horn.
Photo: Mike Hill / Getty Images

PAGE 8
The "Wager" in Extremis. Painting by Charles Brooking, c. 1744. Collection of the late Commander David Joel, reproduced with permission.
Photo: Dave Thompson, courtesy C. H. Layman

SECOND INSERT

PAGE 1
Wager Island.
Photo: David Grann

PAGE 2
(top) Colored engraving by an anonymous artist, from *The Loss of the Wager Man of War, one of Commodore Anson's Squadron . . . and the Embarrassments of the Crew, Separation, Mutinous Disposition, Narrow Escapes, Imprisonment and Other Distresses*, pub. T. Tegg, London, 1809.
Photo: © Michael Blyth

(bottom) Engraved frontispiece by Samuel Wale after Charles Grinion, for John Byron's *The Narrative of the Honourable John Byron. Being an Account of the Shipwreck of The Wager; and the Subsequent Adventures of Her Crew*, pub. S. Baker, G. Leigh & T. Davies, London, 1768.
Photo: Wellcome Collection, London

PAGE 3
(top) Wager Island.
Photo: Chris Holt

(center) Seaweed.
Photo: David Grann.

(bottom) Celery.
Photo: David Grann

PAGE 4
(top) Photograph of a Kawésqar man by Martin Gusinde, 1923–1924.
Photo: © Martin Gusinde / Anthropos Institute / Atelier EXB

(bottom) Photograph of a canoe by W. S. Barclay, *c.* 1904–7.
Photo: Royal Geographical Society / Alamy

PAGE 5
(top) A coastal Kawésqar camp. Photograph by Martin Gusinde, 1923–1924.
Photo: © Martin Gusinde / Anthropos Institute / Atelier EXB

(bottom) Copperplate engraving from George Anson, *A Voyage to the South Seas, and to Many Other Parts of the World*, pub. R. Walker, London, 1745. British Library, London.
Photo: © British Library Board. All Rights Reserved / Bridgeman Images

PAGE 6
(top) *The Capture of the Spanish Galleon "Nuestra Señora de Covadonga."* Painting by John Cleveley, 1756. Shugborough Hall, Staffordshire.
Photo: National Trust Photographic Library / Bridgeman Images

(bottom) Portrait of George Anson attributed to Thomas Hudson, before 1748. National Maritime Museum, Greenwich.
Photo: © National Maritime Museum, Greenwich, London

PAGES 6–7
(bottom, spread) Map of the Strait of Magellan.
Photo: © British Library Board. All Rights Reserved / Bridgeman Images

PAGE 7
(top) A remnant of the *Wager.*
Photo: Chris Holt

(top, left) Title page of John Narborough's *An Account of Several Late Voyages and Discoveries to the South and North*, pub. S. Smith and B. Walford, London, 1694.
Photo: Shapero Rare Books Ltd.

PAGE 8
(top) Painting by John Cleveley, 1760. National Maritime Museum, Greenwich.
Photo: © National Maritime Museum, Greenwich, London

(bottom) Chilean coast.
Photo: Ivan Konar / Alamy

A NOTE ABOUT THE AUTHOR

David Grann is the author of the #1 *New York Times* bestsellers *Killers of the Flower Moon* and *The Lost City of Z*. *Killers of the Flower Moon* was a finalist for the National Book Award and won an Edgar Allan Poe Award. He is also the author of *The White Darkness* and the collection *The Devil and Sherlock Holmes*. Grann's investigative reporting has garnered several honors, including a George Polk Award. He lives with his wife and children in New York.